T0334625

# F. A. Hayek as a Political Economist

Friedrich Hayek is one of the most important economists and social theorists of the twentieth century. His contributions to the social sciences range across cognitive psychology, the history of ideas, the philosophy of law, political philosophy and the theory of liberalism. This book focuses on the links between his economics and the rest of his work, with special attention to normative elements. Topics covered include:

- Hayek's criticism of Cartesian rationalism and the 'engineering spirit';
- his relationship to game theory and his theory of business cycles;
- his theory of the spontaneous social order in his cognitive psychology;
- the relationships between his liberalism and socialism and Austro-Marxism;
- the relationships between spontaneous and organized social institutions;
- the consequences for social stability of the different conceptions of the legislator in his work.

The volume concludes with a discussion of the possibility of a normative economics that is based on objective criteria. Essential reading for all Hayek scholars, this work will also be of interest to historians of economics and social theorists in general.

**Jack Birner** is Professor of Economics in the Department of Sociology, University of Trento. His research interests include capital theory, the theory of business cycles, the evolution of social institutions, the theory of social amplifiers, the history of economic thought, network analysis of markets, the philosophy of science and methodology of economics and the logic of scientific problem solving. He is the author of *The Cambridge Controversies in Capital Theory: A Study in the Logic of Theory Development*, Routledge 2001.

**Pierre Garrouste** is Professor of Economics at the University Lumière–Lyon 2, and researcher at the Centre ATOM (Analytical Theory of Organisations and Market). His research interests include Austrian economics, history of economic thought (he is co-editor of *Path-Dependency and Evolution in Economics: Past and Present*, Edward Elgar, March 2001), and economics of learning in relations with the theories of the firm.

**Thierry Aimar** is Associate Professor of Economics in the Department of Economics at the University of Nancy 2.

# Routledge Studies in the History of Economics

# F. A. Hayek as a Political Economist

Economic analysis and values

**Edited by Jack Birner, Pierre Garrouste and Thierry Aimar**

Routledge
Taylor & Francis Group

LONDON AND NEW YORK

First published 2002
by Routledge
4 Park Square, Milton Park, Abingdon, Oxon OX14 4RN
605 Third Avenue, New York, NY 10017

First issued in paperback 2013

*Routledge is an imprint of the Taylor & Francis Group, an informa business*

Typeset in Baskerville by Taylor & Francis Books Ltd

*British Library Cataloguing in Publication Data*
A catalogue record for this book is available from the British Library

*Library of Congress Cataloging in Publication Data*
F.A. Hayek as a political economist : economic analysis and values / edited
by Jack Birner, Pierre Garrouste and Thierry Aimar.
p. cm.
Includes bibliographical references and index.
1. Hayek, Friedrich A. von (Friedrich August), 1899–1992 Congresses. 2.
Economists–History–20th century–Congresses. 3.
Economics–History–20th century–Congresses. 4. Social
sciences–History–20th century–Congresses. I. Birner, Jack 1951– II.
Garrouste, Pierre 1954– III. Aimar, Thierry 1966–

HB101 .H39 F16 2001
330'.092–dc21
                                                                2001019941

ISBN 13: 978-0-415-86278-3 (pbk)

**Publisher's Note**
The publisher has gone to great lengths to ensure the quality of this reprint
but points out that some imperfections in the original may be apparent

# Contents

# Contributors

**Thierry Aimar**, Associate Professor of Economics, Department of Economics, University of Nancy 2.

**Professor Richard Aréna**, LATAPSES, Université de Nice, Valbonne.

**Dr Mohammed Bensaïd**, Maison des Sciences de l'Homme, Paris.

**Professor Jack Birner**, Department of Sociology, University of Trento.

**Professor Theodore A. Burczak**, Department of Economics, Denison University, Granville, Ohio.

**William N. Butos**, Professor of Economics, Trinity College, Hartford, Connecticut.

**Raimondo Cubeddu**, Professor of Political Philosophy, Department of Political Sciences, University of Pisa.

**Bruno Deffains**, Professor of Economics, Department of Economics, University of Nancy 2.

**Professor Pierre Garrouste**, Department of Economics, University Lumière 2 – Lyon, ATOM, Paris.

**Dr Robert F. Hébert**, Department of Economics and Finance, University of Louisiana at Lafayette.

**Dr Thomas J. McQuade**, Department of Economics, Trinity College, Hartford, Connecticut.

**Professor Laurence S. Moss**, Economics Department, Babson College, Babson Park, Massuchusetts; Editor of *The American Journal of Economics and Sociology*.

**Dr Chikako Nakayama**, Graduate School of Area and Cultural Studies, Tokyo University of Foreign Studies.

**Christian Schmidt**, Professeur à l'Université Paris Dauphine, Directeur du LESOD.

# Preface

On the hottest days of May 1999 the newly founded *Association des Historiens de la Tradition Economique Autrichienne* organized its first annual conference in Paris. This volume contains a refereed selection of the numerous contributions. The fact that these were divided roughly equally between French and foreign participants, and that many young French scholars took part, was a first confirmation of the feasibility of two of the *Association*'s purposes, *viz.*, to give an impulse to the study of Austrian economics in France and to stimulate the intellectual exchange with scholars abroad. By the time this collection is published, our third annual conference in Pisa, Italy, will be over. Its theme was the new economy. Austrian economics needs to be awakened from its mainly historical orientation so as to give contemporary economists the opportunity to benefit from its enormous theoretical and methodological potential. That so many economists and others show an active interest in the *Association*'s conferences indicates that they find them a useful platform for launching and discussing their ideas.

This first conference was co-organized by The Austrian Cultural Institute in France, to whom we express our gratitude. We would also like to thank the Austrian National Bank, the Caisse des Dépôts et Consignations, the Institut Carl Menger and the Groupe de Recherche Histoire de la Pensée et Méthodologie Economiques for their organizational, moral and financial support.

Jack Birner
Pierre Garrouste
Thierry Aimar

# Introduction

*Jack Birner*

## Economics and its past

Economics is a peculiar discipline. Even though it studies the phenomena that influence people's lives most pervasively, it does little to anticipate relevant developments. Economists usually notice them when it is too late – or almost. One of the best recent examples is the problem of retirement and pension schemes. Until the beginning of this century, economics textbooks began with a section devoted to demography. The subject subsequently disappeared from economics (for reasons unknown but worthy of investigation), and only now are we painfully rediscovering the necessity of studying the age distribution of the population and its development. Why do economists have such a short memory? Is it because so many urgent political demands are put to them (or because they *think* that is the case)?

The *ex-ante* activities of anticipation and prediction are as much part of science as explanation *ex-post*. Economics can become more scientific by adopting a more forward-looking perspective. A powerful instrument for achieving this is the analysis of its own past. I do not say this for love of paradox, but because I profoundly believe it is true. The history of economics is the collection of attempts to solve problems that may *seem* to have disappeared, but rarely have. Much of this theoretical treasure trove has not been exploited sufficiently, or not at all. The work of the author that is the subject of this volume, Friedrich Hayek, is a good example.[1] Hayek tried to explain many phenomena and to solve many problems that for some reason had, and have, been forgotten. They include disequilibrium growth, the role of expectations, the relationship between money and the economy of production and consumption, and the role of investment and capital in production. Forgotten, yes, but not disappeared. Let us give another example. The theorists of the currently fashionable "real business cycle theory" take up a number of elements that were part of Hayek's approach, often without even knowing it. Had they been more historically aware, aggregate capital, the $K$ of the Cambridge criticism (does anyone remember?), might not have made a renewed appearance. The number of examples could easily be multiplied.

Studying the history of their own discipline is not, as many economists seem to think, a waste of time or an intellectual luxury reserved for retired colleagues. A discipline that calls itself scientific must take *problems* seriously. Problems have their history, both outside and inside the academic's study. If successful solutions have been found previously, they may be adopted; if not, knowledge of why they failed will help us to avoid repeating the mistakes of others. Studying the history of economics is an intellectual investment that increases the rate of return of contemporary economics.

## Austrian economics in France

As it is, however, economics is fashion-prone, dramatically out of touch with its own past, and also out of synch internally. This is what now seems to be the case in France, and that is not entirely unfortunate. Whereas interest in the Austrian tradition in economics (Menger, Wieser, Böhm-Bawerk, Schumpeter, Mises, Hayek) has remained mainly restricted to elderly economists – except, perhaps, in the US – France has recently witnessed a growing interest in this tradition among young academics. This led, in 1998, to the foundation of the *Association des Historiens de la Tradition Economique Autrichienne*. Its objective is not, as the name might suggest, to limit itself to studying ideas from the past as historical relics. The reason for its foundation was the conviction that much of value is left in the Austrian tradition, and that this is waiting to be worked out.

*AHTEA*'s first international conference was organized in Paris on 27–29 May 1999. For students of Austrianism, that year will go down in history as the centenary of Hayek's birth. Many an old hand must have shaken his graying head in occasional despair at seeing so many conferences at which so many colleagues who until recently did not want to be seen dead with Hayek's work showed up to tell the final truth about it. That year has now come to an end, and we can get on with the work. Of course, *AHTEA*'s first conference could only be devoted to Hayek. But we tried to distinguish it from the others. We also wanted to give a signal to the public that the *Association*'s approach intends to be critical and creative instead of interpretative and repetitive. That led to adopting the theme of the relationship between Hayek's analytical economics and his political and moral convictions. In brief, Hayek as a political economist. To underline the importance of the link between social-scientific analysis and the applications of its results through politics, one of the sessions took place in a committee room of the Chambres des Députés, the French Parliament. About half of the participants came from outside France, which demonstrated the feasibility of another of the *Association*'s goals, stimulating international contacts in the field of Austrian economics.

## Hayek as a political economist

Everything that today is called economics (as distinct from business economics) was known until the beginning of this century by the name of political economy. In *The Wealth of Nations* (The Introduction to Book IV) we read:

Political economy, considered as a branch of the science of a statesman or legislator, proposes two distinct objects: first, to provide a plentiful revenue or subsistence for the people, or more properly to enable them to provide such a revenue or subsistence for themselves; and secondly, to supply the state or commonwealth with a revenue sufficient for the public services. It proposes to enrich both the people and the sovereign.

Taken separately, this formulation seems to express Smith's normative conviction. However, one should not forget that he tried to supply scientific explanations for the mechanisms that contribute to and those that obstruct the growth of the wealth of nations. Forty years later, Ricardo had become the incarnation of the political economist in this classical sense. As a member of parliament he tried to forge the scientific arguments with which to justify his political convictions. By that time economics had become the analysis of the forces of production and distribution as the scientific underpinning of economic policy. It adopted Newton's method as its scientific canon. This is most apparent in the work of another classical economist, Jean-Baptiste Say.

When the first impact of Newtonian natural philosophy was over, the time seemed ripe for reflection on the distinction between what today would be called the social sciences and natural science. This added another dimension to political economy. John Stuart Mill took over from the German tradition of thought the idea that social science differs from natural science in that the former deals with mental phenomena. Mill translated the German *Geisteswissenschaften* by *moral sciences*. Yet in doing so he did not introduce something entirely new; he rather revived a tradition that shortly before had come to a temporary halt and whose most prominent exponents are Francis Hutcheson and Adam Smith in his *Theory of Moral Sentiments*.

For the third dimension to the concept of political economy we can hardly do better than to quote Schumpeter: "By a system of political economy I mean the exposition of a comprehensive set of economic policies that its author advocates on the strength of certain unifying (normative) principles such as the principles of economic liberalism, of socialism, and so on. Such systems do come within our range in as far as they contain genuinely analytic work."[2] The intention of the conference of which this volume reports some results was precisely to investigate the possible links between the normative and analytical elements in Hayek's thought.

There is no doubt that Hayek is a political economist in Schumpter's sense of the word. From very early in his career he embraced the principles of classical liberalism and chose the economic problems that he studied in the light of this doctrine. The result is an impressive list of publications on pure and applied economic analysis. Hayek tries to find a scientific explanation for moral rules and gives scientific arguments for political or moral positions. In this Hayek is exemplary: he tries to make as much progress as possible by scientific, or rather, critical means, in fields that had suffered from ideological immovable *parti pris* for too long, viz. legal, political and social philosophy.

Before he started doing economics, Hayek had already been engaged in a scientific endeavour that led to his being a moral scientist as well. We know from autobiographical notes that when he was a student, Hayek hesitated between a career as an economist or as a psychologist. His very first scientific paper was on psychology. The unpublished manuscript, written in September 1920, bears the title "Beiträge zur Theorie der Entwicklung des Bewusstseins". It contains a very advanced theory of cognitive psychology.[3] Shortly afterwards Hayek decided to become an economist. But that did not mean that his interest in mental phenomena had disappeared; it took a different form and a new source of inspiration in the subjectivism of his intellectual mentors, Carl Menger, Friedrich von Wieser and Eugen von Böhm-Bawerk. By emphasizing, from his earliest contributions to economics, the crucial importance of mental phenomena in the sphere of human and social phenomena, perceptions, expectations and subjective valuations, he showed himself to be a moral scientist. In addition to this, he devoted much of his work to the examination of the methodological consequences and the differences from the natural sciences of this position.

Hayek's work is clearly inspired by strong moral or ethical convictions, perhaps even by a utopian ideal. He deserves to be read critically in this light, too. He proposes and gives arguments for a particular type of society, one which merits critical scrutiny: for those who feel attracted by it, in order to examine if it is feasible; for those who prefer a different kind of society, in order to put their own ideal to a critical comparative test.

As Hayek developed his *oeuvre*, the three aspects of political economy became integrated in his concept of order. This is central to Hayek's thought, particularly in his later work, where his insights in economics and epistemology merge into a conception of society as a whole, including its legal and political institutions. Most of the contributions to this volume address themselves to various aspects of Hayek's ideas on social order.

## About this volume

### *Hayek in France*

The volume starts with two contributions that discuss the relationship between Hayek's thought and a particular French intellectual tradition, one he severely criticizes. In "Hayek and the French engineers" Hébert reviews Hayek's criticism of what he had disparagingly baptized the French engineering tradition. Hébert's critical analysis amounts to the accusation that Hayek is a Whig historian who shuts his eyes to relevant historical details. Thus, he pays no attention to the fact that Austrian economics, and particularly the economics of Carl Menger, shares common roots with the rejected Jules Dupuit in the work of Say. Whereas Hayek rightly criticizes Walras and Cournot for their mechanistic methodology, Hébert shows that he wrongly treats Dupuit for applying a similar method.

In "Moral functionalism" Birner gives further arguments why Hayek's whole-sale rejection of French constructivist rationalism is unacceptable, and even inconsistent with his own thought. He compares Hayek's social and moral theory with that of Emile Durkheim, another French author whom Hayek repudiates. Hayek accuses Durkheim of being a social constructivist who argues in favour of imposing social solidarity, which is the binding force of primitive societies, on modern industral society, where stability is the result of the spontaneous mechanism of market forces. The chapter shows that Hayek seriously misrepresents Durkheim's theory of the division of labour. Moreover, it demonstrates that Durkheim's and Hayek's thought are so similar that they are indistinguishable in many important respects. In their theories of society both emphasize the importance of spontaneous organization in an evolutionary process. The ideas individuals have about their social environment, and particularly the social norms they adhere to, play a crucial role in the emergence and the stability of industrial society. Durkheim is as much a moral scientist as Hayek. That includes the objective both authors have: the scientific explanation of the emergence and the role of morality. In their methodology they share the same type of functionalism, which tries to explain the effects of social institutions with the help of conjectural history.

### Economic analysis

The next pair of chapters addresses some analytical matters in Hayek's economics. In "Hayek, Morgenstern and game theory" Schmidt links Hayek to game theory. The missing link that he uncovers is Johan Huizinga's *Homo Ludens*. Schmidt argues that Hayek's methodology and his theory of the market order imply a concept of games that differs from the one that forms the basis of what now travels under the label of game theory. Hayek can be considered as taking up and reinforcing the idea of the early game theoretician Borel to the extent that it is illegitimate to identify the knowledge of the players of the game with that of the game theoretician. The behaviour of the players is the result of their skills and of chance. This is characteristic of most parlour games, which are Huizinga's frame of reference and that of Hayek's cousin, Wittgenstein, who is not mntioned by Schmidt. Game theory may be developed in a different direction – one, incidentally, indicated by Nash – by extending Hayek's analysis of equilibrium as a knowledge-dependent situation towards which an economic system may tend without ever reaching it.

Aréna's "Monetary policy and business cycles: Hayek as an opponent of the quantity theory tradition" traces the differences between Hayek and Irving Fisher and the consequences they have for their positions with respect to monetary policy. His analysis includes a discussion of Friedman's monetarism, which stands in the Fisherian tradition. Hayek rejected the quantity theory because he knew his history of economic thought. His own position in monetary policy issues is based on a careful analysis of Cantillon, the Banking School, and the tradition of free banking.

## Order

The following six contributions concentrate in one way or another on the important concept of order. Nakayama discusses *The Road to Serfdom* in her "An investigation of Hayek's criticism of central planning". That book is the first systematic manifestation of the theme of the conference: the relationship between value judgements and scientific analysis in Hayek. Her discussion of Hayek's role in the debate on central planning may look traditional, but it is richer than the usual treatments in several ways. First of all, she uses it to assess whether Hayek's liberalism is consistent. This is the main objective of the chapter. Second, she describes a number of neglected opponents of Hayek. Here we find a discussion of one of the most interesting intellectual traditions of the twentieth century, Austro-Marxism. A further element that distinguishes this chapter from more traditional discussions is that Nakayama links historical and intellectual developments. She discusses Austrian politics between the two world wars, economics in Austria, liberalism and Austro-Marxism. This episode serves to focus on Hayek's intellectual and human career, which ends with his emigration to the UK and the publication of *The Road to Serfdom.*

Whereas the previous chapter is backward looking, the next, "Hayek's borderless economy: his escape from the household model", by Moss looks to the future. He, too, discusses the debate on socialism, but from a different perspective. Moss investigates the thought of one of Hayek's teachers, Friedrich von Wieser. It is well known that Hayek used Wieser's dictator model as an idealization that served as a methodological device for keeping the complexities of his capital theory within manageable bounds. Moss argues that for Wieser himself the benevolent dictator also represented an ideal with realistic connotations. In that respect he is not unlike the socialists whom Hayek criticized for considering the dictator model to be a feasible economic system instead of a methodological idealization. Moss argues further that an unintended effect of Hayek's intellectual development (certainly unforeseen by himself) is his emancipation from another of Wieser's concepts, that of an economy as a geographically coherent and limited entity. (A topic that has consequences also for monetary theory, as Aréna correctly argues). One of the logical consequences of Hayek's thought on economic order is the idea of an economy without borders where coordination depends on language, shared meanings and the adherence to certain common customs and rules. In short, as one might add to Moss's conclusion, the sort of system that is nowadays often referred to as the New Economy – incidentally the subject of *AHTEA*'s annual conference in 2001.

The next two chapters deal with the relationships between social order and knowledge. More specifically, they discuss the links between Hayek's *Sensory Order* and his theory of social order. Butos and McQuade in their "Mind, market and institutions: the knowledge problem in Hayek's thought" concentrate on Hayek's theory of markets as the link between the sensory and the social order. In Cubeddu's "Uncertainty, instituions and order in Hayek", what constitutes the link is Hayek's philosophy of science.

The element that according to Butos and McQuade is common to Hayek's psychology, his theory of markets and his theory of social order, is the idea of constrained knowledge. By that they mean that knowledge is the result of the imposition of restrictions in the form of classifications by the mind, of the distributed character of information and skills and their restrictions to local situations in an economic framework, or of the limits on uncertainty imposed by social institutions. Hayek's generalization of the idea of constrained knowledge from a psychological to a market framework led to rather plausible conclusions. However, when he tried a further generalization to the framework of a social order, he ran into problems. One of these concerns the fact that a social order is more complex than a market order because the former contains the latter as a sub-order. Another question Hayek leaves unanswered is whether the mechanisms of the market are the same as the mechanisms that make an entire society work. This has its methodological dual in the question what is abstracted from in the analyses of a market and a social framework. Finally, it is not clear whether the tendency to equilibrium that in a market context may be interpreted as the normative criterion that individuals want to see their plans realized can be translated to the framework of society in its full institutional complexity, or by what other shared norm, if any, it can be substituted. Hayek filled these gaps in his analysis with normative arguments instead of scientific ones. The attempt to replace the former by the latter poses a challenge for future research of social orders.

Cubeddu develops a very similar argument. Whereas in *The Sensory Order* Hayek had solved the problem of how information (sensory inputs) is transformed into knowledge, he failed to do so in his theory of the social order. Cubeddu observes that Hayek's and Menger's concept of the function of institutions is identical to that which is the core of the transaction cost literature: to allow the greatest number of individual expectations to come true in the least time at the lowest cost and with the least unintended consequences. In this context Cubeddu addresses the role of the state. Contrary to what was argued by, for example, Bruno Leoni, Hayek thinks that the state has a legitimate role in reducing uncertainty by imposing new legal rules. He argues that in certain instances of rapid change it may be necessary to prevent a limited number of individuals to take advantage of their position. This leads Cubeddu to propose a criterion by which to judge social orders: the best order is the one that allows the greatest number of individual expectations to be fulfilled without obstructing the achievement of the greatest number of objectives by others. This interpretation of Hayek is a variant of the utilitarian criterion. The proposal is also similar to the treatment by Aimar in the last chapter of this volume in that both aim at an objective criterion, even though the content they give to it is different.

The critical tone of the previous chapters is maintained in the next two. Bensaïd's "The organizational indetermination of spontaneous order in Hayek" and Garrouste's "The difference between order and organization and the foundations of Hayek's liberalism" both analyze Hayek's liberalism. Both start from a comparison between organizations or engineered orders with spontaneous orders. The reason for this confrontation is twofold. First, as both authors notice, Hayek's defence of liberalism is based to a major extent on his criticism of what he considers to be its alternative, socialism. And second, his analysis of liberalism is based on the concept of spontaneous order whereas his criticism of socialism has its foundations in Hayek's theory of deliberately organized institutions.

Bensaïd's vehicle of criticism is an analysis of Hayek's stance in the debate on socialism. Bensaïd observes that, although one often ascribes to Hayek a dichotomous view of orders and organizations, he recognizes that they differ as to the *degree* of intendedness and complexity, and as to the *mix* of types of rules and control mechanisms. What the author criticizes Hayek for instead is his uneven treatment of one of the two factors of production, labour. Hayek's defence of liberalism is based on his defence of spontaneous economic institutions and, more importantly, on his criticism of the centrally planned economy. In the context of the economy as a whole Hayek treats labour as a commodity that is freely bought and sold on the market (without, Bensaïd might have added, being controlled by labour unions). However, in the framework of the business organization labour has to be deliberately and consciously managed and organized. This is apparently because different workers are cognitively complex individuals who have different characteristics and degrees of creativity. Recognizing this would be consistent with Hayek's principle of subjectivism. But then he should not treat labour as homogeneous outside the context of the organization. Moreover, Hayek fails to address the crucial issue of the employment relationship, including the determination of wages and matters of organizational justice. Despite its being a human factor, Hayek treats labour as less complex than capital. This constitutes a serious gap in his analysis of organizations. That analysis underlies his "scientific" critique of socialism, which is the cornerstone of his defence of liberalism. Therefore, Hayek's argument for liberalism is wrong. Whereas Butos and McQuade had explained the normative elements in Hayek's theory of liberal society as attempts to fill the holes in his scientific analysis, Bensaïd reverses the charges: Hayek's theory of liberalism is based on his moral rejection of totalitarianism right from the start.

Garrouste reaches a similar conclusion by different means. He argues that there are two possibilities. One is that Hayek's argument for the superiority of liberalism over socialism is based on an ideal-typical description of both systems. In that case there is conceivably a whole range of intermediate real possibilities, and Hayek's dichotomous and mutually exclusive representation of the two systems must be abandoned. The alternative is that the argument for liberalism is based on the description of real political systems. That description in its turn is based on the contrast between spontaneous orders and engineered organizations, and that again is based on the distinction between abstract and concrete rules. In contrast to Bensaïd, who thinks that for Hayek the differences between orders and organizations are gradual, Garrouste argues that the underlying distinction between concrete and abstract rules is for Hayek mutually exclusive. But that does not stand up to critical scrutiny (he gives a different argument than Watkins, 1976). This dichotomy is linked to others in a deductive argument that reconstructs the way in which Hayek reaches the conclusion that socialism is inefficient and even impossible. Since for Hayek socialism is the only alternative to liberalism, this "proves" the superiority of liberalism. Garrouste has argued that the premises about concrete vs. abstract rules is false. However, that does not imply anything for the truth or falsehood of the conclusion, since any conclusion whatsoever follows deductively from false premises. Hayek's distinction between two types of rules is irrelevant for his defence of liberalism.

## Philosophy of law

Hayek's legal philosophy is the subject of the next two chapters, which both address the consequences for social stability of different conceptions of the legislator and the judge. The title of Burczak's paper, "The contradictions between Hayek's subjectivism and his liberal legal theory", summarizes his argument. Basing himself on the tradition of "legal realism" of authors such as Frank and Llewellyn, he argues that it is wrong to consider the judge, as Hayek does, as a neutral discoverer of the law. A consistent application of the principles of subjectivism to the role of the judge should lead to the conclusion that the judge is a creator of laws who uses his own subjective perceptions in order to arrive at verdicts. For Hayek the non-neutrality of the judge lets in the same undesirable results that lead him, according to Burczak, to oppose the rule by a democratic majority: a loss of predictability in the legal framework and the promoting of special interests. Against this Burczak argues that the democratic platform offers the opportunity for society to come to a shared agreement and commitment on rules and norms for social welfare. As to the creative role of the judge, in a way legal realism comes to a more Hayekian conclusion than Hayek himself; since habits and customs – the crux of Hayek's theory of cultural evolution – are more important in guiding human action than laws, the loss of stability that Hayek feared would follow from creative judges is unlikely to materialize.

Although Deffains makes a similar distinction as Burczak, the judge as referee and the judge as leader, his interpretation of Hayek's opinion on the role of the judge is more lenient. Deffains argues that for Hayek the judge is neither referee nor leader; instead, he is a producer of law within the framework of a legal tradition. He discovers laws in a manner of speaking: he verifies whether new rules are consistent with the legal tradition. The notion of the neutrality of the judge is given an interesting content where Deffains remarks that his impartiality derives from the task, or the ability, to decide the outcome of a case so as to correspond to the expectations of any randomly chosen individual who is in the same position. This, we may add, is the crux of Hayek's ideal of the rule of law. That ideal is very similar to Rawls' construction of the veil of ignorance in the original position, which serves to exclude the influence of special interests in the establishing of the rules of justice. Where Burczak argues in favour of a continuous dialogue about these rules on a democratic discussion platform, it would seem that Deffains is happy to rely on the judge.

## Norms from facts?

The volume concludes with Aimar's "Coordination, survival and normativity: a Hayekian perspective revisited". The chapter examines the extent to which it is possible to escape from ethical anti-naturalism ("normativity without prescriptions"). The author reintroduces an element of objectivity in the domain of human preferences in the form of goods that are necessary for our survival. Following Mises, he calls these praxeological goods. The link with Hayek lies in the criterion for judging the success of a social order proposed in *The Fatal Conceit*: the number of individuals a particular order can keep alive. Aimar takes up Hayek's suggestion in "Economics and Knowledge" that the statement that an economy shows a tendency to equilibrium is what gives empirical content to Hayek's theory. Via Hayek's definition of equilibrium this leads to a social order's capability of coordinating the actions of individuals as the empirical criterion for its success. Whereas Butos and McQuade refer to this criterion as normative and criticize Hayek for giving normative arguments instead of descriptive ones in his passage from markets to the social order, Aimar takes the opposite direction. He argues that survival is the extension of coordination as an empirical measure. He bases this conclusion on a logical argument to the extent that for plans to be coordinated, the individuals in question must stay alive. The central link is that "[i]f individual activities were not coordinated on a wider scale, there would not have been such a degree of specialization of functions and the level of output of goods providing sufficient food for the populations could never have reached present proportions". Although this argument is based on Hayek's work, it is also the logical transposition of Durkheim's theory of the division of labour that is described in Birner's contribution. More interestingly, Aimar's conclusion about the relationship between scientific analysis and value judgements in Hayek's work – the theme of the conference – is a special case of Durkheim's idea that "the antithesis between science and ethics … disappears" (*Division du travail social*, pp. 35–6). We wonder what reaction this would have provoked in the mind of one of Hayek's most eminent and admired precursors in political economy, David Hume …

## Notes

1 Hayek's work itself constitutes a counterexample to the idea that all economists are ahistorical. Each and every time he addresses a problem, his first move is a thorough analysis of its history.

2 *History of Economic Analysis*, p. 38. Cp. also p. 1,139: "Economists moved with the times and a significant change occurred in their views about practical questions. The sum total of these views together with the schema of social values that underlies these views we shall call Political Economy."

3 And of the mind–body problem. In 1952 the manuscript was published, in an extended form, as *The Sensory Order. An Inquiry into the Foundations of Theoretical Psychology*. For the story of Hayek's psychology and its influence on the rest of his work, cp. Birner, 1999.

# Bibliography

Birner, J. (1999) "The Surprising Place of Psychology in the Work of F.A. Hayek", *History of Economic Ideas.*, VII, 1–2, pp. 43–84.

Schumpeter, J.S. (1954) *History of Economic Analysis*, London: Allen & Unwin.

Smith, A. (1776) *The Wealth of Nations*, Everyman's Library, J.M. Dent & Sons (1970).

Watkins, J. (1976) review of F.A. Hayek, *Law, Legislation and Liberty, Vol. I, Philosophy of the Social Sciences, Vol.6, pp. 369–72.* Toronto: York University.

# Part I
# Hayek in France

# 1 Hayek and the French engineers

*Robert F. Hébert*

It is probably no exaggeration to say that every important advance in economic theory during the last hundred years was a further step in the consistent application of subjectivism.

(Hayek, 1952)

## Introduction

In his provocative book, *The Counter-Revolution of Science* (1952), Hayek draws a distinction between the "objective" nature of science and the "subjective" nature of social studies. The object of science is to study things independently of what people think or do about them; whereas the object of social studies is to understand all that people know and believe about themselves, about other people, and about their external world – everything that determines their actions, including science itself. The misappropriation of the method of science to the study of social science is what Hayek calls *scientism*. Hayek identifies scientism with "the characteristic outlook of the engineer, whose conceptions of 'efficiency' constitute one of the most powerful forces through which this attitude has affected current views on social problems" (1952, p. 92). Scratch an engineer, in other words, and you will find a central planner underneath. According to Hayek, the potential mischief that the engineer can wreak in the social sphere is practically boundless, because:

So far as the solution of his engineering problem is concerned, he is not taking part in a social process in which others may take independent decisions, but lives in a separate world of his own. His technique, in other words, refers to typical situations defined in terms of objective facts, not to the problem of how to find out what resources are available or what is the relative importance of different needs. He has been trained in objective possibilities, irrespective of the particular conditions of time and place, in the knowledge of those properties of things which remain the same everywhere and at all times and which they possess irrespective of a particular human situation.

(Hayek, 1952, pp. 168–9)

It is this capacity for mischief that provided the subtitle to Hayek's book: "Studies on the abuse of reason."

Hayek traces the roots of modern socialist thought to nineteenth-century France. His most pointed criticisms are reserved for Claude-Henri Saint-Simon and Auguste Comte. Saint-Simon is said to have inspired the École Polytechnique, a training ground for state planners. Comte, who served as Saint-Simon's secretary and collaborator, is credited with the pernicious doctrine that the entire social order can be changed through revision of the law of property. Together, these two writers launched a kind of social physics that encouraged socialism and other forms of centralized control.

As an examination of the evolution of modern socialism that focuses on the French roots of interventionist thought, *The Counter-Revolution of Science* is a *tour de force*. But as a balanced presentation of the "engineering mentality," a concept that occupies a central role in Hayek's argument, it leaves much to be desired. Hayek's portrait of the engineering profession in nineteenth-century France, and of the influence of French institutions of technical learning that shaped the professional cadre of state engineers, is curiously one-sided. It tars all members of the profession with the same brush. Furthermore, it offers a blanket indictment of an institution, the École Polytechnique, as the breeding ground of socialist thought. It overlooks an opposite intellectual tradition in economic analysis and policy that coexisted alongside the train of thought criticized by Hayek. This other tradition sprang from the same French roots, but was more respectful of the competitive market order. It could be found among the ranks of a select group of state engineers who were associated with the École Nationale des Ponts et Chaussées, the postgraduate school for civil engineers. Key writers among this group of state engineers practically invented microeconomics a generation before the respective efforts of Menger, Jevons and Walras combined to form what we call the neoclassical "revolution." The leader of this small group of proto-neoclassicals was Jules Dupuit. He was the most capable and prominent – but by no means the only – member of an econo-engineering tradition in which state engineers systematically forged new tools of microeconomic theory. Robert Ekelund and I have explored this neglected, micro-analytic tradition in a book entitled *Secret Origins of Modern Microeconomics* (1999), recently published by the University of Chicago Press. In this chapter I would like to review some of the findings of this book and set them against the characterization that Hayek presents in his "Studies on the abuse of reason."

## Menger and Dupuit: was there a French Connection?

Hayek is the putative heir of Menger, the founder of Austrian economics. Any connection, therefore, between Menger and the French econo-engineering tradition may illuminate the genesis of Austrian economics and also bring into sharper focus Hayek's assessment of nineteenth-century French influences on economic method. Surprisingly, the possible filiation between Dupuit, the state engineer, and Menger, the founder of the Austrian School, has never been explored systematically or thoroughly. I am unaware of any citations of Dupuit in Menger's writings, yet Menger was mindful of efforts by Dupuit and his fellow engineers to advance economic theory and policy. At least there is strong circumstantial evidence to that effect. Menger's personal library, which now resides at the University of Hitotsubashi in Japan, contains a number of books by prominent French engineers of his era, including Dupuit.[1]

Dupuit and Menger both founded subjective traditions in value theory. Menger's seed fell on fertile ground and blossomed into what we now call Austrian economics. By contrast, Dupuit was known chiefly to specialists within the state corps of civil engineers in Paris, and to the members of the Société d'Économie Politique, whose preoccupation with the polemics of free trade made them indifferent to Dupuit's contributions to pure theory. As a result, Dupuit had a limited audience for his ideas and he attracted no disciples of any consequence. Unlike Menger, his works were never translated into English – except for fragments of his pioneer treatment of demand and marginal utility – and this inaccessibility of his writings in English has retarded a complete appreciation of Dupuit's position in the development of economic theory.

## The essence of the Austrian approach

The essence of the Austrian approach to economics, and its contrasting stance to orthodox neoclassicism, has been recently outlined by Huerta de Soto (1998), whose main points are these: (1) Economics is a theory of action rather than a theory of decision. (2) As a theory of human action, economics is necessarily based on subjectivism, which establishes our understanding of costs as well as demand. (3) Entrepreneurship is the leading force in economic theory, i.e. competition is a process of rivalry between entrepreneurs. (4) Mathematical formalism is inappropriate to economics, inasmuch as economics consists of human action. (5) The relation of economics to the empirical world is limited and tenuous because the "observing" scientist cannot obtain the practical information that is constantly being created and discovered in a decentralized way by the "observed" actor-entrepreneurs.

Most of these points are consistent with the microeconomic theory invented and advanced by Dupuit and his cohorts in the state corps of engineers. Like Menger, Dupuit advocated a subjective theory of value, a dynamic concept of economic activity, a theory of entrepreneurship that emphasized demand discovery, and a conceptualization of competition as a process of rivalry. His economic analysis also repudiated the idea of a single equilibrium price because it stressed uncertainty and imperfect competition. The basic points of departure consist of Dupuit's notion of cost – which is less systematic and less radically subjective than Menger's – and his view of the relation of economic analysis to the empirical world, which is more elastic than Menger's.

Despite his brilliant originality in developing a theory of demand linked to marginal utility, Dupuit did not develop a robust theory of costs. His writings reveal a basic understanding of opportunity costs, but, in general, Dupuit treated costs more in the manner of Marshall than of Menger, i.e. he thought of costs as objective and measurable. Indeed, attempting to measure the costs of public works was a major undertaking of the state engineers. Moreover, Dupuit advocated the introduction of mathematics to economic analysis, although, as we shall see below, he resisted the purely mechanistic method embraced by Cournot and Walras.

## Common roots

It should be noted at the outset that Dupuit's economics and Austrian economics shared common roots. Both trace their heritage to J. B. Say.[2] The impetus to Dupuit's formal treatment of consumer behavior was a desire to correct the errors of his fellow engineers, who tried to apply Say's demand theory to the economic evaluation of public works. In particular, *ponts* engineers, adopting a literal interpretation of Say's utility measure of value, attempted to gauge the utility of new public works by differences in the cost of transportation introduced by a new mode of transport (e.g. canal, road, etc.). Dupuit argued, in contrast, that the proper measure of utility is the difference in costs of *production* rather than in costs of transportation. Moreover, Dupuit asserted that the increases in quantity taken at lower prices do not take on the same value, but are valued discretely according to the law of diminishing marginal utility. These two insights put him at the cusp of modern demand theory and should have banished forever the classical confusions about value-in-use and value-in-exchange.[3]

Another stark reminder of the similarities between Dupuit and Menger can be found in Dupuit's examples of demand involving a *hierarchy of wants*. One example in particular illustrates how economic and engineering considerations frequently merge. To drive home his point about diminishing marginal utility, Dupuit cited a hypothetical case involving a city on a hillside, to which water must be pumped from below.

> Imagine a city situated at a great height, which has difficulty supplying itself with water. Assume that because of its circumstances, the inhabitants pay a daily rate of 50 francs per hectoliter by annual subscription. It is quite clear that every hectoliter of water consumed under these circumstances has a utility of at least 50 francs. [Suppose that] after recovery of the expenses of putting the pumps in place, the cost of the same quantity of water falls to 30 francs. What happens next? The first effect is that the person who previously bought a hectoliter will continue to do so, and will realize a benefit of 20 francs on the first hectoliter purchased; but it is likely that the reduction of price will induce him to increase his consumption; instead of using water parsimoniously for his personal use, he will use it for needs less essential and less pressing, the satisfaction of which he values ... somewhere between 30 and 50 francs. If new and improved pumps lower the price to 20 francs, the same individual may purchase 4 hectoliters, and

wash his house daily; give him water at 10 francs, he may buy 10 hectoliters, so as to irrigate his garden every day; at 5 francs, he may purchase
20 hectoliters in order to feed an ornamental pond; at 1 franc, he may wish
to buy 100 hectoliters to supply a fountain that flows continuously, etc.
Thus, *every product consumed has a different utility, not only for each consumer but also
for each of the needs he is seeking to satisfy.*

(Dupuit [1853], 1933, pp. 174–5)

It is but a short logical step from this passage to Menger's famous hierarchy-
of-wants approach, in which he outlined the subjective theory of consumer
behavior (cf. Menger [1871], 1981, pp. 131–2).[4]

## The primary role of the entrepreneur

The centrality of the entrepreneur within Austrian economics is well known.
Almost totally overlooked is the extent to which Dupuit's subjective theory of
utility led him to a similar theory of entrepreneurship. Establishing *utility* as the
central feature of his economics, Dupuit gave the entrepreneur a pivotal role in
the competitive marketplace. Dupuit described the entrepreneur's role as that of
demand discovery, which he conceived as a two-stage process. In the first place,
the entrepreneur must devise winning combinations of various utility-laden
*features*, or *characteristics*, that together constitute a desirable product or service.[5] In
the second place, the entrepreneur must estimate the utility that consumers
assign to certain goods or services and establish a pricing scheme that will induce
consumers to pay in proportion to the utility they receive.

In a clear anticipation of Lancaster's contemporary modification of demand
theory, Dupuit argued that competition is not merely about price but also about
the nature of the product itself. The notion that the entrepreneur faces price
uncertainty is one that had been emphasized by a long line of Continental
thinkers, such as San Bernardino, St Antonino, Cantillon, Turgot, and Say.
Dupuit stretched the idea of entrepreneurial uncertainty in a way that opened
the entrepreneur's decision nexus to all manner of product variations: quality,
location, space, time, and so forth. Acknowledging the price uncertainty stressed
by earlier writers, Dupuit also emphasized the uncertainty of the product itself.
He maintained that it is the entrepreneur's function to make consumers pay as
much as possible for the utility they receive. In order to succeed, the
entrepreneur must continually manipulate price *and* product, experimenting to
find profitable combinations of elements that will induce consumers to buy,
thereby increasing the consumer's utility and the entrepreneur's profit. This
"process" view of competition took product differentiation for granted, a fact
made clear in the following passage, in which Dupuit outlined a common sales
strategy.

The same merchandise, disguised in different shops under various forms, is
often sold at very different prices to the rich, the well-off, and the poor.

There is the *fine*, the *very fine*, the *extra fine*, and the *super fine*, which, although drawn from the same barrel, offer no real difference other than a better label and a higher price. Why? Because the same thing has a very different utility for the consumer. If the goods were sold merely at the average price, all those who attached less utility than that measured by this price would not buy, and thus would incur a loss; and the seller would lose because many of his customers would be paying for only a very small part of the utility they receive.

(Dupuit [1853], 1933, p. 177)[6]

This passage underscores Dupuit's thoroughly subjective notion of utility, which is to be found in the consumer's mental state. Dupuit asserted that product differences may be real or imagined, and his utility arguments embraced implicit as well as explicit markets. For example, he used utility to explain the rationale of intellectual and artistic productions, prizes and awards, and even marriage. "It is a serious mistake," he said, "to believe that man attaches a price only to material things" (Dupuit [1853], 1933, pp. 172–3). To Dupuit, all "goods" produce (public) utility, whether real or imagined, tangible or intangible. Menger was a bit more restrained. He refused to grant *goods-status* to *imaginary goods* (e.g. love potions, etc.), but he nevertheless included *useful actions* (e.g. friendship, love, etc.) in his definition of goods. "All goods," Menger wrote, "can, I think, be divided into the two classes of *material goods* (including all forces of nature insofar as they are goods) and of *useful human actions* (and inactions), the most important of which are labor services" ([1871], 1981, pp. 53, 55).

Other interesting contrasts involve qualitative differences in goods and how such differences affect value. From the outset Dupuit treated quality as an essential ingredient of each product, an element conveying utility to each purchaser. Describing the nature of technical improvements in transport, for example, Dupuit proclaimed: "Rarely does a cost-reducing change in production not also change the quality of products ... they become better or worse, larger or smaller, lighter or heavier, faster or slower, and so on ... all these qualities have a value that can be measured by the calculation of utility" ([1844], 1952, p. 54). Menger, too, was concerned with the effect of quality differences on value (Streissler, 1972). Thus he wrote: "If the differences, as to type or kind, between two goods are to be responsible for differences in their value, it is necessary that they also have different capacities to satisfy human needs. In other words, it is necessary that they have what we call, from an economic point of view, differences in *quality*." After careful deliberation, Menger concluded that "there can be no doubt ... that it is the importance of the needs that would remain unsatisfied if we did not have command of a particular good of not only the general type but also the specific quality corresponding to these needs that is, in this case too, the factor determining its value" ([1871], 1981, pp. 142–3).

## Dupuit and his contemporaries

The main departure of the Austrian tradition from the econo-engineering tradition was methodological. Central to Hayek's argument in *The Counter-Revolution of Science* is the distinction between the investigative methods of the physical sciences versus those of the social sciences. Hayek believed it illegitimate to apply the method of the physical sciences to a social science like economics.[7] Because they advanced economics as a branch of rational mechanics, Cournot and Walras are legitimate targets of Hayek's criticism. There is a tendency to include Dupuit among the guilty because of his presumed affinity with Cournot. However, the points of contrast between Cournot and Dupuit are far more instructive than their similarities on this issue.

## The uncoupling of Cournot and Dupuit

There can be little doubt that Dupuit thought seriously about the method appropriate to economic inquiry. He devoted two articles to this subject in 1863, and he peppered many of his earlier papers with asides regarding the promise and prospects of economic analysis, correctly applied (Dupuit, 1863a, 1863b). But he treated the topic rather obliquely, and in piecemeal fashion, so that his ideas must be assembled and evaluated *in toto* before they can be appreciated. Dupuit espoused a holistic method, which sought to integrate theory, institutions, and policy into a cohesive analytical system. His vision of the economic process was not constrained by mechanical notions of static behavior, but took on an organic character akin to the analysis of Say. Dupuit accepted *a priori* knowledge and speculations from Smith, Say, Ricardo, and others, but he pressed it through the sieve of mathematics and statistics in order to refine, and if necessary reformulate, basic principles. I wish to establish three basic points of contrast between him and Cournot.

First, Cournot and Dupuit disagreed on the role of utility in economic analysis. Cournot rejected utility as "unscientific," therefore denying it a legitimate place in economic theory. As a consequence, Cournot emptied his demand curve of any behavioral content. His so-called demand curve is a *sales* curve, as he aptly described it. In other words, it is an empirical, not a theoretical, relationship. By contrast, Dupuit believed that economics could become a science only if it could establish the *motivation* for exchange. As a result, his demand curve took the form of a behavioral law.

The second point is that despite his occasional resort to mechanical and physical analogies, Dupuit did not embrace economics as a branch of rational mechanics. Cournot stressed the abstract, mathematical nature of microeconomic theory, but he merely hinted at its applications. Dupuit stressed the operational nature of his theoretical concept immediately by placing marginal utility within an empirical framework of demand and consumer surplus.[8] He maintained that economic markets were, by nature, continuously evolving. Nevertheless, the vagaries of this world (i.e. constantly shifting demand parameters) require that theory be stated as exactly as possible. To Dupuit, theory was the only way to organize thoughts, and to produce solutions to practical problems. Geometry and mathematics provided useful tools to enhance theoretical precision. This confidence in mathematics did not, however, blind him to the limitations of existing data and empirical methods. Economics should use whatever means are at its disposal to increase precision, but it must not become a slave of mathematics in the blind search for precision. While readily admitting that human action was complex and (sometimes) confusing, Dupuit always insisted that it was only through rigorous mathematical and statistical inquiry that phenomena such as the value of a bridge or the amount of loss due to a new tax could be understood. But statistics and statistical methods should never take the place of theory, and sometimes theory must stand on its own.

The third point is that Cournot's analytical method employed a concept of competition alien to Dupuit. Cournot's view, a logical consequence of the rational mechanics approach, treated all products as homogeneous and emphasized market *structure* over market *process*. Using demand as the backbone of his analysis, Cournot explicated the nature of market adjustments progressively, beginning with the absence of competition (monopoly) and moving through the intermediate stage of *limited* competition (duopoly) to the final stage of *unlimited* competition. In the first two instances, demand is given; producers simply adjust to the nature of demand and the number of sellers in the market. The defining characteristic of the demand curve in the case of *unlimited* competition is that its slope becomes increasingly flat as the number of competitors increases, so that, in the limit of *pure* competition, no single firm has any appreciable impact on market price: as we say today, each firm is a price taker rather than a price maker.[9] This leads to a highly stylized notion of competition in which rivalry loses its ordinary meaning because competition takes on a *situational* rather than a *procedural* context. Dupuit developed a contrasting view of competition as a dynamic process in which entrepreneurs confront and deal with full market uncertainty as regards both product and price.

The outward similarities between Cournot and Dupuit have no doubt encouraged historians of economics to link them together. But in light of their important differences, the continued homogenization of Cournot and Dupuit is ill advised. Their kinship springs from the facts that they shared a national patrimony; they both favored mathematical economics; each in his own fashion pioneered the theory of demand and profit maximization; and both were neglected by their countrymen, so that their efforts bore little fruit during their lifetimes. But their differences were more dramatic, and they provide more insight into the subsequent development of economic theory. Later economists who walked in Cournot's footsteps gradually refined economics as an increasingly narrow branch of rational mechanics. Prominent successors (e.g. Jevons, Walras, Marshall) refused to be bound by Cournot's strictures against incorporating utility considerations into demand theory, but adopted Cournot's narrow definition of competition, which confined itself to homogeneous products and emphasized structure over process. This has led to the contemporary treatment of competition as a *situation* in which all rivalry disappears. The alignment of "orthodox" neoclassicists with Cournot established Cournot as an intellectual leader among the major architects of neoclassical economics, and effectively severed Dupuit's robust notion of competition from the mainstream. As the neoclassical era unfolded, only Menger bucked this tide, which makes him more like Dupuit than his contemporary neoclassicals.

## Conclusion

Despite certain fundamental differences between the Austrian tradition in economic theory founded by Menger, and the econo-engineering tradition that spawned Dupuit, there are also strong similarities. Dupuit persisted in raising the issue of whether economics is a science, and to what extent engineers could contribute to that science and use its principles in the service of the public. The essence of Dupuit's economics may be set out in relatively simple terms. Economics is fundamentally a process involving human behavior, and can be fully understood only as such. Vital to the ultimate understanding of the market process is the development of a body of deterministic economic analysis that uses mathematics as a *tool* and empirical verification as a check on the accuracy and relevance of results. Within this paradigm, Dupuit treated price discrimination and heterogeneous products and services (constantly developing through the stratagems of entrepreneurs) as commonplace, in contrast to the Anglo-Saxon habit of treating them as special cases. Dupuit realized that *net* surpluses emerge in the production and distribution of goods and services, and therein lies the key to understanding all the main issues of economics: production, distribution, and exchange. Because the creation and destruction of some of these surpluses occur within a political process, an understanding of the interface between political and market behavior is an essential accouterment of economic analysis. This view is decidedly not a preamble to socialism.

Perhaps we can never know fully the measure of influence that Dupuit might have had on Menger, but the possibility remains alive. It is therefore surprising that in *The Counter-Revolution of Science* Hayek issued a blanket condemnation against nineteenth-century French engineers. Not only does this assign guilt by association; it also ignores possible filiations between the respective contributions of Dupuit and Menger. In light of this discovery, should Hayek's indictment against the nineteenth-century French engineers be revised? In this chapter I have not challenged Hayek's assertions about the putative method to be followed by the social sciences, but I have raised some questions as to the nature and scope of his historiography.

## Acknowledgements

I wish to express my gratitude to R. B. Ekelund, Jr., my research partner of several decades, who developed many of the arguments in our recent book, *Secret Origins of Modern Microeconomics: Dupuit and the Engineers* (Chicago: University of Chicago Press, 1999), from which this chapter draws freely.

## Notes

1 Menger may have been more tolerant of the "engineering mentality" which Hayek excoriates in *Counter-Revolution*. At least he collected a sampling of the economic contributions of the *ponts* engineers. Among his personal holdings were the *Annales des Ponts et Chaussées*, from 1844 to 1849 (the years when Dupuit's major contributions appeared there), and books by Isnard, Dutens, Cazaux, Du Mesnil-Marigny, Dupuit, and Foville, all state engineers. For more detail on the place of these writers within the econo-engineering tradition, see Jaffé (1969) and Ekelund and Hébert (1999).

2 On Say as a forerunner of the Austrian method, see Rothbard (1995, II, pp. 12–18). Streissler (1990) provides a cogent review of distinctively German influences on Menger.

3 Dupuit ([1853], 1933, p. 167) chided the classical economists, and Say in particular: "J. B. Say, after having perfectly defined what was to be understood by the utility of wealth, has often confused it with value, pretending that this value in exchange was the measure of utility. Now, the nature of a measure is to increase or decrease proportionately with the measured quantity. ... In order that Say's opinion be admissible, it would then be necessary that value always be proportionate to utility. But that is not the relation that exists between these two quantities."

4 See also Menger's discussion of the "water-diamond paradox" on pp. 140–1, which is also strongly reminiscent of Dupuit.

5 The compatibility of this perspective with the characteristics-based demand theory of Kelvin Lancaster has been noted in Ekelund and Hébert (1991).

6 In practice, the entrepreneur's role is even more complicated, because all exchange involves transaction costs, such as relative convenience, location and waiting. Dupuit said that the entrepreneur must account for these factors in setting nominal prices. In transport markets, for example, he advised that nominal rates might be lowered to offset the transaction costs imposed by slow-moving trains, inconvenient schedules, railway congestion, and the opportunity costs associated with alternative modes of transport (see Dupuit [1849], 1933, pp. 159–62; 1852–3, 2, p. 343).

7 This argument, of course, goes beyond Hayek. It has been reprised more recently by Mirowski (1988, 1989) and others.

8 The full consequences of this development are spelled out in Ekelund and Hébert (1999), Chapter 5.

9 As Cournot ([1838], 1960, p. 90) phrased it: "The effects of competition have reached their limit, when each of the partial productions $D_k$ is inappreciable, not only with reference to the total production $D = F(p)$, but also with reference to the derivative $F'(p)$, so that the partial production $D_k$ could be subtracted from $D$ without any appreciable variation resulting in the price of the commodity."

## Bibliography

Cournot, A. A. ([1838] 1960) *Researches into the Mathematical Theory of the Principles of Wealth*, trans. Nathaniel Bacon. Reprint, New York: Augustus Kelley.

Dupuit, Jules ([1844] 1952) "On the Measure of the Utility of Public Works," trans. R. M. Barback, *International Economic Papers*, 2, pp. 83–110.

—— ([1849] 1933) "De l'influence des péages sur l'utilité des voies de communication." in *De l'utilité et de sa mesure: Écrits choisis et republiés par Mario de Bernardi*. Torino: La Riforma Sociale.

—— (1852–3) "Péage," in *Dictionnaire de l'économie politique*, ed. Charles Coquelin, 2, pp. 339–44. Paris: Guillaumin.

—— ([1853] 1933) "De l'utilité et de sa mesure: De l'utilité publique," in *De l'utilité et de sa mesure: Écrits choisis et republiés par Mario de Bernardi*. Torino: La Riforma Sociale.

—— (1863a) "L'économie politique est-elle une science ou n'est-elle qu'une étude?" *Journal des Économistes*, 2nd ser., 37, pp. 237–48.

—— (1863b) "Réponse de M. Dupuit à M. Baudrillart au sujet de l'article 'L'économie politique est-elle une science ou une étude?'" *Journal des Économistes*, 2nd ser., 37, pp. 474–82.

Ekelund, R. B., Jr. and Hébert, R. F. (1991) "Dupuit's Characteristics-Based Theory of Consumer Behavior and Entrepreneurship," *Kyklos*, Vol. 44, Fasc. 1, pp. 19–34.

—— (1999) *Secret Origins of Modern Microeconomics: Dupuit and the Engineers*. Chicago: University of Chicago Press.

Hayek, F. A. (1952) *The Counter-Revolution of Science: Studies on the Abuse of Reason*. Glencoe, IL: The Free Press.

Huerta De Soto, Jesus (1998) "The Ongoing Methodenstreit of the Austrian School," *Journal des Économistes et des Études Humaines*, 8 (1), pp. 75–113.

Jaffé, William (1969) "A. N. Isnard, Progenitor of the Walrasian General Equilibrium Model," *History of Political Economy*, 1, pp. 19–43.

Menger, Carl ([1871] 1981) *Principles of Economics*, trans. J. Dingwall and B. F. Hoselitz, introduction by F. A. Hayek. Glencoe, IL: The Free Press.

Mirowski, Philip (1988) *Against Mechanism: Protecting Economics from Science*. Totowa, NJ: Rowman & Littlefield.

—— (1989) *More Heat than Light: Economics as Social Physics, Physics as Nature's Economics*. New York: Cambridge University Press.

Rothbard, M. N. (1995) *Classical Economics: An Austrian Perspective on the History of Economic Thought*. Aldershot, Hants: Edward Elgar, Vol. II.

Streissler, Eric (1972) "To What Extent Was the Austrian School Marginalist?" *History of Political Economy*, 4, pp. 426–41.

—— (1990) "The Influence of German Economics on the Work of Menger and Marshall," in *Carl Menger and His Legacy in Economics*, Annual Supplement to Volume 22, *History of Political Economy*, ed. B. Caldwell. Durham, NC: Duke University Press, pp. 31–68.

# 2 Moral functionalism

*Jack Birner*

## Introduction

The abandonment of the idea that rules of behaviour and morality are given for all time by some supreme divine or human being or, more neutrally, that they are unalterable owes much to the philosophers of the Scottish Enlightenment. I will discuss the theories of the emergence and function of morality of two authors who, each in his own way, place themselves in this tradition: Friedrich Hayek and Émile Durkheim. Durkheim challenges a part of the intellectual tradition that Hayek strongly identifies himself with, and Hayek takes up the challenge. A discussion of their different approaches will lead us to some fundamental issues concerning the role of moral rules in society.

Durkheim's challenge consists in his attempt to create a place for sociology as a social science in its own right, independent from economics. That is what he does in his first book, *De la division du travail social* (*DTS*, 1893).[1] Durkheim's strategy relies on a comparison of the two pillars of the thought of the father of the then dominant political economy, Adam Smith. The message of *The Wealth of Nations* is that the pursuit of self-interest together with the division of labour lead to increased efficiency and economic growth. *The Theory of Moral Sentiments* argues that what makes a civil society possible is sympathy, the human capability of imagining the other's position. So, sympathy is based on the similarity of human beings. The division of labour, on the other hand, presupposes that humans are different. The new science of sociology will have justified itself if it succeeds in resolving this contradiction. This is what Durkheim sets out to do. He seeks an open confrontation with classical political economy by declaring that *the most important* consequence of the division of labour is not efficiency, but solidarity: "les services économiques qu'elle peut rendre sont peu de chose à côté de l'effet moral qu'elle produit, et sa véritable fonction est de créer entre deux ou plusiers personnes un sentiment de solidarité" (*DTS*, p. 19) ["the economic services that it can render are picayune compared to the moral effect that it produces, and its true function is to create in two or more persons a feeling of solidarity", p. 56].[2]

Half a century later, Hayek responds to the challenge, putting knowledge and its limits forward as the principal explanatory factors:

All the possible differences in men's moral attitudes amount to little, so far as their significance for social organization is concerned, compared with the fact that all man's mind can effectively comprehend are the facts of the narrow circle of which he is the center; that, whether he is completely selfish or the most perfect altruist, the human needs for which he *can* effectively care are an almost negligible fraction of the needs of all members of society.
("Individualism: True and False" (*ITF*), p. 14)[3]

In a later work, he even denies sociology's right to exist as a scientific discipline:

however grateful we all must be for some of the descriptive work of the sociologists, for which, however, perhaps anthropologists and historians would have been equally qualified, there seems to me still to exist no more justification for a theoretical discipline of sociology than there would be for a theoretical discipline of naturology apart from the theoretical disciplines dealing with particular classes of natural or social phenomena.

(*LLLIII*, p. 173)[4]

Not only is economics enough to explain why the interaction of millions of individuals creates an orderly and stable social structure instead of resulting in total chaos; it is also the *only* discipline that is capable of showing how the rules governing property and honesty have evolved so as to create a stable system of cooperation that maximizes the amount of information that is accessible to these individuals.[5] The pursuit of self-interest in a market society is the rule of behaviour that is both necessary and sufficient for this. Hayek criticizes Durkheim's explanation of coordination and cooperation in terms of morality interpreted as altruism: "This confusion [of identifying altruism with morality] stems in modern times at least from Emile Durkheim, whose celebrated work *The Division of Labour in Society* ... shows no comprehension of the manner in which rules of conduct bring about a division of labour and who tends, like the sociobiologists, to call an action 'altruistic' which benefits others" (*LLLIII*, p. 205). Hayek also attributes to Durkheim the "constructivist" idea that the faculty of reason enables man to successfully design and change social institutions and processes according to his desires.[6]

The severity of Hayek's criticism might lead one to expect that his theory of society is radically different from Durkheim's. But that is far from the truth. On the contrary, they have many elements in common. For instance, both share the idea that most social institutions evolve spontaneously, and that their evolution has consequences that no one ever intended. For both, the relationship between the individual and society is an important item on their research agenda. Both dwell at length on the relationship between scientific analysis and morality, and both come to the conclusion that a moral system is the outcome of an evolutionary process, and that imposing rules of conduct that are not adapted to the individuals with their specific capacities in their specific historical situation has a destabilizing effect.[7] The question why Hayek nevertheless brands Durkheim as one of the *bêtes noires* of social theorizing will be discussed at the end of this chapter. Let us first give a summary of Hayek's and Durkheim's theories of society, in preparation of a comparison between their views on morality.

## The spontaneous evolution of social institutions

Even though in the 1940s Hayek abandons technical economics and starts developing a theory of society, this does not constitute a clean break in his thought. From his economics he retains the emphasis on coordination. The idea of the market as a coordinating device is generalized to all social institutions as coordinating devices. They have evolved as the unintended consequences of individual actions. Another idea from his economics, viz. that individuals have only limited knowledge – they only know their immediate environment, and most of that knowledge is implicit – comes to play an increasingly important role.[8] What he preserves from his earlier work in psychology[9] is the concept of self-organization. Hayek adds to this an evolutionary perspective that becomes more prominent from about 1960, when *The Constitution of Liberty* was published, but whose origin can also be traced back to his psychology. In many articles[10] and in the three volumes of *Law, Legislation and Liberty* Hayek constructs a theory that describes social institutions as mostly spontaneously evolved, relatively stable patterns of behaviour or rules that coordinate the interaction among individuals. Institutions embody the accumulated, mainly implicit and temporally and spatially limited knowledge of individuals and their ancestors. These institutions are the survivors of a selection process. That is why they contain more knowledge than any single human being can ever dispose over or make explicit. That is how institutions enable individuals to survive in a highly complex environment. Deliberate interventions risk destroying this accumulated experience of the past.

In the course of social evolution, individuals have become used to, or, through adaptation, practically forced to, suppress a large part of the behavioural instincts that were adequate to the small and primitive groups of hunters and gatherers whose members all know each other personally. Interaction through markets has taught individuals (in an implicit, non-theoretical way) to accept the anonymous interaction patterns that are characteristic of modern society. This "Great Society", as Hayek calls it, relies on abstract rules that regulate the behaviour of millions of individuals who all pursue the interests of themselves and of their immediate friends and relatives. The modern market society has evolved in a process of variation and selection. In *The Constitution of Liberty* the process of variation is presented as originating with courageous individuals trying out, at their own risk, new forms of behaviour that may go against the norms and laws of their social environment. This is the same process that we find in Mandeville.[11] As to selection, Hayek rejects social Darwinism on the grounds that it builds upon the selection of innate capacities of individuals instead of culturally transmitted rules embodied in institutions. In its stead he proposes group selection. This has been criticized as being inconsistent with

Hayek's own methodological individualism. I will not go into this criticism here, except for pointing out that group selection solves a problem that arises within the Hayekian framework: it explains why certain moral rules were adopted despite the fact that they were "infringing or repressing some of the innate rules and replacing them by new ones which made the co-ordination of activities of larger groups possible" (*LLLIII*, pp. 160–1).[12]

Hayek's last contribution to social science, *The Fatal Conceit* (1988), is often referred to as the place where he presents his theory of cultural evolution. However, it is announced by that name in the Epilogue of the final volume of *Law, Legislation and Liberty* (1979). One of its earliest appearances is in "Notes on the Evolution of Systems of Rules of Conduct" (*Notes*, Hayek, 1967b). I will for the moment discuss it as it can be found in the first chapter of *The Fatal Conceit* (*FC*) of 1988. In biological evolution acquired features cannot be inherited. In social evolution, however, they can. Cultural evolution involves the transmission of behaviour patterns and information to offspring, not only from parents, but from innumerable other ancestors as well. This Lamarckian process of instruction makes cultural evolution much faster than biological evolution. Another difference is that in cultural evolution selection does not function through "the immediately perceived effects of actions that humans tend to concentrate on" but "rather, selection is made according to the consequences of the decisions guided by the rules of conduct in the long run [which depend] chiefly on rules of property and contract securing the personal domain of the individual" (*FC*, p. 76). This leads Hayek to the idea of group selection. On the other hand, biological and cultural evolution are similar in that both consist of a continuous adaptation to unforeseeable circumstances. There are no laws of biological and cultural evolution, and both involve the same principles of selection, viz. survival or reproductive success.

The comparison with biology leads Hayek to the conclusion that there are three main types of evolution in human affairs: genetic evolution, which produces instincts and instinctive behaviour, the evolution of rational thought, and cultural evolution. In time, culture comes after instinct and before reason.[13] Instinctive behaviour is sufficient for the coordination of the actions of individuals within small primitive groups, the members of which have common perceptions and objectives and are motivated by the instinct of solidarity. On the other hand, within the advanced or "abstract" society (the "extended order"), which is too complex to be fully understood by the human mind, coordination is ensured by abstract rules that have developed gradually. These rules govern private property, honesty, contracts, exchange, commerce, competition, profit, and the protection of privacy. They are transferred by tradition, learning, and imitation. There is a continuous tension between the rules governing individual behaviour and those governing the functioning of social institutions. The formation of supra-individual systems of coordination have forced individuals to change their natural or instinctive reactions: "Disliking these constraints so much, we can hardly be said to have selected them; rather these constraints selected us: they enable us to survive" (*FC*, p. 14).[14] The institutions that emerge are the result of certain individuals stumbling upon solutions to particular problems in a process of competition. Every type of evolution operates through competition, which acts as a process of discovery. However, each type of environment or stage of society requires its own type of rules, and following the rules that were adapted to one environment in a different one may lead to disaster. This is particularly the case with small, primitive groups and modern extended society. "If we were to apply the unmodified, uncurbed rules of the micro-cosmos ... to the macro-cosmos (our wider civilisation) ... we would destroy it. Yet if we were always to apply the rules of the extended order to our intimate groupings, we would crush them" (*FC*, p. 18).

Let us now turn to Durkheim's theory of society of *De la division du travail social*. A summary will do for now as we will come back to his sociology in the section on functionalism. Whereas for Hayek, at least until 1960, the individual is the methodological starting point of all social theorizing, for Durkheim it is the social framework. Without it, all the individualistic elements that classical economics has adduced for explaining the rise and success of industrialized market societies, such as the pursuit of self-interest and competition, are centrifugal forces. Society is based on "association", the sharing by individuals of hereditary or geographical characteristics. Social density makes for cooperation, and not until a cooperative framework exists can the market and other social institutions start playing their coordinating role. In a piece of conjectural history that has a similar function as in Hayek, Durkheim shows the evolution of society from the primitive tribe, whose members are completely similar and which is ruled by the same collective consciousness that is orientated towards concrete circumstances, to the highly diversified modern industrial society, where individuals identify themselves with their professional group rather than with society as a whole. In the beginning were the *hordes*, homogeneous primitive tribes. They are kept together by a type of social cohesion that rests on similarity. The second stage in the development is *primitive society*, which consists of a repetition of identical hordes. Next in the course of evolution are *segmentary societies*. They arise due to a diversification that takes place as soon as one individual (by a mutation that Durkheim does not explain) distinguishes himself from his fellow-men by his leadership capacities. Even though the authority of these clan chiefs is a new element, similarity is still the only basis of social cohesion or solidarity. These societies are regulated by *repressive law*, which imposes sanctions on infringements of the values and rules that are shared by all members. There is no place for individual personality. The form of social cohesion that rules these societies is *mechanical solidarity*.

This starts to change with the increase in geographical and social density. The fact that the members of society now have to keep track of a greater number of individuals makes it necessary for collective consciousness to come to terms with more abstract spatial and social relationships. This involves a weakening of the hold of tradition. It also marks the birth of abstract thought, which is an additional source of variations among individuals. It also creates greater individual liberty which together with the rationalization of society underlies the process of specialization, in which mechanical solidarity is gradually replaced by a different form of cohesion, *organic solidarity*. The transition is reflected in the legal system; *repressive law*, which punishes infractions on the common social code, gives more and more way to *restitutive law*, a system of rules that regulate how torts can be put right.[15]

Although the analysis of law has an important place in the work of both, its function is different. Durkheim arrives at it via a methodological consideration. Solidarity is a moral concept, and as such it cannot be observed. It can only be investigated *indirectly* (cp. *DTS*, p. 28), through the legal system. It is the empirical manifestation of the state of solidarity in society because it is the system of binding rules that have been developed to suppress conflicts. In Hayek's work, the legal system is important for two different reasons. First, because it constitutes the body of rules that enables the market order to function. Second, because it is a prime example of a spontaneously evolved system of rules. The legal system is the set of "institutions that Western man has developed to secure individual liberty" (*The Constitution of Liberty* (*CL*), p. 5). Hayek's treatment of law is also more limited than Durkheim's in that he concentrates almost exclusively on property law. For Durkheim property law belongs to the part of restitutive law which he calls negative: it is based on abstention and links a thing to a person. Positive restitutive law, or the law of cooperation, is the set of the rules that regulate cooperation. It is this positive restitutive law that increases in importance as we come closer to modern society.

Durkheim wants to explain how the complex process of the division of labour and the concomitant emergence of social cohesion could have taken place without anyone, or any central organ, consciously organizing it so as to result in a relatively stable social system. His fascination by spontaneous evolution is shared by Hayek, who arrives at the same cautious, non-interventionist consequences as Durkheim, as we will see in the next section.

## A social science of morality

The relationship between scientific analysis and morality is something Durkheim is concerned with from the very beginning of his scientific career. He writes in *DTS* that the scientific explanation of norms and values is his main objective; morality is "un ensemble de faits acquis qu'il faut étudier" (*DTS*, p. XL) ["a collection of facts to study", p. 35] and not "une sorte de législation toujours révocable que chaque penseur institue à nouveau" (ibid.) ["a sort of revocable law-making which each thinker establishes himself", p. 35]. Durkheim harnesses this legal and moral anti-positivism to his strategic goal of launching sociology. *DTS* is an investigation into the moral effects of the division of labour. The concept of morality not only involves the study of rules of behaviour, it also encompasses the idea of J.S. Mill of social science as moral science, the disciplines that involve the mental attitudes of individuals.[16] For Durkheim, "moral" refers to the linking of conscience (or consciousness) among individuals, something which economics with its narrow focus on self-interest as the source of human action cannot explain:

> [S]i l'intérêt rapproche les hommes, ce n'est jamais que pour quelques instants; il ne peut créer entre eux qu'un lien extérieur. Dans le fait de l'échange, les divers agents restent en dehors les uns des autres, et l'opération terminée, chacun se retrouve et se reprend tout entier. Les consciences ne sont que superficiellement en contact; ni elles se pénètrent, ni elles n'adhèrent fortement les unes aux autres. Si même on regarde au fond des choses, on verra que toute harmonie d'intérêts recèle un conflit latent ou simplement ajourné. ... L'intérêt est, en effet, ce qu'il y a de moins constant au monde.
>
> (*DTS*, pp. 180–1)

> [If interest relates men, it is never for more than a few moments. It can create only an external link between them. In the fact of exchange, the various agents remain outside of each other, and when the business has been completed, each one retires and is left entirely on his own. Consciences are only superficially in contact; they neither penetrate each other, nor do they adhere. If we look further into the matter, we shall see that this total harmony of interests conceals a latent or deferred conflict. ... There is nothing less constant than interest.]
>
> (pp. 203–4)

But there is more to the meaning of morality. Moral is what serves a certain social function: "tout fait d'ordre vital – comme sont les faits moraux, – ne peut généralement pas durer s'il ne sert à quelque chose, s'il ne répond à quelque besoin" (p. XLI) ["each vital fact – and a moral fact is vital – cannot endure if it is not of some use, if it does not answer some need", p. 35]. The "quelque chose", the need the satisfaction of which is the function of morality, is the subject of *DTS*. Durkheim summarizes it at the end of the book: "Est moral ... tout ce qui est source de solidarité, tout ce qui force l'homme à compter avec autrui, à régler ses mouvements sur autre chose que les impulsions de son égoïsme, et la moralité est d'autant plus solide que ces liens sont plus nombreux et plus forts" (*DTS*, p. 394). ["Everything which is a source of morality is moral, everything which forces man to take account of other men is moral, everything which forces him to regulate his conduct through something other than the striving of his ego is moral, and morality is as solid as these ties are numerous and strong", p. 398.]

The various connotations of the concept of morality are merged in Durkheim's idea that attempts to improve the social world are conditional on a scientific analysis of the mechanisms by which it is ruled. This leads him to be very cautious about the possibility of intervention. One must start by presuming that a certain status quo responds to a particular need: "tant donc que la preuve contraire n'est pas faite, il a droit à notre respect" (*DTS*, p. XLI) ["until the opposite is proved true, such vital facts are entitled to our respect", p. 35]. If we must intervene in the moral sphere, it is better to do so piece-meal, basing ourselves upon scientific analysis: "l'intervention est ... limitée: elle a pour objet, non de faire de toutes pièces une morale à coté ou au-dessus de celle qui règne, mais de corriger celle-ci ou de l'améliorer partiellement. Ainsi disparaît l'antithèse que l'on a tenté d'établir entre la science et la morale" (ibid.) ["the intervention is ... limited; it has for its object, not to make an ethic completely different from the prevailing one, but to correct the latter, or partially to improve it. Thus, the antithesis between science and ethics ... disappears", pp. 35–6].

In the case of Hayek, the scientific explanation of the emergence of moral rules appears rather late as an explicit item on the research agenda. In his published work it is mentioned for the first time in the concluding chapter of Volume III of *Law, Legislation and Liberty* of 1979. However, he had discussed the subject at least as early as 1944, in *The Road to Serfdom* (particularly in chapter 10), and more extensively in 1945, in "Individualism: True and False" (*ITF*). There, his main premise is that "without principles we drift" (*ITF*, p. 2). The question "Is there anywhere a consistent philosophy to be found which supplies us not merely with the moral aims but with an adequate method for their achievement?" (ibid.) is answered affirmatively. The philosophy is that of the Scottish Enlightenment, which Hayek distinguishes sharply from the French constructivist tradition to which he reckons Durkheim belongs. In the Introduction I have already mentioned that Hayek's rejection of Durkheim is odd in view of the many parallels with his own thought. They extend to Hayek's thought on morality. Hayek shares with Durkheim the idea that the peculiarity of the social sciences lies in the fact that they deal with mental phenomena. The whole of *The Counter-Revolution of Science* (*CRS*) is devoted to exploring the consequences of the fact that they are moral sciences. Another important point of agreement is that morality is a gradually and spontaneously evolved system of rules of conduct that we must not intervene with at all, or at the most piecemeal.

The emergence of rules of behaviour is the subject of *Notes*. By studying rules of behaviour in an evolutionary context the link between science and morality is tightened. The article focuses on the function of moral rules for increasing the predictability and hence the stability of the social environment:

> The knowledge of some regularities of the environment will create a prefer-
> ence for those kinds of conduct which produce a confident expectation of
> certain consequences, and an aversion to doing something unfamiliar and
> fear when it has been done. This creates a sort of connection between the
> knowledge that rules exist in the objective world and a disinclination to
> deviate from those rules commonly followed in action, and therefore
> between the belief that events follow rules and the feeling that one "ought"
> to observe rules in one's conduct.
>
> (Hayek, 1967a, p. 80)

This leads to the conclusion that "[t]he factual belief that such and such is the only way in which a certain result can be brought about, and the normative belief that this is the only way in which it ought to be pursued, are thus closely associated" (ibid., p. 80). That Hayek does not defend a moral naturalism can be concluded from the last footnote. It contains the suggestion (interesting but not elaborated) that the descriptive or explanatory rules on which individuals base their behaviour in society "may be meaningful only within a framework of a system of normative rules" (Hayek, 1967a, p. 81, n. 20).

Hayek intended to work out the project of a scientific explanation of morals in *The Fatal Conceit*. As we have seen above, it contains the elements of a theory of cultural evolution that tries to develop the ideas in *Notes*. The most important additions are that culture, and hence morality, constitutes a level of evolutionarily emerged rules that is situated between instinct and reason, and that the success of a particular social order can be measured by the number of individuals it can keep alive. The project was never finished; *FC* is a patchwork of brief chapters and appendices without the sense of unity that characterizes Hayek's earlier books. No doubt this is due to the fact that Hayek's health was deteriorating and that the book was written together with Bill Bartley.[17] I will therefore discuss a text that was certainly written by Hayek himself, and that shows more coherency, the *Origins* manuscript referred to above.[18] Hayek writes there that the problem of the scientific study of cultural evolution (and hence, we may add, of morality) threatened to become unmanageable until he introduced group selection. Cultural evolution depends on it. This explains why our morals provide us with the means of adapting to unforeseen and unforeseeable conditions for which reason is insufficient. In this context, Hayek refers to the collective mind in the sense of the moral rules the members of a social group have in common. Even though this collective consciousness remains in permanent interaction with the minds of the individuals, it is different from the contents of individual minds, and it has an autonomous existence. This is very similar to Durkheim's idea of collective consciousness. Hayek chooses a non-Darwinian evolutionary framework for dealing with the complexity of the origin of morals. Durkheim, too, is critical of an application of Darwinism to social processes.[19] Hayek addresses the same problem as Durkheim: how social evolution in a non-Darwinian process creates moral rules.

## Functionalism

*La division du travail social* is as much a methodological manifesto as a theory of society. I have already mentioned that it serves to establish sociology as an independent discipline. The other sense in which the book is methodological is that it is intended as an exercise in functional explanation. On the first page of Book I Durkheim defines function as

> le rapport de correspondance qui existe entre ces mouvements [vitaux] et les besoins de l'organisme. ... Se demander quelle est la fonction de la division

du travail, c'est donc chercher à quel besoin elle correspond; quand nous aurons résolu cette question, nous pourrons voir si ce besoin est de même nature que ceux auxquels correspondent d'autres règles de conduite dont le caractère moral n'est pas discuté.

(*DTS*, p. 11)

[the relation existing between these [vital] movements and corresponding needs of the organism. ... To ask what the function of the division of labor is, is to seek for the need it supplies. When we have answered this question, we shall be able to see if this need is of the same sort as those to which other rules of conduct respond whose moral character is agreed upon.]

(p. 49)

This might suggest that Durkheim subscribes to a theory in which final causes are a central element. He also distinguishes between normal and abnormal forms of social life. Usually, such a distinction immunizes a theory against falsifications, turning it into a piece of metaphysics, or worse, a tautology. This suspicion is fed, for instance, by what Durkheim writes on p. 343: "Si, normalement, la division du travail produit la solidarité sociale, il arrive cependant qu'elle a des résultats tout différents ou même opposés." ["Though normally the division of labor produces social solidarity, it sometimes happens that it has different, and even contrary results", p. 535.] Does Durkheim's functionalism make his theory empirically empty? To see whether that is the case, let us examine his procedure in more detail. Durkheim discusses three examples of an anomalous division of labour. The first is that of *industrial or economic crises*. They represent a case where the division of labour fails to produce solidarity. In general, if the relationships among the various organs that make up society are not regulated in the sense that the division of labour has created a sufficiently developed system of rules, then that society is in a state of *anomie*. This is due to the fact that these organs have not been in contact with one another sufficiently or for a sufficiently long period. Another possible cause is that the organs are separated by a dark zone, a "milieu opaque", so that the rules cannot establish in sufficient detail the conditions of equilibrium. In that case,

les relations, étant rares, ne se répètent pas assez pour se déterminer; c'est à chaque fois nouvelle de nouveaux tâtonnements. Les lignes de passage suivies par les ondes de mouvements ne peuvent pas se creuser parce que ces ondes elles-mêmes sont trop intermittentes.[20] Du moins, si quelques règles parviennent cependant à se constituer, elles sont générales et vagues; car, dans ces conditions, il n'y a que les contours les plus généraux des phénomènes qui puissent se fixer. Il en sera de même si la contiguïté, tout en étant suffisante, est trop récente ou a trop peu duré.

(*DTS*, pp. 360–1)

[Relations, being rare, are not repeated enough to be determined; each time there ensues new groping. The lines of passage taken by the streams of movement cannot deepen because the streams themselves are too intermittent. If some rules do come to constitute them, they are, however, general and vague, for under these conditions it is only the most general contours of phenomena that can be fixed. The case will be the same if the contiguity, though sufficient, is too recent or has not endured long enough.]

(p. 369)

In those conditions, with the growth of industry and the market becoming practically unlimited, producers can no longer see all relevant factors directly, and production proceeds unfettered and gets out of control; it can only proceed by random "tâtonnements".[21] The different organization of industry that would be needed to cope with this has not kept pace with the very rapid changes, so that the various conflicting interests have not yet found the time to find a new equilibrium (*DTS*, p. 362). In order for the division of labour to have a non-disequilibrating effect, the worker must not lose his fellow workers from sight, so that he is aware of the effects he has on them and they on him. The labourer is thus not a machine that repeats itself,[22] but he feels that he is useful ("sert"). In order for that to be possible, he need not be able to survey large parts of the social horizon; it is sufficient that he sees enough of it to understand that his actions have a goal that lies outside himself (an external goal, *DTS*, p. 365).[23]

The second example of an anomalous division of labour is "la division du travail contrainte", *forced division of labour*.[24] Durkheim observes that the existence of rules is not enough, for sometimes the rules are the *cause* of the anomaly, for example in the case of class struggle (*DTS*, p. 368). In order for the division of labour to create solidarity, it is not enough that everybody performs his task, but also that that task suits him ("convient"). The division of labour must be adapted to the natural distribution of talents: "La seule cause qui détermine alors la manière dont le travail se divise est la diversité des capacités. ... Ainsi se réalise de soi-même l'harmonie entre la constitution de chaque individu et sa condition" (*DTS*, 369). ["The only cause determining the manner in which work is divided, then, is the diversity of capacities. ... Thus, the harmony between the constitution of each individual and his condition is realized of itself", p. 376.] Compare also *DTS*, p. 370, where he writes: "La contrainte ne commence que quand la réglementation, ne correspondant plus à la nature vraie des choses, et, par suite, n'ayant plus de base dans les moeurs, ne se soutient que par la force." ["Constraint only begins when regulation, no longer corresponding to the true nature of things, and, accordingly, no longer having any basis in customs, can only be validated through force", p. 377.] Durkheim speaks in this context of *spontaneity*: "par spontanéité, il faut entendre l'absence, non pas simplement de toute violence expresse et formelle, mais de tout ce qui peut entraver, même indirectement, le libre déploiement de la force sociale que chacun porte en soi" (*DTS*, p. 370) ["by spontaneity we must understand not simply the absence of all express violence, but also of everything that can even indirectly shackle the free unfolding of the social force that each carries in himself", p. 377]. And "le travail ne se divise spontanément qui si la société est constitutuée de manière à ce que les inégalités sociales expriment exactement les inégalités naturelles" (*DTS*, p. 370) ["labor is divided spontaneously only if society is constituted in such a way that social inequalities exactly express natural inequalities", p. 377].

The third anomalous type of the division of labour is the *lack of functional activity*, which can be characterized as a lack of a particular type of coordination of the functions. The continuity with which the various functions interact and need one another has to keep pace with the increased division of labour; they must feel their interdependence (*DTS*, p. 387). To specialize more means to work harder (ibid.). However, if – for instance as a consequence of a wrong central organization within an enterprise or a society – the various specialized functions do not have enough to do, this causes defects in their coordination. Working harder constitutes

> une nouvelle raison qui fait de la division du travail une source de cohésion sociale. Elle ne rend pas seulement les individus solidaires, comme nous l'avons dit jusqu'ici, parce qu'elle limite l'activité de chacun, mais encore parce qu'elle l'augmente. Elle accroît l'unité de l'organisme, par cela seul qu'elle en accroît la vie; du moins, à l'état normal, elle ne produit pas un de ces effets sans l'autre.
>
> (*DTS*, pp. 389–90)

> [a new reason why the division of labor is a source of social cohesion. It makes individuals solidary, as we have said before, not only because it limits the activity of each, but also because it inceases it. It adds to the unity of the organism, solely through adding to its life. At least, in its normal state, it does not produce one of these effects without the other.]
>
> (p. 395)

This passage makes it particularly clear that the main function of Durkheim's anomalies is to clarify the content of his theory of social cohesion. The conclusion of the discussion of Durkheim's anomalous forms is therefore that they serve to give his theory more rather than less empirical content. Nor do final causes have a role to play in Durkheim's functionalism. Functional is that which arises spontaneously, as a solution to the complexity of life in society. The division of labour

> consiste … dans le partage de fonctions jusque là communes. Mais ce partage ne peut être exécuté d'après un plan préconçu; on ne peut dire par avance où doit se trouver la ligne de démarcation entre les tâches, une fois qu'elles seront séparées; car elle n'est pas marquée avec une telle évidence dans la nature des choses, mais dépend, au contraire, d'une multitude de

circonstances. Il faut donc que la division se fasse d'elle-même et progres-
sivement.

(*DTS*, p. 260)

[consists in the sharing of functions up to that time common. But this
sharing cannot be executed according to a preconceived plan. We cannot
tell in advance where the line of demarcation between tasks will be found
once they are separated, for it is not marked so evidently in the nature of
things, but depends, on the contrary, upon a multitude of circumstances.
The division of labor, then, must come about of itself and progressively.]

(p. 276)

Let us now turn to Hayek's method. Above, in the discussion of his theory of
society and moral rules, I have indicated the importance of the concept of social
institutions as the unintended consequences of individual actions, and of the
contribution of both individuals and institutions to the maintenance of the social
framework as a whole. Even though Hayek never puts these ideas in terms of
individuals and institutions serving the goal of stability, his theory has a strong
functionalist ring to it. Is it functionalist? Since Hayek is always very explicit
about his own methodology, the first place to turn to for an answer is his many
articles on methodology, and, of course, *CRS*. Hayek never describes himself as a
functionalist.[25] However, chapter 8 in *CRS* on "'Purposive' social formations"
leaves no doubt that he accepts the main tenets of functionalism. He mentions
the notion of unintended consequences, i.e. the fact that human actions often
have functions different from the one for which they were undertaken.
Furthermore, phenomena such as individual freedom and tacit knowledge are
mentioned as serving to maintain a particular social framework:

If we survey the different fields in which we are constantly tempted to
describe phenomena as "purposive" though they are not directed by a
conscious mind, it becomes rapidly clear that the "end" or "purpose" they
are said to serve is always the preservation of a "whole", of a persistent
structure of relationships, whose existence we have come to take for granted
before we understood the nature of the mechanism which holds the parts
together. The most familiar instances of such wholes are biological organ-
isms. Here the conception of the "function" of an organ as an essential
condition for the persistence of the whole has proved to be of the greatest
heuristic value.

(*CRS*, pp. 81–2)

By emphasizing the as-if character of many social explanations, Hayek
defends a sophisticated functionalism. He does not reject the use of explanations
that employ purposive or functionalist concepts: "It is easily seen how paralyzing
an effect on research it would have had if the scientific prejudice had banned the
use of all teleological concepts in biology and, e.g., prevented the discoverer of a

new organ from immediately asking what 'purpose' or 'function' it serves" (*CRS*, p. 82). He is against using them in an anthropomorphic sense:

> As the terms of ordinary language are somewhat misleading, it is necessary to move with great care in any discussion of the "purposive" character of spontaneous social formations. The risk of being lured into an illegitimate anthropomorphic use of the term purpose is as great as that of denying that the term purpose in this connection designates something of importance. In its strict original meaning "purpose" indeed presupposes an acting person deliberately aiming at a result. The same, however, ... is true of other concepts like "law" or "organization", which we have nevertheless been forced, by the lack of other suitable terms, to adopt for scientific use in a non-anthropomorphic sense. In the same way we may find the term "purpose" indispensable in a carefully defined sense.
>
> (*CRS*, p. 81)

The analogy with biology is recommended as useful for social science. This does not imply an endorsement of organicism, as is shown by his rejection of historicism in *CRS*.[26] This is closely related to Hayek's use of conjectural history, which is a typically functionalist device.[27] Hayek calls it *reconstruction*.[28] Every reconstruction is a reconstruction in the light of some point of view, or of some *function*; without this anchoring device, a reconstruction would be pointless (if not impossible). Hayek is very clear about this in *Notes*. There the method of conjectural history is described as

> the reconstruction of a hypothetical kind of process which may never have been observed but which, if it had taken place, would have produced the phenomena of the kind we observe. The assumption that such a process has taken place may be tested by seeking for as yet unobserved consequences which follow from it, and by asking whether all regular structures of the kind in question can be accounted for by that assumption.
>
> (Hayek, 1967a, p. 75)

This is yet another defence of a counterfactual or as-if approach, one that even aims at producing testable implications. This method is merged with a functionalist approach in two intervening steps. One is the argument that the social sciences differ from the natural sciences in that the complex structures which they study are in their turn composed of other complex structures, viz. the sets of rules which govern the behaviour of individuals who are equipped with a mind. The second step is the introduction of an evolutionary process in which rules of behaviour have been selected by their adaptedness to the system. Again, Hayek's conclusion is a defence of functionalism:

> This implies a sort of inversion of the relation between cause and effect in the sense that the structures possessing a kind of order will exist because the

elements do what is necessary to secure the persistence of that order. The "final cause" or "purpose", i.e. the adaptation of the parts to the requirements of the whole, becomes a necessary part of the explanation of why structures of the kind exist: we are bound to explain the fact that the elements behave in a certain way by the circumstance that this sort of conduct is most likely to preserve the whole. ... A "teleological" explanation is thus entirely in order so long as it does not imply design by a maker.

(Hayek, 1967a, p. 77)

The conclusion is that Hayek is a functionalist.[29] Not only that, but also, like Durkheim, he is a sophisticated functionalist who is fully aware of the dangers a literal interpretation of the notion of function or purposiveness has, and who for that reason relies on the tools of counterfactual reconstruction and evolutionary explanation. Now we have the ingredients to examine Durkheim's and Hayek's theories of morality.

## Functional morality

But before proceeding to a comparison between Hayek's and Durkheim's thoughts on morality, a problem must be addressed that has been left open so far. It concerns the question what it is that we compare. In the case of Durkheim I have limited myself mainly to *DTS*, whereas in the case of Hayek the picture is composed of elements borrowed from various episodes in his development that vary from *ITF* of 1945 to *FC* of 1988. On a number of issues Hayek's thought seems to evolve (for instance on the importance of individual freedom as a moral value), whereas on others he seems to be more constant. I "solve" this problem radically by reconstructing Hayek's thought on morality in the most coherent way possible, even though I shall occasionally discuss its evolution where I think it useful to do so. This may not be satisfactory from a purely historical point of view. However, I think the possible disadvantages of this approach are compensated by the gains in understanding of the role of morality in society as a problem in its own right that I hope will result from the comparative discussion of Durkheim and Hayek.

Let us begin by comparing the methods Hayek and Durkheim employ in developing their theories of morality. Both attempt to find an uncontestable, or at least an uncontested, basis for morality. For Durkheim it is the rule that commands us to realize *the essential characteristics of the collective type* (*DTS*, p. 393). Since these have been defined by Durkheim as solidarity, it follows that moral rules "énoncent les conditions fondamentales de la solidarité sociale" (*DTS*, p. 393) ["enunciate the fundamental conditions of social solidarity", p. 398]. And since solidarity rests on the division of labour, the latter "devient du même coup la base de l'ordre moral" (*DTS*, p. 396) ["becomes, at the same time, the foundation of the moral order", p. 401]. So, because it is a fundamental characteristic of man that he is a social being, morality is that which is conducive to the establishment and strengthening of social cohesion. Hayek shares the idea that morality is that which rests on, or follows from, human nature. He adopts this idea from the philosophy of the Scottish Enlightenment, or, as he calls it, "true individualism": "The great concern of the great individualist writers was ... to find a set of institutions by which man could be induced, by his own choice and *from the motives which determined his ordinary conduct*, to contribute as much as possible to the need of all others ..." (*ITF*, pp. 12–13, emphasis added). In later writings this is elaborated into the criterion of the survival of the greatest number of individuals as the value by which a particular social order should be judged. Underlying this idea is a peculiar logical argument: since morals regulate human relationships, there can be no morality without human beings. This is supplemented by two arguments that we find in *origins*. The first is that morals are rules of behaviour that have been accepted by individuals because they have been exposed to them long enough, even though they do not understand their rationale. If a sufficiently large number of individuals accepts the moral rules, keeping to them becomes an advantage because of the network externalities (as they would now be called) they create. The second argument is aimed against all egalitarian moral systems. If, says Hayek, we had enforced social justice in the sense of an equitable distribution of property, we would never have reached the current state of development in which many more people are born and survive than would have been possible in an egalitarian society. So, those who defend an equitable distribution of property and income (i.e. the socialists) have not understood that the apparently unjust principle of "several property" is more beneficial than an equal distribution, under which the masses of the poor would have been far smaller, not because more people would belong to the haves instead of the have-nots, but simply because many fewer people would be alive.[30] So, the existence of morality logically presupposes the existence of (at least two) human beings, and therefore life is a necessary condition for morality. Hayek concludes from this that morals are not idealistic but materialistic, since their function is to keep us alive.[31]

Durkheim uses the same type of argumentation. It can be summarized as follows. All social science is moral science; its basic ingredients are intentionality and relatively stable mental constructs individuals somehow share. This presupposes that they interact regularly. This in turn presupposes the existence of a social framework, which again presupposes the existence of solidarity, which implies the existence of rules of behaviour that allow individual mental attitudes to be made compatible with one another. So in the case of both authors we have a peculiar mix of logical, methodological, and theoretical arguments that sustain their theories of morality. But even though their procedures for finding the foundations of morality are very similar, Hayek and Durkheim come to different conclusions as to its content. For Durkheim morality is everything that keeps man from being selfish[32] and favours cooperation. Hayek *rejects* unselfishness, at least as a moral value of the market order,[33] and emphasizes the value of coordination.[34] For Durkheim, society has a mitigating effect on egoism.[35] For Hayek self-interest (in the extended sense of caring also for one's immediate social environment[36]) is the value that holds the order of the market together and makes it work. Everything that is aimed at taking away this motivation (and Hayek singles out all proposals that are based on the promotion of altruism) jeopardizes the continued functioning of the market order.

In summary, Hayek and Durkheim both explain the function of moral rules by using *conjectural history*. Both are *moral functionalists*. They share the central idea that *the function of moral rules is to preserve the stability of the social framework*,[37] though they give it a different content. For Hayek, the system of morals serves to keep the greatest possible number of people alive. For Durkheim morality has the function of maintaining social cohesion. In addition to these similarities, let me indicate several others. For both authors *moral rules rest on the way in which our fellow citizens judge our behaviour*.[38] A further common element is that *moral rules involve a cognitive dimension*.[39] Another shared characteristic is their *empiricism* in the sense that a theory of morality should be empirically testable. For instance, in *Origins* Hayek criticizes hedonism, utilitarianism and egalitarianism by saying that they have never been put to the test of determining whether they help to maintain or to improve the survival of the group.[40] The ultimate test for any system of moral rules lies in the number of individuals it can keep alive.[41] In Durkheim we find a similar empiricist strand. Scientific method relies on observation. Solidarity is a moral concept, and as such it is unobservable. That is why Durkheim studies its most important empirical manifestation, the legal system. There is also a second sense in which Durkheim and Hayek share an empiricist approach. Both emphasize that in order for individuals to accept moral rules, they must be exposed to them long enough.[42]

## The cement of the social universe

In the above, Durkheim's emphasis on solidarity and altruism has repeatedly been contrasted with Hayek's idea that the pursuit of self-interest is the force that keeps society together. It is now time to go into the details of what Hayek means by self-interest, and what its place is. In *ITF* Hayek stresses "the value of the family and all the common efforts of the small community and group ... local autonomy and voluntary associations ..." (p. 23). In short, the intermediate groups, whose "grip"on the individual is negatively correlated with the rate of suicide in Durkheim's *Suicide*. So, the integration of the individual in the inter- mediate groups is a direct empirical measure of *social cohesion*. For Hayek, however, the function of these groups lies in their greater *efficiency* in making individuals achieve their goals than the state. Hayek's idea of solidarity is more restricted than Durkheim's, and he rejects it as the factor that keeps larger social aggregates together:

> Even today the overwhelming majority of people, including, I am afraid, a good many supposed economists, do not yet understand that this extensive division of labour, based on widely dispersed information, has been made possible entirely by the use of those impersonal signs which emerge from the

market process and tell people what to do in order to adapt their activities to events of which they have no direct knowledge.

(*LLLIII*, p. 161)

So, it is the pursuit of the interests of oneself and the members of one's immediate social environment together with the anonymous price system that makes for coordination and social stability. The market order has co-evolved with the system of moral rules that sustains it: "This exchange society and the guidance of the coordination of a far-ranging division of labour by variable market prices was made possible by the spreading of certain gradually evolved moral beliefs which, after they had spread, most men in the Western world learned to accept" (*LLLIII*, p. 164).[43] The content of these rules is economic: providing for the future, accumulating capital, and seeking the esteem of fellow-men.

There are *differences* between Hayek and Durkheim. What they have *in common* is the problem of explaining social stability. Their theories of morality have to be seen in that light. The function of moral rules is to preserve a stable social framework. More specifically, the moral rules that have co-evolved with the market order serve to suppress or transform the individual instincts that still belong to the era of the primitive tribe and that have failed to co-evolve with the increase of the complexity of society. Both Hayek and Durkheim propose functional theories of morality. They use a mixed logical-explanatory analysis that starts from an attempt to find the system of rules that is accepted by everyone. They both employ the method of conjectural history without abandoning the possibility of putting their theories to the test. Finally, both add a cognitive dimension to this empiricism. However, they propose *different* fundamental factors that explain social stability. For Durkheim they are cooperation and altruism; Hayek emphasizes coordination and the pursuit of self-interest. They also differ in their preferences for the political system that is conducive to social stability. This is discussed in the next section.

## Moral theories

The whole of Durkheim's intellectual career is inspired by his concern to put sociology in the service of morality. One of the last sentences of *DTS* reads: "notre premier devoir actuellement est de nous faire une morale" (p. 406) ["our first duty is to make a moral code for ourselves", p. 409]. Even though the phrasing would be too constructivistic to Hayek's taste, the idea is very similar to Hayek's objective. It is to make man understand that in order to maintain the social order that brings so many benefits, we must change our moral attitudes, and in particular abjure the morals of socialism, since they are based on descriptively false premises. This conditionality of moral prescriptions on facts, which we also find in Durkheim,[44] alerts us to an important feature of morality that is often forgotten: moral rules and value judgements are not isolated entities, but they are always embedded in judgements of fact. Each and every moral judgement has implicit or explicit factual premises and presuppositions. It is therefore more appropriate to speak of moral *theories*. One advantage is that this widens the scope of a rational and critical discussion of moral rules. Hans Albert has elaborated this proposal.[45] A principle on which probably all human beings agree[46] is that it is not reasonable to impose moral rules that one cannot keep to as a matter of fact: "ought" ought to imply "can". Hayek and Durkheim add a dimension to this by placing morality in an evolutionary perspective, introducing the emergence of moral rules and the consequences they may have for future social developments as legitimate objects of scientific inquiry. The two authors also agree on the general function of morality, which is to preserve the stability of the social framework.

However, studying moral judgements as part of moral theories does not alter the fact that every moral theory has at least one value judgement among its premises, since moral judgements cannot be derived from factual ones.[47] So this raises the question about Durkheim's and Hayek's moral premises. Rather casually Durkheim introduces the brotherhood of man as a universal moral ideal: "C'est un rêve depuis longtemps caressé par les hommes que d'arriver enfin à réaliser dans les faits l'idéal de la fraternité humaine" (*DTS*, p. 401). ["Men have long dreamt of finally realizing in fact the idea of human fraternity", p. 405.] This is linked to solidarity by a conditional argument: if we want brotherhood, then solidarity is a necessary intermediate social norm. This is reminiscent of Hayek's defence of liberty. In *CL* the freedom of the individual is presented first and foremost as instrumental to the functioning of the market. Its most important effect is that it creates the conditions under which information and the creative powers of society are mobilized. Hayek is aware that his emphasis on instrumental freedom might be considered as insufficient for the defence of a liberal society:

> Some readers will perhaps be disturbed by the impression that I do not take the value of individual liberty as an indisputable ethical presupposition and that, in trying to demonstrate its value, I am possibly making the argument in its support a matter of expediency. This would be a misunderstanding. But it is true that if we want to convince those who do not already share our moral suppositions, we must not simply take them for granted. We must show that liberty is not merely one particular value but that it is the source and condition of most moral values.
>
> (*CL*, p. 6)

However, when we look for those other moral values, again we find an enumeration of factors that are instrumental to the functioning of the market order: abstract rules governing private property, honesty, contracts, exchange, commerce, competition, profit, and the protection of privacy (cp., for instance, *FC*, p. 76). So, Hayek does not really seem to have changed his mind between *CL* and *FC*. What he has done instead is to unwrap, or render explicit, an idea that had always been a premise of his system of ideas: that the market is the economic system that favours the material opportunities for sustaining the greatest number, and that liberal society is the best socio-political framework for the market.

Durkheim does not pronounce himself openly in favour of any political system; perhaps he would have found that incompatible with his conception of sociology as the positive science of morality and of himself as a social scientist.[48] But it is clear that he favours a system in which professional groups play an important role, without either the state or unfettered competition being dominant.[49] In other words, Durkheim opposes both liberalism and socialism. If Hayek's liberalism and Durkheim's anti-liberalism followed logically as conclusions from their method and analysis, which as I have argued are very similar, these different preferences would be hard to explain. So the conclusion seems inevitable that here we have arrived at different political value judgements that inspire the two authors.

## A historical puzzle

This leaves us with one last question. Hayek accuses Durkheim of constructivism and of being opposed to accepting the outcome of spontaneous social evolutionary processes. He attributes to Durkheim the idea that solidarity is to be obtained by consciously creating and imposing the conditions under which all members of a society could pursue the same goal on which they all agree,[50] and that moral is that which furthers altruism. We have seen that a closer reading of Durkheim reveals a picture that is almost the exact opposite. Most differences between the functional moral theories of Hayek and Durkheim are differences of degree, not of kind. Spontaneous social orders, the importance of free associations, the emphasis on the emancipation of the individual and on individual freedom are prominent features of the theories of both. So, why does Hayek reject Durkheim's ideas?[51]

I propose two alternative explanations. The first is that Hayek interpreted Durkheim's emphasis on the role of professional groups as a defence of corporatism. For Hayek, corporatism, whether of the socialist or of the fascist kind, is the embodiment of hostility to competition.[52] This made him decide that a further study of Durkheim would be a waste of time. Consequently, all the details and subtleties of Durkheim's analysis were lost on him. The second explanation is that Hayek remembered that Durkheim stands in the tradition of Comte – without knowing or remembering that he is critical of Comte – and that he is critical of Spencer, who advocates a particular brand of liberalism. For Hayek, criticizing liberalism is tantamount to advocating socialism. Hayek attributed this presumed defence of socialism to Durkheim's scientific analysis. In both cases, in order to make Durkheim's presumed defence of corporatism or socialism coherent with that author's scientific analysis, Hayek truncated Durkheim's analysis of society to the description of solidarity in primitive society. So, in the end, Hayek's misrepresentation of Durkheim is due to Hayek's attempt to make Durkheim's scientific analysis of society and the defence of corporatism or socialism which he, Hayek, wrongly attributed to him, consistent with one another. This would explain why Hayek developed and presented many of his own ideas as if they were a critical reaction to Durkheim. In reality, he rejects many of the very ideas Durkheim rejects, too. This "double negation" explains why Hayek's theory of society is so similar to Durkheim's.

## Notes

1  Except when stated otherwise, in the case of Durkheim page references are to Durkheim, 1893 (1994). The translation is taken from Durkheim, 1933 and is given in square brackets. References to Hayek's three volumes of *Law, Legislation and Liberty* (1973–9) will be given as *LLLI*, *II*, or *III*.

2  Because the doctrine that specialization leads to more efficient production derives from *The Wealth of Nations*, Durkheim's project is also a provocation of economists in that it implies that they "did not know their Smith" in the sense that they neglected *The Theory of Moral Sentiments*.

3  Both the content and the phrasing of *ITF* (for instance, "amount to little" is an almost literal translation of Durkheim's "sont peu de chose") strongly suggest that it is a direct reaction to Durkheim. If this is the case – as I think it is – the question remains why Hayek does not refer to him. (Due to the speed with which Birner and Ege, 1999 was written and published, we failed to eliminate the sentence on p. 764 in which we wrongly say that he does.)

4  This is very similar to Menger's idea about the relationship between his own ("exact") economic theory and the historical and statistical methods of the German Historical School, which only produce descriptions of concrete phenomena and processes. For a discussion, cp. Birner, 1990.

5  Hayek says so explicitly in a text that will be discussed more at length below, "The Origins and Effects of our Morals: A Problem for Science", an unpublished ms. in Box 96/126 of the Hayek Archives at the Hoover Institution of War, Revolution and Peace, Stanford. It is the text of a lecture, which was apparently delivered between the publication of the third volume of *Law, Legislation and Liberty* in 1979 and *The Fatal Conceit* in 1988. I will refer to it as *Origins*.

6  Saying that this is shown by his insistence on social solidarity. Cp. *LLLII*, p. 186, n. 9. What Hayek means by solidarity is discussed below, in the section beginning on p. 45.

7  The question of the relationship between Hayek's and Durkheim's theories of society is discussed further in Birner and Ege, 1999.

8  Hayek's contribution to the debate on socialism in the 1930s is the platform where he first elaborates the importance of limited knowledge.

9  Which dates from 1920. Hayek's theory of perception is an early precursor of neural network models. Hayek explains the human mind as a self-organizing system of decentralized, parallel distributed neural connections. For more details about the relationships between Hayek's psychology and the rest of his work, cp. Birner, 1999 and 1999a.

10  Cp. the collections *Individualism and Economic Order* (1948a) and *Studies* (1967a).

11  For an excellent discussion, cp. Bianchi, 1994.

12  The criticism that Hayek's theory of group selection is non-individualistic can be found, for instance, in Vanberg, 1986. The solution proposed in the text (and in Birner, 1999b) constitutes also a reply to the criticism that Hayek does not propose a mechanism through which individuals are motivated to cooperate when this is not in their immediate self-interest. Cp. Bianchi, 1994, Shearmur, 1994, and Witt, 1994.

13  Hayek writes that this is also the case logically and psychologically (*FC*, p. 23). It is not entirely clear what he means by this.

14  This neglects the problem of incentives. Cp. Witt, 1994 and Shearmur, 1994. Cp. also the conclusion of Birner and Ege, 1999.

15  What Hayek has to say on the passage from primitive to modern society is very similar. He even speaks of the role of magic and ritual in passing from one economic order to another through the relaxation of prohibitions (*LLLIII*, p. 161). Cp. also what he says about sharing in primitive societies: "But these habits had to be shed again to make the transition to the market economy and the open society possible. The steps of this transition were all breaches of that 'solidarity' which governed the small group and which are still resented. Yet they were the steps towards almost all that we now call civilization" (*LLLIII*, p. 161).

16  Cp. for instance the passage further on in the book to the extent that "[t]oute société est une société morale" (*DTS*, p. 207), which clearly reveals the influence of Mill, whose "moral sciences" is the translation of the German "Geisteswissenschaften".

17  Bartley's influence shows for instance in the relatively prominent place given to religion, something Hayek had never paid much attention to.

18  Cp. note 5.

19  Cp. *DTS*, p. 174: "Si les hypothèses de Darwin sont utilisables en morale, c'est encore avec plus de réserve et de mesure que dans les autres sciences. Elles font, en effet, abstraction de l'élément essentiel de la vie morale, à savoir de l'influence modératrice que la société exerce sur les membres et qui tempère et neutralise l'action brutale de la lutte pour la vie et de la sélection. Partout où il y a des sociétés, il y a de l'altruisme, parce qu'il y a de la solidarité." ["If the hypotheses of Darwin have a moral use, it is with more reserve and measure than in other sciences. They overlook the essential element of moral life, that is, the moderating influence that society exercises over its members, which tempers and neutralizes the brutal action of the struggle for existence and selection. Wherever there are societies, there is altruism, because there is solidarity", p. 197.]

20  The association that the reader may make with a neurophysiological metaphor would be justified. Durkheim devotes several sections to this. A discussion of the relationship between Durkheim's and Hayek's theories of society with neurophysiological models goes beyond the scope of the present chapter. For the case of Hayek, the reader is referred to Birner, 1996.

21  The use of the term is probably a deliberate evocation (provocation?) of Walras.

22  Cp. the contribution of Bensaïd, this volume, who takes up this issue in a criticism of Hayek.

23  Durkheim's triumphant criticism of "the economists" that they failed to see this certainly does not apply to Hayek, who emphasizes the limited scope of individuals' perceptions and the division of knowledge: "Les économistes n'auraient pas laissé dans l'ombre ce caractère essentiel de la division du travail et, par suite, ne l'auraient pas exposée à ce reproche immérité, s'ils ne l'avaient réduite à n'être qu'un moyen d'accroître le rendement des forces sociales, s'ils avaient vu qu'elle est avant tout une source de solidarité" (*DTS*, p. 365). ["The economists would not have left this essential character of the division of labor in the shade and, accordingly, would not have exposed it to this unmerited reproach, if they had not reduced it to being merely a means of increasing the produce of social forces, if they had seen that it is above all a source of solidarity", p. 373.] For further discussion, cp. Birner and Ege, 1999.

24  An attempt to incorporate an element of Marx's economics?

25  Nor do any of his commentators. Only Vanberg, 1986 mentions it.

26  Cp. also his rejection of the idea of society as mind-like in Hayek, 1967a, p. 74.

27  Pettit calls this the missing mechanism type of explanation. Cp. Pettit, 1996.

28  Cp. *CRS*, p. 85.

29  Cp. also *LLLI*, p. 149, n. 15.

30  Basically, this is the same argument as in Hayek's introduction to *Capitalism and the Historians* of 1954.

31  Cp. *Origins*, p. 17.
32  Cp. the passage from *DTS*, p. 394 which was quoted on p. 32. Cp. also *DTS*, p. 404: Morality "nous demande seulement d'être tendres pour nos semblables et d'être justes, de bien remplir notre tâche, de travailler à ce que chacun soit appelé à la fonction qu'il peut le mieux remplir, et reçoive le prix juste de ses efforts" ["only asks that we be thoughtful of our fellows and that we be just, that we fulfill our duty, that we work at the function we can best execute, and receive the just reward for our services", p. 407].
33  Cp. *LLLIII*, p. 165: "Its mores involved withholding from the known needy neighbours what they might require in order to serve the unknown needs of thousands of unknown others. Financial gain rather than the pursuit of a known common good became not only the basis of approval but also the cause of the increase of general wealth." The criticism of social justice is the subject of *Law, Legislation and Liberty*.
34  Cp. *LLLIII*, p. 164: "This exchange society and the guidance of the coordination of a far-ranging division of labour by variable market prices was made possible by the spreading of certain gradually evolved moral beliefs which, after they had spread, most men in the Western world learned to accept." For a discussion of Hayek and Durkheim as representatives of explanations of social stability that are based on coordination and cooperation, cp. Birner and Ege, 1999.
35  *DTS*, p. 396: "cette pression salutaire de la société, qui modère son égoïsme [de l'homme] et qui fait de lui un être moral" ["this salutary pressure of society which moderates his egoism and makes him a moral being", p. 401]. On p. 401 Durkheim generalizes the argument: "La seule puissance qui puisse servir de modérateur à l'égoïsme individuel est celle du groupe; la seule qui puisse servir de modérateur à l'égoïsme des groupes est celle d'un autre groupe qui les embrasse" (*DTS*, p. 401). ["The only power which can serve to moderate individual egotism is the power of the group; the only power which can serve to moderate the egotism of groups is that of some other group which embraces them", p. 405.]
36  Cp. the section which follows.
37  Thus, they both qualify as functionalists also in the second sense Pettit distinguishes.
38  Cp., for instance, *LLLIII*, p. 171: "All morals rest on the different esteem in which different persons are held by their fellows according to their conforming to accepted moral standards. It is this which makes moral conduct a social value." And Durkheim: "Voilà ce qui fait la valeur morale de la division du travail. C'est que, par elle, l'individu reprend conscience de son état de dépendance vis-à-vis de la société ... puisque la division du travail devient la source éminente de la solidarité sociale, elle devient du même coup la base de l'ordre moral" (*DTS*, p. 396). ["This is what gives moral value to the division of labor. Through it, the individual becomes cognizant of his dependence upon society ... since the division of labor becomes the chief source of social solidarity, it becomes, at the same time, the foundation of the moral order", p. 401.]
39  Durkheim observes that solidarity, the main social value, is only operative if individuals are aware of its existence (*DTS*, pp. 259–60). Hayek's idea that a major function of moral rules is to create a more predictable social environment has already been discussed.
40  Cp. *Origins*, p. 11.
41  This corroborates the idea of Shearmur, 1996, ch. 5, and Aimar, this volume, that Hayek looks for a testable criterion by which to judge a social order, and that this criterion is biological.
42  For Hayek's empiricism in the second sense cp. Birner, 1999a and 2001. Durkheim's empiricism is apparent from our discussion of the first anomalous type of division of labour in the section beginning on p. 34.
43  On the idea of the co-evolution of morals and institutions, cp. also *LLLIII*, p. 170: "But as moral views create institutions, so institutions create moral views."

44 Cp. above, the first paragraph of section beginning on p.31.

45 Cp. Albert, 1979, pp. 76–9, where he takes up an idea of Popper's; cp. Popper, 1945, ch. 24, para. III.

46 All humans, that is, who do not subscribe to a romantic heroism that considers as the highest value to demand and do the impossible.

47 Notice, however, that Durkheim denies that there is a fundamental difference between moral and factual statements. Cp. the next note.

48 On the other hand, he should not have shrunk from making his political preferences explicit. Cp. Durkheim, 1911, in particular pp. 138–9: "Comment faut-il donc concevoir le rapport des jugements de valeur aux jugements de réalité? De ce qui précède il résulte qu'il n'existe pas entre eux de différences de nature." ["How must the relationship between value judgements and descriptions of reality be conceived of? From the preceding discussion it follows that there is no difference of kind between the two", my tr.]

49 Cp., for instance, the preface to the second edition of *DTS*, and the preface to Durkheim, 1928 by Marcel Mauss.

50 Cp. also *LLLII*, p. 11, where Hayek writes that the "Great Society" has nothing to do with solidarity in the "true" sense of conscious unitedness in the pursuit of common goals.

51 Hayek's misrepresentation of Durkheim is repeated by Popper: "It is the analysis of these abstract relations with which modern social theory, such as economic theory, is mainly concerned. This point has not been understood by many sociologists, such as Durkheim, who never gave up the dogmatic belief that society must be analysed in terms of real social groups" (Popper, 1945, Vol. 1, p. 175).

52 Cp. Hayek, 1944, p. 30. Cp. also Nakayama, this volume, note 52.

## Bibliography

Aimar, T. (2000) "Coordination, survival and normativity: a Hayekian perspective revisited", in this volume, pp. 217–36.

Albert, H. (1979) *Traktat über kritische Vernunft*, Mohr (Siebeck).

Bensaïd, M. (2000) "The organizational indetermination of spontaneous order in Hayek", in this volume, pp.153–70.

Bianchi, M. (1994) "Hayek's Spontaneous Order: the 'Correct' versus the 'Corrigible' Society", in Birner and van Zijp (1994).

Birner, J. (1990) "A Roundabout Solution to a Fundamental Problem in Menger's Methodology and Beyond", *History of Political Economy*, suppl. to Vol. 22, pp. 241–61.

—— (1996) "Mind, Market and Society: Network Structures in the Work of F.A. Hayek", working paper Computable and experimental economics laboratory, WP 1996–02, Department of Economics, University of Trento, Italy.

—— (1999) "Making Markets", in S.C. Dow and P.E. Earl (eds), *Economic Organisation and Economic Knowledge: Essays in Honour of Brian Loasby*, Cheltenham, UK and Brookfield, US: Edward Elgar.

—— (1999a) "The Surprising Place of Cognitive Psychology in the Work of F.A. Hayek", *History of Economic Ideas* 7 (1–2), pp. 43–84.

—— (1999b) "An Austrian Approach to the Evolution of Knowledge and Social Institutions", paper presented at the annual Allied Social Sciences Association conference, January, New York.

—— (2001) "The Mind–Body Problem and Social Evolution", paper presented at the workshop "The Nature and Evolution of Institutions", Max Planck Institute for Research into Economic Systems, Evolutionary Economics Unit.

Birner, J. and Ege, R. (1999) "Two Views on Social Stability. An Unsolved Question", *American Journal of Economics and Sociology* 58 (4), pp. 749–80.

Birner, J. and van Zijp, R. (eds) (1994) *Hayek, Co-ordination and Evolution: His Legacy in Philosophy, Politics, Economics and the History of Ideas*, London: Routledge.

Durkheim, E. (1893) *De la division du travail social*, Paris: Presses Universitaires de France, 1994; quoted as *DTS*.

—— (1895) *Les règles de la méthode sociologique*, Paris: Presses Universitaires de France, 1997.

—— (1911) "Jugements de valeur et jugements de réalité", in Durkheim (1924).

—— (1924) *Sociologie et philosophie*, Paris: Presses Universitaires de France, 1996.

—— (1928) *Le socialisme – Sa définition, ses débuts, la doctrine saint-simonienne*, Paris: Librairie Félix Alcan.

—— (1933) *The Division of Labor in Society*, tr. by George Simpson, New York: The Free Press.

Hayek, F.A. (1944) *The Road to Serfdom*, London: Routledge & Kegan Paul, 1976.

—— (1945) "Individualism: True and False", in Hayek (1949); quoted as *ITF*.

—— (1949) *Individualism and Economic Order*, London: Routledge & Kegan Paul.

—— (ed.) (1954) *Capitalism and the Historians*, London: Routledge & Kegan Paul.

—— (1955) *The Counter-Revolution of Science. Studies in the Abuse of Reason*, New York: Free Press of Glencoe.

—— (1960) *The Constitution of Liberty*, London: Routledge & Kegan Paul, quoted as *CL*.

—— (1962) "Rules, Perception and Intelligibility", in Hayek (1967a).

—— (1967a) *Studies in Philosophy, Politics and Economics*, Chicago, IL: University of Chicago Press.

—— (1967b) "Notes on the Evolution of Systems of Rules of Conduct", in Hayek (1967a), referred to as *Notes*.

—— (1973–9) *Law, Legislation and Liberty* (3 vols), London: Routledge & Kegan Paul; quoted as *LLLI, II*, or *III*.

—— (1988) *The Fatal Conceit*, London: Routledge; quoted as *FC*.

—— (no date) "The Origins and Effects of our Morals: A Problem for Science", unpublished ms., 21 pp., Box 96/126 of the Hayek Archives, Hoover Institution of War, Revolution and Peace, Stanford, referred to as *Origins*.

Nakayama, C. (2001) "An investigation of Hayek's criticism of central planning', in this volume, pp. 81–96.

Pettit, P. (1996) "Functional Explanation and Virtual Selection", *The British Journal for the Philosophy of Science* 47, June, pp. 291–302.

Popper, K.R. (1945) *The Open Society and its Enemies*, London: Routledge & Kegan Paul, fifth rev. edn, 1966.

Shearmur, J. (1994) "Hayek and the Case for Markets", in Birner and van Zijp, (1994).

—— (1996) *Hayek and After. Hayekian Liberalism as a Research Programme*, London: Routledge.

Smith, A. (1759) *The Theory of Moral Sentiments*, published 1984, Liberty Fund.

—— (1776) *The Wealth of Nations*, Everyman's Library, J.M. Dent & Sons (1970).

Vanberg, V. (1986) "Spontaneous Market Order and Social Rules: A Critical Examination of F.A. von Hayek's Theory of Cultural Evolution", *Economics and Philosophy Vol 2, pp. 75–100*.

Witt, U. (1994) "The Theory of Societal Evolution", in Birner and van Zijp (1994).

# Part II
# Economic analysis

# 3 Hayek, Morgenstern and game theory

*Christian Schmidt*

## Introduction

Linking Hayek's economics and social thought to game theory seems *prima facie* a real challenge.[1] First of all, there is a lack of evidence about this alleged connection in the writings of Hayek. Therefore, the hypothetical statement of a relationship between game theory and Hayek requires a prior reconstruction. Two major objections arise. The first objection is general and well known. It concerns the consistency between the very Austrian principle of methodological individualism and game theory. As Nozick rightly pointed out, situations characterized by the interdependence of the players' expectations, which are modelled by game theory, cannot entirely be reduced to any theory of individual action whatever, plus a contextual statement upon the interactions through convenient parameters (Nozick, 1977).[2] Now, in spite of some variations on methodology, Hayek has remained continuously attached to the methodological individualism option. The second objection is more specific to Hayek's personal approach to social phenomena. Hayek continuously defended a position that he probably conceived in 1945: a social order which is generated by individual action cannot be deduced from the design of these individual actions (Hayek, 1945, 1949, 1967). Such an opposition to constructivism is difficult to combine with the consequentialism which provides the prevailing interpretation of game theory as a branch of a general theory of decision, even if the consequentialist axioms cannot be directly applied to game theory (Hammond, 1996). Anyway, for a majority of game theorists, the solution of any game is understood as the expected consequences of the strategies exclusively chosen by the players on the grounds of their pay-off values associated with the end of the games (Harsanyi, 1977; Aumann, 1985, 1987).

The purpose of this chapter is to challenge this apparent opposition between the Hayekian views on social interactions and the corpus of game theory. We argue on the contrary that there is room for game theory in Hayek's construction and that its investigation offers the opportunity to sketch an alternative interpretation of game theory. We start by comparing what Hayek called the game of "catallaxy" (Hayek, 1976) to game theory. Game theory provides a relevant framework for clarifying the Hayekian distinction between rules and actions.

Such a clarification enables us to understand the respective roles of chance and players' skill in the acting process of such a catallactic game. In addition to this, Hayek's original approach to the problem of embedded expectations leads to a dynamic treatment (Hayek, 1952). At variance with Morgenstern's acceptance of the Von Neumann solution (Von Neumann and Morgenstern, 1944), it fits into the tradition of evolutionary games in the light of Nash's interpretation of his equilibrium in terms of "mass actions" (Nash, 1950).

## Games, rules and actions

The term "game" and the reference to game theory only appears in the last writings of Hayek, namely in an appendix especially devoted to this topic in *The Fatal Conceit* (Hayek, 1988, appendix E, p. 209) and in the analysis of the market order (on "catallaxy") developed in *Law, Legislation and Liberty* (Hayek, 1976, vol. II, pp. 139–54). It proves that the link between Hayek's representation of economics and game theory is not the result of a purely speculative hypothesis. These late references suggest in addition that such a relationship does not follow an historical filiation through Morgenstern. Indeed, Hayek shared with Morgenstern a sceptical view on the possibility of a person making exact predictions about future events including the behaviour of all the persons concerned (Hayek, 1935), but contrary to Morgenstern, this reflection on the cognitive side of economic phenomena did not lead Hayek to the mathematical solution proposed by game theory in the spirit of Von Neumann. This difference between Hayek and Morgenstern on the valuation of the problem raised by the assumptions of agents' knowledge and the accessibility of an economic equilibrium will be studied later. It explains why Hayek was not attracted by the game theory approach for the same reason as Morgenstern was, in spite of their common Austrian patterns of thinking economics.

Let us proceed backwards and start with the end of the story. At that time, Hayek's main purpose was the refinement of his explanation of the relation between the individual actions which express the free will of the person and an economic order which is at one and the same time natural and social (Hayek, 1952). The difficulty can be summarized as follows: This "order" is the exclusive result of individual actions. While actions are goal-oriented and rational within the limits of incomplete and imperfect information, the social order cannot be produced by the design of individual decision-making. Parlour games give sense to such a situation through the sociological interpretation given by Huizinga (Huizinga, 1938). Thanks to Huizinga, the game offers the picture of a social order where the individual actions of each player take place in a system of rules commonly accepted by all the players. In the specific universe of the game, a clear distinction emerges between the actions freely decided on by individuals on the basis of their own interests, and the rules which become social as accepted by the individuals. The rules of the game frame the actions of individuals and this process justifies for Hayek the characterization of the resulting order as "natural" (Hayek, 1973).

In an unexpected way, Huizinga's *Homo Ludens* was the actual intermediary between Hayek and game theory. Still more interesting is the striking parallelism between Hayek's utilization of some concepts derived from game theory to explain the problem previously raised and Morgenstern's interpretation of the solution of a game, developed more than thirty years earlier, in the really different context of the elaboration of *Theory of Games and Economic Behavior* (*TGEB*) (Von Neumann and Morgenstern, 1944).

Let us recall *TGEB* on this point. The system of imputations which characterizes a solution of the game in the sense of Von Neumann, describes, according to Morgenstern, "an established order of society", sometime labelled as an "accepted standard of behaviour" by the players (Von Neumann and Morgenstern, 1944, p. 41). Translated in Hayek's words, this order generated by the solution of the game is tantamount to the economic order. It is directly derived from the standards of behaviour which correspond to the rules of the game in parlour games. Morgenstern is still more precise. The standards of behaviour allow the transformation of strategies freely chosen by the players of the game into a social organization for all those who accept the standard. Such a social organization can be considered as "natural", because its main characteristic is to reflect a possible order of things. Putting together these two views shows that beyond a great diversity of ideas, there exists an Austrian point of view for considering the notion of a game and the theory which has been elaborated on the topic. Roughly speaking, game theory is seen with Austrian eyes as a powerful operator for explaining how individual actions can be consistent with different social orders without any kind of exterior constraints (as a central plan or an organized market *à la* Walras).

On further examination, several differences appear. The order that Morgenstern had in mind does not exactly correspond to Hayek's order. Indeed, Morgenstern invokes tradition and human experience as a background of all kinds of social orders. "According to all traditions and the experience human beings have a characteristic way of adjusting themselves to such a background" (Von Neumann and Morgenstern, 1944, p. 41). But the very foundation of its natural feature is to be found elsewhere, on the grounds of formal logic. Therefore stability, understood as an application of the non-contradiction principle, is, for Morgenstern (and Von Neumann), the ultimate criterion to justify such orders (non-self-defeating organization). Hayek never shared this logistic conception. His catallactic order does not refer to logic, but is defined as one of the specific applications of a "spontaneous order" (Hayek, 1976). What Hayek called a "spontaneous order" is not a metaphor, but a real phenomenon. It designates in the pure Mengerian tradition the process which explains at one and the same time the institutional organization as a temporary solution of the game, and its evolution corresponding to an evolutionary trajectory of the game.

Another major difference concerns the rules of the game in their relation to the notion of "standards of behaviour" as described in game theory by Morgenstern. At first sight, both seem to refer to the same idea. This is, however, a spurious vision. In a parlour game, as observed by Morgenstern, the rules of the game are laid down. Consequently, the standards of behaviour of the game are no more than the available information of the set of its rules for their players. Things are different when we move from zero-sum two-person parlour games to non-zero-sum social games, where the rules are not laid down and coalitions of players are allowed. Thus, a distinction is now required between the standard of behaviour which tells the players how to behave in every possible situation of the game and the rules of the game which describe the social organization. Therefore, Morgenstern proposes translating the content of the standard of behaviour in terms of players' strategy (Von Neumann and Morgenstern, 1944, p. 44).

The distinction between the rules, understood as standards of behaviour for the players, and the actions, which means players' strategies in the language of game theory, is crucial in Hayek's vision of a game to be used as a social paradigm. This is the reason why Hayek remains attached to parlour games in Huizinga's spirit. Assimilation of the rules of the game with players' strategies leads, in Hayek's view, to a serious mistake, because it is a way to reintroduce a form of rationalism that he always bitterly criticized (Hayek, 1952). A strategy in game theory is defined as a complete plan of actions, decided by the players at the beginning of the game. According to Hayek's conception, the "established order" provided by the solution of the game cannot be derived from the rational choice of the players' strategies. Therefore, Hayek, while he can sympathize with Morgenstern's institutional interpretation of the "standards of behaviour" which prevail in parlour games, necessarily rejects Von Neumann's basic intuition on strategic games. The solution of a game is basically, for Von Neumann, the mathematical result of strategies chosen by players by reference to a well-defined criterion of rationality, i.e. the Minimax (Von Neumann, 1928). To sum up, the "standard of behaviour" is an elastic notion used by Morgenstern as a compromise between the Austrian approach to a game and the mathematical topic of Von Neumann. Hayek's insight could lead to a real alternative conception of game theory. Let us recall the historical background of the story.

## Hayek versus Morgenstern

At the end of the twenties and the beginning of the thirties, the condition of the possibility of relaying predictions on future events to any economic equilibrium whatsoever was the principal research programme for Morgenstern as well as for Hayek.[3] Morgenstern published his first major book, *Wirtschaftsprognose* (1928), which was never translated into English, just one year before Hayek's paper, "Geldtheorie und Konjunkturtheorie" (1929) in *Zeitschrift für Nationalökonomie*, the journal edited by Morgenstern. In 1935, one of Morgenstern's most famous papers appeared, translated into English under the title of "Perfect Foresight and Economic Equilibrium", at the same time as another paper by Hayek, "Preiserwartungen, monetäre Störungen und Fehlinvestitionen", in *Nationalökonomisk Tidskrift* (1935). More important for our topic is Hayek's "Economics and Knowledge" (1937), reprinted in *Individualism and Economic Order* (1949).

These materials offer a basis of evidence large enough to illuminate Hayek's and Morgenstern's respective analyses of the role of knowledge in economic predictions. Our purpose here is to use some of their features to explain the very foundations of their future divergence about game theory.

Let us start with a forecasting paradox due to the endogenous expectations of the agents in a situation of complete information discussed by Morgenstern (Morgenstern, 1935), and expressed for the first time in the famous story of Sherlock Holmes against Professor Moriarty (Morgenstern, 1928). Sherlock Holmes, pursued by Professor Moriarty, leaves London (Victoria Station) for Dover. At a station between Victoria and Dover, Sherlock Holmes sees Moriarty. He takes for granted that Moriarty has recognized him. What must he do? The answer depends on the level of Sherlock Holmes' expectations about Moriarty's behaviour. The situation can be summarized as follows from Sherlock Holmes' point of view:

### Level 1

Sherlock Holmes knows (or believes) that Moriarty knows that he is on the way to Dover, therefore he must stop at the station;

### Level 2

Sherlock Holmes knows (or believes) that Moriarty knows his expectations about him, therefore he must continue on his way to Dover;

### Level 3

Sherlock Holmes knows (or believes) that Moriarty knows (or believes) that he knows his expectations, therefore he must stop at the station; and so on to level $+\infty$. At each level the answer reiterates in the opposite direction the answer which was previously given at the former level.

Framed in this way, the problem seemed at that time to Morgenstern inextricable because the self-references of both expectations generate an intrinsic instability. Such a situation is not consistent with any social order whatever (Morgenstern, 1928).

Twenty years later, Sherlock Holmes and Professor Moriarty appear again in *TGEB*, but the question that Morgenstern has put into Sherlock Holmes' mind is now solved, thanks to the game theory reformulation. The structure of the situation with which Sherlock Holmes is faced is really very simple. Sherlock Holmes' and Moriarty's interests are strictly opposite. The purpose of each is to avoid being discovered by the other. Thus, the structure of the problem is the same as for the game of matching penny and its solution is provided by mixed strategies and the resumption of a probability reasoning through the reappearance of hazard, as quoted in Von Neumann's 1928 seminal article (Von Neumann, 1928; Von Neumann and Morgenstern, 1944, pp. 176–8).

Reviewing Sherlock Holmes' and Moriarty's story in the light of the standards of behaviour is informative. First, a common reference to the standards of behaviour derived from the solution concept can stop the regression *ad infinitum* generated by the situation of mutual expectations. Second, this example shows that such a reference to standards of behaviour is disconnected from individual rationality. If, according to the theoretical solution, Moriarty chooses his corresponding mixed strategy, Sherlock Holmes does not have any personal incentive to oppose to Moriarty his mixed strategy. He will obtain the same outcome in choosing any other pure strategy. The reason why Sherlock Holmes must, however, choose the mixed strategy recommended by the solution of the game is elsewhere. Moriarty will choose rationally his mixed strategy if, and only if, he is confident in Sherlock Holmes' choice of his own mixed strategy (and vice versa). As soon as this confidence is destroyed, the vicious circle previously described reappears, which means instability and the absence of a social order. On the contrary, the "established order" through the standards of behaviour support the mutual confidence of the players even in spite of their opposing interests. Von Neumann and Morgenstern were themselves perfectly aware of this feature when they pointed out the necessity of rejecting imputations outside the solution although preferable to an effective set of players, in order to maintain among all the players of the game their faith in the solution concept which has been "accepted" (Von Neumann and Morgenstern, 1944, pp. 265–6). In that sense, Sherlock Holmes and Moriarty illustrate an extreme case where the social order invoked by the standards of behaviour is self-fulfilled. It does not matter as long as this order is consistent, which is tantamount to stability. Let us relax the assumption of strictly opposite interests, i.e. the narrow structure of a two-person zero-sum game and the Von Neumann solution based on the Minimax theorem, then the interpretation of mixed strategies in terms of chance quickly vanishes.

According to Hayek's position on individual knowledge and what he calls the "patterns of prediction", the *deus ex machina* acting in Von Neumann's machinery for solving the problem cannot be accepted. Indeed, the mixed strategies of equilibrium cannot be understood as patterns of prediction in Hayek's sense (Hayek, 1935), because they are derived from the concept of solution which reverses the causal chain. As we know now, this solution is a special case of a Nash equilibrium, where the basic problem, in spite of the strictly opposing interests of the players, is a problem of coordination. But the coordination of this game is provided by the equilibrium itself, which for the sake of convenience is supposed to be integrated in the players' mind. This way of reasoning implies for Hayek a vicious circle which he precisely tries to avoid, thanks to his idea of "tendency towards equilibrium".

The nature of the knowledge necessary to implement the game theory solution in Morgenstern's example raises an additional difficulty. Indeed, the solution of the game must be "common knowledge" between the players. Suppose for a moment that Sherlock Holmes and Moriarty both know game theory, but that they do not share the equilibrium solution as "common knowledge". Thus Sherlock Holmes could rightly wonder why he should choose his equilibrium mixed strategy, since he knows that if Moriarty chooses it, he could choose rationally any one of his strategies (and symmetrically for Moriarty). In other words, Von Neumann's two-person zero-sum game solution is not "self-enforcing" as in the case of a Nash equilibrium. Therefore, Morgenstern's standards of behaviour cannot serve as "patterns of prediction" in Hayek's sense. Furthermore, as previously underlined, the definition of the players' strategy, which, for Morgenstern, incorporates all the relevant information on the rules of the game, is not sufficient in itself to guarantee their coordination. Those arguments seem sufficient to explain Hayek's rejection of Von Neumann and Morgenstern's construction, as well as Nash's later framing of game theory, at least in its static interpretation. It does not, however, entail a definite contradiction between Hayek's approach to economic problems and every kind of game theory reasoning, as we shall try to show.

## A "catallactic order" between chance and the skill of players

The distinction between the rules of the game and the players' strategies clarifies the reason why a distance necessarily separates the social market order from the individual plans of its participants. Like the rules of the game in a parlour game, the market prices operate as guidelines for the decision-makers. They provide the framework of information necessary to play the game. But the allocation of wealth corresponding to this price system never coincides with the individual expected pay-offs which determined their strategic choices. Why? The price system identifies the allocation which could be obtained if the players made their choice as they should, but, due to their imperfect knowledge, they cannot (Hayek, 1976, p. 144). Let us suppose that they can. In such a situation, no difference would exist between the standard of behaviour and the players' strategies, which was precisely disputed by Hayek.

Hayek's approach to catallactic games seems at variance with game theory teaching, at least in its classical version. This does not mean that it precludes any form of game theory reasoning. Further investigations on the game of catallaxy bring a new surprise to the historians of ideas. The two major components of this game are chance and the skill of the players, which, for Hayek, are intricately linked. This introduction of catallaxy immediately suggests the early beginnings of game theory with the most important note of Borel on the topic entitled "on games that involve chance and the skill of the players" (Borel, 1924). Indeed, Borel elaborated a mathematical theory for two-person zero-sum games whilst Hayek's game of catallaxy is a non-zero-sum game with a large number of players. Beyond these differences emerges a much more important similarity. Borel, contrary to Von Neumann, tried to build a mathematical theory of games from the exclusive point of view of the players. His guiding assumption was that the knowledge of the players of the game could not be assimilated with the knowledge of the theoretician (Schmidt, 2001).

The qualification of a game by the combination of a chance element and of an element of players' skill can be understood at two different levels. At a first level, the rules of some parlour games are based on such a combination, as for example in packs (bridge, poker, etc.). Second, playing a game independently of its rules requires from the players both chance and skill in a sense to be specified. In Hayek's game of catallaxy, these two levels are mixed. As the rules of the game imply chance and skill for reasons explained by Hayek, the players are obliged to take account of these two elements when they plan their actions, skill partly reducing uncertainty, but only partly (Hayek, 1976, p. 151). Borel thought, for his part, that the combination of chance and skill can be found in almost all parlour games, whatever their rules, due to the position of the players *vis-à-vis* the relevant information for their decision.

An analysis of the knowledge of the players in the line of Borel's intuitive thought provides a bridge between Hayek's representation of individuals in a situation of interaction with many players and the cognitive constraint of a player in game theory. The major problem is no longer a lack of information but rather a contradiction between two kinds of knowledge which are both necessary for choosing a strategy: (a) an adaptive knowledge *vis-à-vis* the other players; (b) a rational knowledge, which is by definition rigid to a certain extent. Thus, the problem can be formulated as follows: does such a knowledge exist which combines (a) and (b)? Borel's answer was negative. With a flavour of mathematical humour, he summarized the situation in these terms:

> Strictly speaking, a complete incoherence of mind would be needed, combined of course with the intelligence necessary to eliminate those methods we have called bad.
>
> (Borel, 1921, p. 203)[4]

Borel's conclusion harks back to Hayek's analysis of the game of catallaxy where chance and skill of players are necessary together in the market process (Hayek, 1976). The arguments developed by Borel at a micro level are extended by Hayek to a larger system with a different terminology. What Borel calls "intelligence" is "skill" in Hayek's vocabulary. In both cases a part of reason is required to identify the best combination (or the right action). On the other hand, individuals are faced with a complete ignorance *vis-à-vis* the others, due to their interdependent expectations. The chance dimension comes in here. To authors who propose to mimic hazard, Borel bravely replies that nobody can imitate hazard (Borel, 1938). This position sounds at least as radical as Hayek's own views on uncertainty, recalling that Borel was the actual precursor of the mixed strategy concept (Borel, 1921).

This unexpected revisitation of Hayek's game of catallaxy through Borel's original vision of a mathematical theory of games is fruitful for our quest. Borel's attempt to construct a game from the exclusive point of view of the individual players gives some hope for conciliating game theory with methodological individualism. This statement, however, is to be compared with his negative conjecture on a general solution for game situations. Ten years after Von

Neumann demonstrated the Minimax theorem, Borel still remained sceptical about its real interest on the grounds of two considerations: first, the extreme complexity of the cognitive side of the problem for the players; second, the fact that if the players of a game could successfully apply this type of solution, the game would rapidly be abandoned by the players because it would eradicate its chance dimension (Borel, 1938). Those remarks are quite relevant for a game theory approach of catallaxy in the Hayek mode. They confirm that Hayek's thoughts on games open the way to an alternative conception of game theory, which takes its source from the very origin of game theory.

## Towards a connection with evolutionary games

Borel's dissatisfaction with Von Neumann's Minimax theorem for solving game theory is to be related to his scepticism about a purely deductivist approach of game situations. He emphasizes many times the role of information that a player can infer from the repetition of the game. Unfortunately, this prospect remains limited because Borel, as well as Von Neumann, primarily worked on zero-sum games, corresponding to almost all parlour games. If we relax this narrow assumption, the time dimension which even Borel has suggested as meaningful for the understanding of a game, becomes prominent. Thus, thanks to Borel's initial design, Hayek's game of catallaxy as a dynamic process mixing together chance and the skill of players (Hayek, 1976, chap. 10) is no longer a metaphor but a domain where a revised theory of games is to be applied.

Let us conclude by another comparison. Fifty years after Borel, Nash submitted a Ph.D. dissertation on "Non-co-operative games" which became the core of a seminal article (Nash, 1951). In addition to its mathematical content, a stimulating section entitled "Motivation and interpretation" suggested an alternative interpretation of his concept of equilibrium points which was named "mass action" interpretation (Nash, 1950). Instead of focusing on a few players, Nash assumed the existence of populations of participants for each position of the game. No individual player has a complete knowledge of the total structure of the game and the process of reasoning of each of them is not very elaborated in the sense of rational expectations. On the contrary, all the players have the opportunity to accumulate empirical information for guiding the adjustment of their strategic moves during the game. Uncertainty and then chance are modelled as an "average playing" selected at random.

Except for this probabilistic treatment of the populations' strategic behaviour, Nash's mass interpretation of a game appears quite consistent with the game of catallaxy derived by Hayek from the division of knowledge among economic agents and from their cognitive adjustment to some kind of social order. More precisely, Nash observed that according to his "mass actions" interpretation, the notion of equilibrium as a solution of the game has no great significance (Nash, 1950, p. 21). Due to the necessary lack of perfect information, the best to be expected is some sort of approximate equilibrium. Such a diagnosis, which can be understood as the starting point of the evolutionary approach to game theory, sounds like the equilibrating tendency formulated by Hayek since 1937 to challenge the orthodox acceptance of economic equilibrium.

Does this mean that Hayek's work on economic knowledge and market processes anticipated volutionary game theory? Certainly not, but rather that there is no definite gap between the Hayekian approach to those phenomena and this branch of game theory recently rediscovered by the economists and which has rapidly grown in the last ten years. A cross-fertilization is now to be expected from their mutual recognition.

## Notes

1  For a survey of the broader topic of Austrian Economics and game theory, see Foss, 2000, pp. 11–58.
2  For an elaborated analysis of such a difficulty in the Austrian perspective of methodological individualism, see Nozick, 1977, pp. 354–8.
3  The relation between foresight and economic equilibrium during this period was the topic of an active debate between Hayek and Morgenstern. Both were attracted by the possibility and the limits of economic forecasting for practical reasons. At that time, the *Oesterreichisches Institut füer Konjunkturforschung* was created. Hayek was its first director, just before Morgenstern. For a substantial analysis of the comparison between Hayek's and Morgenstern's views on "perfect", "correct" and "relevant" foresight, see Zappia, 1999, pp. 833–46.
4  Borel's argument is relevant for our purpose. Indeed, the player should vary his strategy in such a way that the probabilities attributed by an outside observer to his different manners of playing can *never* be defined, which means that the function defining the dynamics of the game varies *at each instant* without following any law whatsoever (Borel, 1921).

## Bibliography

Aumann, R.J. (1985) "What is Game Theory Trying to Accomplish?" in K. Arrow and Y. Yhonkapohja (eds), *Frontiers of Economics*, Oxford: Basil Blackwell.
—— (1987) "Game Theory" in J. Eatwell, M. Milgate and P. Newman (eds), *The New Palgrave*, London: Macmillan.
Borel, E. (1921) "La théorie du jeu et les équations à noyau symétrique gauche", *Comptes-rendus de l'Académie des Sciences*, Paris.
—— (1924) "Sur les jeux où interviennent le hasard et l'habileté des joueurs", *Comptes-rendus de l'Académie des Sciences*, Paris.
—— (1938) "Applications aux jeux de hasard", cours professé à la Faculté des Sciences de Paris, Paris: Gauthier-Villars.
Foss, N. (2000) "Austrian Economics and Game Theory: A Stocktaking and Evaluation", *Review of Austrian Economics*, 13.
Hammond, P. (1996) "Consequentialism, Structural Rationality and Game Theory" in K. Arrow, C. Colombatto, M. Perlmann and C. Schmidt (eds), *The Rational Foundations of Economic Behaviour*, London: Macmillan.
Harsanyi, J.C. (1977) *Rational Behaviour and Bargaining Equilibrium in Games and Social Situations*, Cambridge: Cambridge University Press.
Hayek, F.A. (1929) "Geldtheorie und Konjunkturtheorie", *Zeitschrift für Nationalökonomie*.
—— (1935) "Preiserwartungen, monetäre Störungen und Felhinvestitionen", *Nationalökonomisk Tidskrift*, Vol. 73.

—— (1937) "Economics and Knowledge", *Economica*, Vol. IV.

—— (1945) "The Use of Knowledge in Society", *American Economic Review*, 25, 4.

—— (1949) *Individualism and Economic Order*, London: Routledge & Kegan Paul.

—— (1952) *The Sensory Order. An Inquiry into the Foundations of Theoretical Psychology*, London: Routledge & Kegan Paul.

(1967) *Studies in Philosophy, Politics and Economics*, London: Routledge & Kegan Paul.

—— (1973) *Law, Legislation and Liberty: Rules and Order*, (Vol.1), London: Routledge & Kegan Paul.

—— (1976) *Law, Legislation and Liberty: The Mirage of Social Justice* (Vol.2).

—— (1988) *The Fatal Conceit: The Errors of Socialism*, London: Routledge.

Huizinga, J. (1938) *Homo Ludens*, Haarlem: Tjeenk Willink.

Morgenstern, O. (1928) *Wirtschaftsprognose, Eine Untersuchung der Voraussetzungen und Möglichkeiten*, Vienna: Springer.

—— (1935) "Perfect Foresight and Economic Equilibrium", translated from the German, *Zeitschrift für Nationalökonomie*, Vol. V.

Nash, J. (1950) "Non-Cooperative Games", Ph.D. thesis, Princeton University.

—— (1951) "Non-Cooperative Games", *Annals of Mathematics*, 2, Vol. 54.

Nozick, R. (1977) "On the Austrian Methodology", *Synthèse*, 36, pp. 354–8.

Schmidt, C. (2001) "De la théorie des jeux", *Essai d'interprétation*, Paris: P.U.F. (to be published).

Von Neumann, J. (1928) "On the Theory of Games of Strategy", translated from German, *Mathematische Annalen*, 100.

Von Neumann, J. and Morgenstern, O. (1944) *Theory of Games and Economic Behavior*. Princeton: Princeton University Press.

Zappia, C. (1999) "The Assumption of Perfect Foresight and Hayek's Theory of Knowledge", *Revue d'Economie Politique*, 6.

# 4    Monetary policy and business cycles

## Hayek as an opponent of the quantity theory tradition

*Richard Aréna*

## Introduction

On 12 March 1970, at University College, in London, Nicholas Kaldor gave a public lecture which was originally published in the *Lloyds Bank Review* some months later (Kaldor, 1970/1989, chapter 20). This lecture was devoted to the characterization of what the author called the "new monetarism" and became later Friedmanian monetarism. Amongst the main propositions attributed by Kaldor to this "new" monetary approach, he especially mentioned the long-run neutrality of money, namely a neutrality which could only be disturbed temporarily. Referring to this assertion of monetarism, Kaldor noted that

> all this part of the Friedman doctrine is closely reminiscent of the Austrian School of the twenties and the early thirties – the theories of Von Mises and Von Hayek – a fact which so far (to my knowledge) has received no acknowledgement in Friedmanite literature. (Very few people these days know the works of the Mises–Hayek school; unfortunately, I am old enough to have been an early follower of Professor Von Hayek, and even translated a book, particularly from the German language, to force you to come to grips with an argument.) Friedman differs from Von Mises and Von Hayek in being more literally spiced with the new-empiricism. On the other hand, he misses some of the subtleties of the Hayekian mechanism, and of the money-induced distortions in the "structure of production".
>
> (Kaldor, 1970/1989, pp. 476–7)

This quotation from Kaldor gives a significant flavour of a widespread opinion on Hayek's economic theory, four years before the author of *Prices and Production* was awarded the Nobel Memorial Prize in economic sciences. On one side, it shows the relative oblivion into which Hayek's contribution to economics had sunk, in those days. This situation remarkably contrasts with the substantial interest it arouses today, at least amongst contemporary historians of economic thought. On the other side, Kaldor's quotation stresses the fact that, at the beginning of the seventies, Hayek's theory was too often assimilated to a preliminary and tortuous version of modern monetarism.

This is not the view we shall support in this contribution. On the contrary, we intend to argue that Hayek's theory of money and business cycles essentially *differs from the quantity theory tradition.* These differences are not only *analytical.* They also appear in Hayek's monetary *doctrine* or, to be more precise, in his successive proposals for a reform of the monetary system. From this point of view, the long life of Friedrich Von Hayek provided him with a far from scarce opportunity: he was indeed given the possibility to read the authors belonging to the various generations of the Chicago School, from Irving Fisher to Milton Friedman, and to react to their contributions. We shall emphasize this quasi-unique singular case, building our chapter on the contrast Hayek's economic theory presents with the successive constructions of Fisher and Friedman within the quantity theory tradition.

## Fisher and Hayek

Irving Fisher proposed one of the earliest versions of the quantity theory of money and strongly contributed to the monetary doctrines of the Chicago School. We shall consider the relations between his monetary views and those of Hayek, distinguishing successively economic analysis and doctrine.

### *Economic analysis*

It is sometimes argued that there exists some complementarity between the quantity theory and Hayek's approach, the former focusing on the states of equilibrium while the latter would point out the disequilibrium dimensions of the relation between the real and the monetary magnitudes of the economic system. This view is however superficial. Both Fisher and Hayek tried to build an economic theory able to cope with both equilibrium and disequilibrium situations.

There indeed exists a tendency to limit Fisher's contribution to the pure quantity theory described in the *Purchasing Power of Money* and to neglect further contributions devoted by the author to the analysis of economic crises and fluctuations. For our purpose, it is however crucial to take both aspects of Fisher's economic analysis into account.

On the one hand, Fisher indeed describes equilibrium situations revealed by the equation of exchange in the cases of a stability of the velocity of circulation and the volume of trade. We all know Fisher's basic assertion:

> The so-called "quantity theory", i.e., that prices vary proportionately to money, has often been incorrectly formulated but (overlooking checks) the theory is correct in the sense that the level of prices varies directly with the quantity of money in circulation, provided the velocity of circulation of that money and the volume of trade which it is obliged to perform are not changed.
>
> (Fisher, 1911, p. 14)

In this framework, Fisher explicitly excludes any confusion which would result from a simultaneous change in the relative prices *and* in the general level of prices. Referring to a situation in which the quantity of money in circulation is supposed to double, Fisher notes that

> whether all prices increase uniformly, each being exactly doubled, or some prices increase more and some less (so as still to double the total money value of the goods purchased) the prices *are* doubled *on the average*. This proposition is usually expressed by saying that the "general level of prices" is raised twofold.
>
> (Fisher, 1911, p. 15)

Such an approach to the effects of the variation of the quantity of money on prices implies two necessary requirements. We must first be able to define precisely – both theoretically and empirically – what money and "the" quantity of money are. We must also consider that average economic magnitudes make sense and, even more, that they form the main concern of monetary theory.

If these requirements are supposed to be fulfilled, it is then necessary to point out the main forms of variation of the quantity of money in circulation.

One of them is related to the metallic system which still prevailed at the epoch of Irving Fisher. Within this system, the import or export of metals from foreign countries contributed to a variation in the volume of circulation of money. The same effect is obtained in the cases of minting operations or changes in the production or consumption of precious metals.

Fisher also considers, however, the possible effects of monetary systems which differ from mono-metallism. Thus, the introduction in a metallist system of a second type of metal, cheaper than the previous one, for instance, also exerts an influence on the volume of circulation. Moreover, Fisher does not exclude the use of paper money at the issue of central bank notes and these circumstances also contribute to changes in the quantity of money in circulation.

Finally, Fisher does not only consider magnitude M, namely the volume of circulating money, but also magnitude M′, namely the total deposits subject to transfer by check. If this second magnitude is permitted to vary, the ratio between circulating and deposited money will change and exert its effects on the general level of prices. The variation of deposits is related by Fisher to both the "extension of the banking system" and the "use of book" credit (Fisher, 1911, p.149).

Therefore, Fisher takes various types of change of the volume of money in circulation into account but changes are always considered at a macroeconomic level, emphasizing the effect of the variation of an aggregate magnitude on the general level of prices.

However, Fisher did not only develop a theory of the value of money. He also faced what he called, in his *Purchasing Power of Money*, the "temporary effect during the period of transition" (Fisher, 1911, pp. 55–6). These "periods" are especially investigated in the books that Fisher dedicated to business cycles. They indeed suppose that neither the velocity of circulation nor the volume of trade remain constant. Therefore, an analysis of economic *processes* becomes necessary. From this point of view, *Booms and Depressions*, published in 1932, offers a good flavour of the Fisherian approach to business cycles.

The origin of the cycle lies in the occurrence of a difference between the rate of interest paid to the banks and the expected rate of profit on investment. This origin can be related to "new opportunities to invest at a big prospective profit" generated by various types of innovation (new products, new techniques, new resources, new markets, etc.). These new opportunities lead entrepreneurs to an over-investment phase of expansion: contrary to Hayek, Fisher does not exclude a further increase of the bank rate of interest but he supposes this increase is less than the initial rise of the expected rate of profit (Fisher, 1911, pp. 56–60). Therefore, as long as a positive difference exists between both rates, real costs remain minor and, therefore, contracted debts are more easily reimbursed to banks. The turning point of the cycle is not analysed with sufficient care by Fisher. However, the relation of banking policy and banks' behaviours with the mass psychology of agents plays a central role: at a certain point of time, the confidence of entrepreneurs begins to vanish and the economy enters into a slump. The Fisherian slump is not only a phase of output contraction. It also implies a real process of debt deflation, which reduces the volume of money in circulation. When debts have been liquidated through reimbursement or through firms or banks' bankruptcies, a new period of expansion becomes possible.

This description of the business cycle presents some similarities with Hayek's approach, in which the beginning of the cycle also lies in the emergence of a difference between the natural and the monetary rates of interest: these similarities are only apparent, however.

First, Hayek expresses strong doubts about the validity of using aggregate magnitudes such as the quantity of money in circulation or the general level of prices. We cannot avoid quoting here a famous passage from *Prices and Production*, which questions the relation between macromagnitudes and microdecisions. Let us first note that this passage begins with an explicit reference to the Fisherian version of the quantity theory of money (Hayek, 1931, p. 2). In this framework, Hayek notes:

> What I complain of is not only that [the Fisherian quantity] theory in its various forms has unduly usurped the central place in monetary theory, but that the point of view from which it springs is a positive hindrance for further progress. Not the least harmful effect of this particular theory is the present isolation of the theory of money from the main body of general economic theory. For so long as we use different methods for the explanation of values as they are supposed to exist irrespective of any influence of money, and for the explanation of that influence of money

on prices, it can never be otherwise. Yet we are doing nothing less than this if we try to establish *direct* causal connections between the *total* quantity of money, the *general level* of all prices and, perhaps, also the *total* amount of production. For none of these magnitudes *as such* ever exerts an influence on the decisions of individuals; yet it is on the assumption of a knowledge of the decisions of individuals that the main propositions of non-monetary economic theory are based. It is to this "individualistic" method that we owe whatever understanding of economic phenomena we possess; that the modern "subjective" theory has advanced beyond the classical school in its consistent use is probably its main advantage over their teaching.

If, therefore, monetary theory still attempts to establish causal relations between aggregates or general averages, this means that monetary theory lags behind the development of economics in general. In fact, neither aggregates nor averages do act upon one another, and it will never be possible to establish necessary connections of cause and effect between them as we can between individual phenomena, individual prices, etc. ... I would even go so far as to assert that, from the very nature of economic theory, averages can never form a link in its reasoning.

(Hayek, 1931, pp. 3–5)

This passage expresses the fundamental opposition between Fisher's and Hayek's theories of money. As the Walras of the first edition of the *Eléments d'Economie Pure*, Fisher isolates, at least partially, the theory of money from the rest of the microtheory of his epoch. To put it in other words, he builds a theory of the relation between money and prices which is not microfounded. On the contrary, Hayek completely excludes such a possibility. Monetary theory has to be a part of general economic theory; it cannot be conceived independently from the theory of relative prices.

A significant illustration of the empirical problems implied by Hayek's critique is given by the geographical space in which we define *a* given quantity of money or general level of prices. According to Hayek, the use of a national quantity or index is, for instance, equivalent to the belief in the "illusion, based on the accident that the statistical measures of price movements are usually constructed for countries as such" (Hayek, 1937, p. 7). Hayek raises here, in fact, the problem of the spatial validity of the aggregate concepts of quantity theory (pp. 21–4): policies of control of the quantity of money may cumulatively generate international inflation, if there is no coordination of the variations of the different national quantities (pp. 42–6).

The rejection of aggregate magnitudes from the group of the explanatory variables of monetary theory obviously implies the use of relative prices. This is why, characterizing Hayek's contribution to economics, Machlup noted that, at the time of Fisher,

Hayek rejected three generally accepted positions:

(1) that money acts upon prices and production only if the general price level changes
(2) that a rising price level always causes an increase in production, and
(3) that monetary theory was mainly, if not exclusively, the theory of how the value of money is determined.

(Machlup, 1974/1992)

Concerning proposition (1), Hayek showed that almost any change in the quantity of money or credit influences relative prices, whether or not it changes the general level of prices. Proposition (2) is unintelligible in Hayek's framework, since the notions of aggregate output and general price level have no meaning for individual agents. Proposition (3) shows that the very purpose of economic theory and, within it, of monetary theory is to point out the influence of credit creation by banks upon the relative prices and, later, upon the allocation of resources to the production of different goods. Now, in spite of some analogies between Fisher's and Hayek's theories of business cycles, the former hardly distinguished between consumers' and producers' goods while the latter introduced all the successive stages of production from the earliest (namely, those which are at the most remote level of production) to the latest ones (namely the level of the consumers' goods). We know the role these successive stages of production played in Hayek's structural theory of business cycles and money and it is then easy to understand why, in spite of some analogies relative to the impulsions in both Fisher's and Hayek's approaches, the two respective business cycle theories strongly differ in their analysis of propagative mechanisms.

A last difference must be stressed, which might help us to understand still better why Hayek's and Fisher's approaches did not really converge. When Fisher refers to the quantity of money in circulation, it is indeed clear that he is coping within an outside money type of explanation. This remark is easy to confirm when we consider the changes in the quantity of money in circulation related to metal variations: in this case, we immediately see that this quantity changes according to purely non-economic factors. When metallic influences no longer appear, changes remain, however exogeneous, either through a discretionary decision of monetary authorities or through a change in the money/bank deposits ratio.

With Hayek's approach, the scenario is completely different. Following his Wicksellian inspiration, Hayek explicitly considers money supply as an endogenous variable. The role devoted to bank credit in Hayek's scheme is indeed to fill the gap between saving and investment. Therefore, according to Hayek's conception, money supply follows money demand and this is precisely the reason why a cyclical phase of expansion appears: under the pressure of entrepreneurial credit requirements, banks tend to attribute credits beyond what would be necessary to ensure capital market equilibrium.

These differences clearly appear when one considers the origin of impulsion in Hayek's business cycle theory. According to the version considered, the impulsions might be various: changes in the income distribution, existence of a difference between the natural and the monetary rates of interest; changes in costs and prices; new opportunities for investment; changes in the credit policy of banks; inventions; entrepreneurial increase of optimistic expectations, etc. These impulsions do not necessarily imply a deliberate change of the central money in circulation decided by monetary authorities. Money, therefore, plays a very different role in Fisher and in Hayek.

### Economic doctrine

The analytical differences we have reviewed had substantial consequences in the respective views Hayek and Fisher developed concerning monetary policies. The instance of the "Chicago Plan" might be here recalled. This plan was elaborated during the early thirties at the University of Chicago, by Simons and Fisher. It was also called the "100 per cent money" plan in compliance with the title of the book in which Fisher developed his proposals (Fisher, 1935).

The purpose of the "100 per cent money" plan was to reduce the strength and the length of slumps through a monetary reform able to stabilize the economy. As Seccareccia (1994, p. 63) emphasized, its essence was to break the link between money and credit. On the one hand, a part of the existing banks were destined to become "deposit" or "check" banks. These financial institutions had to cover deposits by 100 per cent reserves; these reserves were supposed to be obtained by transforming a large part of the assets of commercial banks into cash. On the other hand, the remaining part of banks would become "investment banks"; they were assumed to form their capital through security issue and perform the pure intermediary function of lending institutions on the capital market. Therefore, in this system, hopefully, banks do not create money beyond the gap between saving and investment. Investment banks do indeed only offer means of financing using their own resources, namely the capital they obtained through security issue. Check banks, on the contrary, are unable to play this financial role since they can no longer create credit *ex nihilo* to finance firms. Moreover, the capital market rate of interest cannot differ from the financial one. Fisher's solution thus appeared to favour the nationalization of money combined however with a reduction in the discretionary powers of monetary authorities.

The distinction proposed by Fisher between investment and check banks or investment and check departments in a given single bank; the reduction of the discretionary powers of monetary authorities and the objective of an equality between the natural and the monetary rates of interest were all themes compatible with Hayek's view of monetary problems. However, Hayek did not support the "100 per cent" money plan. Analytical arguments already developed provided the foundations of his critiques of the Chicago Plan.

On one side, Hayek denied the possibility of "drawing a sharp line [today] between what is money and what is not" (Hayek, 1937, p. 83). Here again, we meet the distrust of Hayek as regards the possibility and also the meaning of controlling a given quantity of money.

On the other side – and that is, in a sense, a corollary of the first argument – Hayek was strongly sceptical about the possibility of "abolishing deposit banking" (p. 82). Referring to the historical example of the Act of Peel of 1844, Hayek noted that any restriction placed on the expansion of bank deposits would lead individual agents to monetary innovations or towards specific forms of "near-money", both able to provide new types of money substitutes to banking deposits. It was therefore hopeless to try to control a monetary aggregate.

Finally, Hayek also contested the monopolistic role given to a governmental currency commission proposed in the Fisher plan for the process of transformation of commercial banks' assets into cash. He considered the state still had too strong discretionary powers in the monetary domain.

We know what Hayek proposed in the thirties in order to stabilize the economy: the policy of "neutral money". However, Hayek did not consider the objective of "neutral money" as a real precept of monetary policy. He knew perfectly well that this was only a pure analytical concept and, therefore, that, in reality, the condition of neutrality could only be approached. Moreover, he was also aware that, in concrete economies, the condition of instantaneous price flexibility was hardly fulfilled. This is why the practical objective for neutral money was considered to be a constant quantity of money (under the assumption of a given velocity of circulation and a given volume of trade). Here again, Hayek's critique of monetary aggregates explains the choice of the neutral money objective.

## Hayek and Friedman

In the fifties, Friedman proposed a revised version of the quantity theory of money, which avoided some of the limits of the Fisherian version.

### *Economic analysis*

First, as Bellante and Garrisson (1988/1992, p. 313) noted, Friedman refined Fisher's argument in favour of a structure of aggregation including only one single capital good. Friedman indeed referred to the Chicago theory of capital which was built in 1934 by Knight. According to this theory, the problem of the intertemporal structure of capital could be ignored, the more as the Austrian theory suffered from a certain number of logical inconsistencies. Moreover, distribution effects and differential income effects were explicitly excluded:

> Friedman's heuristic device for short-circuiting the distribution effects is to assume that increases in the money supply are brought about by a one-time dropping of money from an helicopter in such a way that each individual picks up new money in direct proportion to the amount already in his

possession. The differential income effects of "helicopter money" – as it has come to be called – are assumed away. This mode of theorizing reflects the implicit assumption that differential income effects are in fact negligible on the heuristic assumption that indifference curves are both identical across agents and homothetic.

(Bellante and Garrisson, 1988/1992, p. 313)

This framework obviously implies that any injection of money exerts an homothetic influence on economic activities. Thus, if the variation of the quantity of money in circulation exerted by chance an influence on relative prices, the divergence in the pattern of prices between the initial monetary injection and the variation of the general level of prices would be purely stochastic. Bellante and Garrisson note that

disequilibrium relative-prices movements within the markets for both capital goods and final products are taken to be unsystematic. No generalizations about such movements can be made.

(Bellante and Garrisson, 1988/1992, p. 313)

The market of capital goods is not therefore at the heart of Friedman's views on money and business cycles. A major role is given to the labour market and we are reminded how expectational mistakes may be committed by both employers and workers in confusing relative price and general level of price movements. These mistakes explain how the short-run fluctuations of macromagnitudes and their corrections permit the return to former levels that characterized the economy before the money injection.

This form of money injection – based on the image of the "helicopter" – is more Fisherian than Hayekian. In contrast with both authors of the quantity theory tradition, in the Hayekian framework money is indeed injected through credit markets. We retrace here a major difference between outside and inside money approaches.

As Bellante and Garrisson also noted, Hayek's approach is easier to generalize than Friedman's (Bellante and Garrisson, 1988/1992, pp. 323–4). We indeed know that in his characterization of cycles, Hayek distinguished the cases of forced and voluntary savings. In the first situation, prices of capital goods and labour rise relatively to the prices of consumer goods and this tendency leads entrepreneurs to invest in the "new", more capital-intensive processes. Then, sooner or later, the output of consumption goods declines, individual preferences remaining stable. Shortages of consumer goods thus drive up their prices and this process constitutes the mechanism of forced saving. Thus, new money is first falling into the hands of producers and only later into the hands of consumers. In the situation of voluntary saving, consumers change their time-preference such that they are willing to sacrifice an additional part of their claims to current output in exchange for more consumption in the future. Here, new money first falls into the hands of consumers, as is the case in Fisher's analysis. The main difference is here that both stories can be told and, therefore, that Hayek's approach appears to be more general than Friedman's.

Now, Hayek's approach is not easily compatible with Friedman's views. First, in the seventies, Hayek went deeper into his critique of economic aggregates. He wrote:

> I have always found it useful to explain to students that it has been rather a misfortune that we describe money by a noun, and that it would be more helpful for the explanation of monetary phenomena if "money" were an adjective describing a property which different things could possess to varying *degrees*.
>
> (Hayek, 1976, p. 47)

According to this quotation, money appears to be a "continuum" rather than a precise object. It is thus hopeless to try to measure *the* quantity of money. Friedman's empiricism leads him to focus on the necessity of measurement but, far from increasing the scientific contents of the concept, it might sometimes reduce it (Hayek, 1976, p. 48, note 1). These new critiques of the quantity theory tradition permitted Hayek to associate both Fisher and Friedman in the formulation of his objections against the discretionary powers of monetary authorities:

> I wish I could share the confidence of my friend Milton Friedman who thinks that one could deprive the monetary authorities, in order to prevent the abuse of their powers for political purposes, of all discretionary powers by prescribing the amount of money they may and should add to circulation in any one year. It seems to me that he regards this as practicable because he has become used for statistical purposes to draw a sharp distinction between what is to be regarded as money and what is not. The distinction does not exist in the real world. I believe that, to ensure the convertibility of all kinds of near-money into real money, which is necessary if we are to avoid severe liquidity crises or panics, the monetary authorities must be given some discretion.
>
> (Hayek, 1991, p. 279)

Another important divergence between Friedman and Hayek is familiar to us. It is related to the stress Hayek put on the role of capital goods within the process of economic fluctuation. In clear contrast with the Knightian theory of capital, capital goods in the Austrian view are fundamentally heterogeneous and, therefore, the structure of capital provides an unavoidable element in the Hayekian explanation of monetary and real short-run disturbances.

The last difference between Hayek's and Friedman's analytical structures is related to the respective characterizations of money involved by their approaches to business cycles. Again, we shall not spend much time on it since what we told about Hayek and Fisher's different conceptions can be retraced here without substantial changes. The image of the "helicopter" is significant from this standpoint since it clearly points out that Friedmanian money is typical outside money. On the contrary, even if the necessity of a confrontation with monetarism often leads Hayek to redefine his position in the framework of an outside money issue, fundamentally, his concern remained the creation process of credit and therefore supposed an approach in terms of inside money.

It is thus important to emphasize the permanent distrust expressed by Hayek of the quantity theory tradition, from Fisher to Friedman. This opposition does not mean, however, that Hayek condemned this theory with the same strength from both analytical and empirical standpoints. In one of his seventies papers, Hayek indeed reiterated his analytical critique of the quantitativist tradition and repeated his wish to connect monetary theory and the theory of relative prices (Hayek, 1978, p. 215). He did not deny however that, "for most practical purposes", "the simple form of the quantity theory" offers "a decidedly helpful guide" (p. 215). These remarks were not new and Hayek himself reiterated in 1978 what he wrote in 1931, namely that "it would be one of the worst things which could befall us if the general public should ever again cease to believe in the elementary propositions of the quantity "theory" (Hayek, 1931, p. 3 quoted by Hayek, 1978, p. 216).

This ambiguity with respect to the practical utility of quantity theory also appears when we consider the respective Hayekian and Friedmanian approaches to monetary policy.

### Economic doctrine

Since the fifties, Friedman's position concerning monetary policy never varied. The origin of his doctrine is simple:

> All in all, perhaps the only conclusion that is justified is that either rising prices or falling prices are constant with rapid economic growth, provided that the prices changes are fairly steady, moderate in size, and reasonably predictable. The mainsprings of growth are presumably to be sought elsewhere. But unpredictable and erratic changes of direction in prices are apparently as disturbing to economic growth as to economic stability.
> (Friedman, 1958/1965, p. 103)

Now the discretionary powers given to monetary authorities play a crucial role in the Friedmanian explanation of those "unpredictable and erratic changes". For Friedman, "fine tuning" policies provide the typical way to create inflation or deflation. The only solution, therefore, consists in replacing "discretion" with automatic rules. In order to stabilize the general level of prices, the total amount of money has to grow to accommodate itself to the growth in output and in population. However, a steady rate of growth of the money supply does not mean perfect stability, even though it prevents substantial economic fluctuations. According to Friedman, the observation of historical series shows that monetary changes take a fairly long time to exert their influence and that the time taken is highly variable. This is why Friedman suggested that an announcement should be made concerning the long-run permanence of a given rate of growth of money: this permanence had to be accepted by the public and it had to acquire some credibility in order to exert real effects on the economy.

Hayek undoubtedly shared with Friedman the idea that monetary policy was a major cause of inflation and depressions. He pointed out the reasons which prevented any "monopolistic governmental agency", to take his own words (Hayek, 1976, p. 80), from stabilizing the economy.

First, this agency is perfectly unable to possess the information which should govern the supply of money. In this prospect, no government can efficiently replace the market:

> Money is not a tool of policy that can achieve particular foreseeable results by control of its quantity. But it should be part of the self-steering mechanism by which individuals are constantly induced to adjust their activities to circumstances on which they have information only through the abstract signals of prices.
>
> (Hayek, 1976, p. 80)

Secondly, even if the government would be perfectly informed upon the possible effects of its decisions, it would not be able to act "in the general interest" (p. 80). The democratic system indeed imposes the necessity of being supported by a majority of the electors and, within this context, a government will often be unable to resist the pressure of "particular groups or sections of the population". Governments will try to decrease "local or sectional dissatisfaction by manipulating the quantity of money" (p. 80).

In the first part of this contribution, we saw that, in the thirties, Hayek proposed a policy which would approach the situation of "neutral money". This objective does not exactly correspond to a Friedmanian one since Hayek translated it, for practical purposes, as the necessity of reaching "the stabilization of some average prices of the original factors of production" (Hayek, 1933/1984, p. 161) and then, later, the stabilization of the domestic prices of a given standard basket of commodities (Hayek, 1943). We however know that, finally, Hayek renounced the idea of a national monopolistic currency and pleaded in favour of the "denationalisation of money" (Hayek, 1976). In 1976, Hayek himself explained how he came to this solution and it is interesting to quote fully his own interpretation of the transition from "neutral" to "denationalised money":

> Although I have myself given currency to the expression "neutral money" ... it was intended to describe this almost universally made assumption of theoretical analysis and to raise the question whether any real money would ever possess this property, and not as a model to be aimed at by monetary policy. I have long since come to the conclusion that no real money can ever be neutral in this sense, and that we must be content with a system that

rapidly corrects the inevitable errors. The nearest approach to such a condition which we can hope to achieve would appear to me to be one in which the average prices of the "original factors of production" were kept constant.

I will readily admit that such a provisional solution ... though giving us an infinitely better money and much more general economic stability than we have had leaves open various questions to which I have no ready answers. But it seems to meet the most urgent needs much better than any prospect that seemed to exist while one did not contemplate the abolition of the monopoly of the issue of money and the free admission of competition into the business of providing currency.

(Hayek, 1976, pp. 69–70)

We know the main characteristics of Hayek's project of denationalization of money. Individual agents must be given the choice of their currency. In other words, they must have the possibility of only using the money in which they have confidence and of refusing the ones they distrust. The government monopoly of money must be abolished in order to permit private banks to be on an equal level, able to create their own instruments of circulation and to compete in order to obtain the confidence of their customers. In this framework, the expected value of a bank currency will be the decisive factor determining how much of it the public will hold. Any bank will have two methods of changing the quantity of its own currency in circulation: either exchanging its currency against other currencies; or varying the level of its lending activities. To assure the constancy of its currency value, a given bank has never to increase its volume beyond the public demand to hold the currency; and never to reduce its supply below it. In practice, it therefore regulates its behaviour according to the rates of exchange of its currency against other ones (Hayek, 1976, chapter 11). Therefore, competition among banks is supposed to regulate the different quantities of currencies in circulation. It is therefore easy to understand why Hayek wrote that "the past instability of the market economy is the consequence of the exclusion of the most important regulation of the market mechanism, money, from itself being regulated by the market process" (Hayek, 1976, p. 79).

It is also interesting to note that Hayek's solution is compatible with his assumption of considering money supply as an endogenous variable. Hayek indeed noted the importance of money creation by credit in modern economies:

First, bank deposits subject to cheque, and thus a sort of privately issued money, are today of course a part, and in most countries much the largest part, of the aggregate amount of generally accepted media of exchange. Secondly, the expansion and contraction of the separate national super-structures of bank credit are at present the chief excuse for national management of the basic money.

(Hayek, 1976, p. 18)

It is thus easy to understand how the project of denationalization of money could fit with Hayek's view of the saving/investment adjustment process through credit: if competition prevails among banks, it is hoped that they will only issue the accurate volume of credit which permits a strict equalization of saving and investment and excludes any overbanking tendency. Obviously, the efficiency of the competitive process is at the heart of Hayek's solution and this is why it provoked so many critiques. Some authors found it "messianic" more than "analytic" (Fisher, 1986, p. 434): very few historical examples existed, which gave an idea of what would happen in a private monetary system. Others raised strong doubts concerning the crucial applicability of the theory of price competition to the case of money production activity (Howard, 1977, p. 485).

Anyway, Hayek's monetary doctrine clearly differs from Friedman's. It proposes the denationalization of money, while Friedman developed his reasoning in a system of nationalized money. The distance between Hayek's approach and the quantity theory therefore increased in the seventies and reinforced his objections against it.

## Some concluding remarks

Our conclusion is simple: Hayek was and remained, during his whole life, an opponent of quantity theory. This observation might surprise those who are still convinced by the view expressed in Kaldor's quotation at the beginning of the present contribution. It is, however, easy to accept if we remember that Hayek was a remarkable historian of economic thought and found some inspiration while reading the authors of the past. From this standpoint, it makes sense to note that, in a way, Hayek took three developments of the classical age and mixed them to build his own construction. One is Cantillon's view of the relation between money and values. In *Prices and Production* Hayek indeed notes that "Richard Cantillon ... provided the first attempt known to me to trace the actual chain of cause and effect between the amount of money and prices" (Hayek, 1931, p. 79). The second development is due to the Banking School which coped with money supply as an endogenous variable. The third corresponds to the Free Banking tradition which questioned the utility of the monopoly of the state as an issuer of money. Now, it is clear that these three sources of inspiration are not the closest to the quantity theory tradition. To some extent, it could even be shown that, at least, a part of the analysis they contributed in building, contradicts this tradition. From his standpoint, Hayek's knowledge of the history of economic thought certainly contributed to the "subtleties" that Kaldor attributed to the Hayekian mechanism, in contrast with the Friedmanian version of modern quantity theory.

## Acknowledgements

I would like to thank R. Van Zijp, N. Janson, A. Leijonhufvud, J. Magnan de Borgnier and P. Nataf for their valuable comments, critiques and suggestions. The usual disclaimer applies.

## Bibliography

Bellante, D. and Garrisson, J. (1988/1992) "Philips Curves and Hayekian Triangles: Two Perspectives on Monetary Dynamics", *History of Political Economy*, vol. 20, Summer 1988, republished in Woods and Woods (1992).

Fisher, I. (1911) *The Purchasing Power of Money*, New York: Macmillan.

—— (1932) *Booms and Depressions, Some First Principles*, New York: Adelphi..

—— (1935) *100% Money*, New York: Adelphi.

—— (1986) "Friedman Versus Hayek on Private Money: Review Essay", *Journal of Monetary Economics*, vol. 17, May.

Friedman, M. (1958/1965) "The Supply of Money and Changes in Prices and Output", in US Congress Joint Economic Committee, *The Relationship of Prices to Economic Stability and Growth: Compendium of Papers Submitted by Panelists* Washington, DC, 1958, republished in Dean, E. (ed.) (1965) *The Controversy Over the Quantity Theory of Money*, Lexington: Heath & Company.

Hayek, F. (1931) *Prices and Production*, London: Routledge & Kegan Paul.

—— (1933/1984) "On 'Neutral' Money", republished in Hayek, F. (1984) *Money, Capital and Fluctuations, Early Essays*, London: Routledge & Kegan Paul.

—— (1937) *Monetary Nationalism and International Stability*, London: Longman, Green & Co.

—— (1943) "A Commodity Reserve Currency", *Economic Journal*, 53 (210), June–September.

—— (1976) *Denationalisation of Money*, Hobart Paper Special, London: Institute of Economic Affairs.

—— (1978) *New Studies in Philosophy, Economics and the History of Ideas*, London and Henley: Routledge & Kegan Paul.

—— (1991) *Economic Freedom*, London: Basil Blackwell.

Howard, D. (1977) "Review of Denationalisation of Money", *Journal of Monetary Economics*, vol. 8, October.

Kaldor, N. (1970) "The New Monetarism", *Lloyds Bank Review*, July, republished in Targetti, F. and Thirlwall, A. (eds) (1989) *The Essential Kaldor*, chapter 20, New York: Holmes & Meier.

Machlup, F. (1974) "Friedrich von Hayek's Contribution to Economics", *Swedish Journal of Economics*, vol. 76, December, republished in Woods and Woods (1992).

Seccareccia, M. (1994) "Credit Money and Cyclical Crises: the Views of Hayek and Fisher compared", in Colonna, M. and Hagemann, H. (eds) *Money and Business Cycles, vol. 1, The Economics of F.A. Hayek*, Aldershot, Hants: Edward Elgar.

Woods, J. and Woods, C. (eds) (1992) *Critical Assessments*, Aldershot, Hants: Edward Elgar.

# Part III
# Order

# 5 An investigation of Hayek's criticism of central planning

*Chikako Nakayama*[1]

## Introduction

The Austro-Marxist, Eduard März, has suggested that *"The Road to Serfdom*, the anti-socialist treatise published by Friedrich von Hayek, shortly after the Second World War, was anticipated in its main points by Mises's book."[2] Hayek's *Serfdom* tends to agree with Mises's *Die Gemeinwirtschaft* and with the ideas of the Socialist Calculation debate of the 1920s, and indeed appears to be directly influenced by Mises. I would like here to investigate this point: that in the twenties Hayek had already evolved the basic arguments of *Serfdom*, most especially his criticisms of central planning.[3] That is, I hope to reappraise *Serfdom* in the context of Hayek's earlier career – in particular, in terms of his advocacy of the Austrian or Viennese School of Economics. However, the scope of *Serfdom* is not limited to the values of this specific historical context; it is a product not only of Hayek's Austrian background but of his adoption of English, or rather classical, rational liberalism as well.[4] Hayek's text is clearly sharp in its general criticisms of totalitarian tendencies, criticisms which originate, allegedly, in Hayek's fear that "it is Germany whose fate we [people in England] are in some danger of repeating".[5] I will try to assess the consistency of Hayek's political and economic liberalism. März, after all, points out that Hayek concludes his book with an argument which directly connects a society's economic system and political situation:[6] one might therefore usefully compare Hayek's own political and economic perspectives. In doing so, one may witness the characteristics and the consequences of Austrian liberalism.

It is a cliché to suppose that human reason distinguishes our species from any other "beast devoid of reason"; and that a life based on reason is not necessarily the same as a merely (ergonomically or economically) "rational" existence. This common notion seems consistent with Hayek's theory of values (and with Austrian value theories in general). Questions of freedom are extremely pertinent to this Austrian idealism; the urgency of such questions might be challenged, however, when a nation-state is faced with hunger and hardship, to test the limits and to expose the inadequacies of this breed of liberalism. This perspective may illuminate the ways in which attitudes to Hayek's liberal theories have differed and changed in the years between the publication of *Serfdom* and the present day.[7]

We may finally see the fate of liberalism – just one of its fates – in the light of Hayek's personal history: a sentence of exile, liberated from the constraints of home or birthplace, an individual reduced to the status of those human labour commodities he espoused. Yet this liberation from the responsibilities and preconceptions of place limits the capacity of this brand of liberalism to address the problems which accrue to the issue of nationalism: Hayek's placelessness, while politically liberating, at the same time undermines his perspective on the politics of any particular place.

## What was at stake immediately after the First World War in Austria?

In the immediate wake of the First World War, the most urgent concern of the people of the newly born Austria was to construct their own nation-state. The Habsburg monarchy had not survived the end of the war, and many of the nations within its dominion gained independence. The western part of this empire, consisting mainly of Germanic populations,[8] could have solved the problem of this political vacuum in a variety of ways.[9] Austria eventually chose a solution, establishing a coalition between the Social Democratic Party (SDP) and the Christian-Socialist Party (CSP) in an attempt to invent autonomy and nationhood, which turned out to be imperfect. The survival of this new independent nation-state seemed uncertain: the chances of Austria's success were debated publicly and pessimistically.[10] This pessimism was underlined by the country's economic problems.[11]

A contemporary newspaper article analysed Austria's problematic position in terms of the separation of state and society, quoting the leader of the CSP.[12] The view of the state, the perspective of power, was emphatically divorced from society in general. The wishes of the state were informed and performed by the SDP and by its leadership. Although the SDP leader, Otto Bauer, had not originally supported Austrian independence,[13] he was obliged to argue the viability of the new nation-state. He was an Austro-Marxist; it thus became the lot of this political group to improve the odds that Austria might prosper.[14]

The Austro-Marxists tried to establish a system which might comprehensively supervise their citizens' lives in the words of their slogan, "from the cradle to the grave": a socio-political system which afforded a special emphasis to the notion of enlightenment through education.[15] However, the prevailing economic opinion around the turn of the century was the very different perspective of the liberal Austrian School of Economics, which not only espoused radically different methods but also witnessed quite different problems. Although liberalism was out of favour in Austrian politics, it remained dominant in economic theory.[16] As a result of the fecundity of the controversies between Marxists and liberals, Austria, and especially Vienna, enjoyed something of a belle époque, a blossoming of intellectual activity in the field of economics.[17]

This particular ideological conflict can be traced as far back as Eugen von Böhm-Bawerk's 1896 polemic on Marxist economic theory (focusing specially on value theory), which was countered by Rudolf Hilferding's[18] argument in 1904; and so the debate ensued. From the end of the nineteenth century this school of liberal economics dominated Austrian economic thought, pricked though it was by the tireless critiques and challenges of the Marxists.[19]

According to Hayek, the liberal school maintained a strong (if perhaps diminished) influence.[20] However, Hayek adds, rather ambiguously, that, while the liberal position had become Austria's economic orthodoxy, the peak of that school's success had been before the First World War.[21] The fact that in 1919 and in 1923 the University of Vienna chose not to fill academic vacancies with such liberal economists of the Austrian School seemed to signal the School's decline.[22] The economic hardships of the 1920s inspired harsh and apparently unanswerable attacks upon the liberal economists.[23]

When Hayek entered the debate between the liberals and the Marxists, its central controversy lay in the question of the socialization of Austria's economic, social and political systems. In 1919 the Marxist Bauer[24] published a pamphlet in favour of socialization,[25] and three years later the powerful liberal, Ludwig von Mises, penned an article, later anthologized in a book, against this proposed programme.[26] In fact, the socialization committee, led by Bauer, soon foundered, and Mises's essay passed virtually unnoticed.[27] Although the debate was neither lively nor particularly long lived, this issue was significant as a rare convergence of the interests, methods and researches of the two schools.

The essence of this debate seems to lie in the two schools' different notions of rationality and rationalization. Mises had already stated that the establishment of a socialist system could make no concessions to the criteria of rationalization.[28] This issue was to prove even more important to Hayek, as a crucial factor in his argument against totalitarianism. He believed that totalitarianism required a process of absolute rationalization, and that the consequences of this process were contrary to the conditions necessary for human happiness.

## The attack on central planning

Before we examine Hayek's ideas on totalitarianism in detail, we might profit from a brief foray into his early academic activity in Vienna, a period of his life which seems less well known than his later achievements.[29] In 1918, after coming back from the First World War, Hayek began to study law[30] at the University of Vienna. From 1920 Ludwig von Mises organized a series of private seminars in which Hayek was one of the more active participants. It would appear that Hayek was fascinated by the books and articles Mises published around this time. From 1921 Hayek himself founded another intellectual circle: the "Geistkreis".[31] Between 1923 and 1924 he visited the United States where he met W. C. Mitchell and other American Institutionalists. In 1927, thanks to Mises, Hayek became the head of the *Österreichisches Institut für Konjunkturforschung* (Austrian Institute of Trade Cycles), where he remained until 1931, when he travelled to England to take a position at the London School of Economics. Hayek was still active in Mises's seminar group in 1928, reporting on his recent research.[32] In

1929, he had completed his "Habilitation" under the supervision of Hans Mayer, and since then he had been teaching as a private lecturer at the University of Vienna.

Hayek's contribution to the so-called "Socialist Calculation Debate" can be seen in his roles as editor and analyst. He published a collection of articles on this subject in 1935; this book included two articles of his own,[33] delineating the problems and offering his own solutions. The fact that these same articles reappeared – alongside some new ones – in another book on the subject of political epistemology and economics, which he published in 1948, suggests that he found this topic important.[34]

As he consistently maintained his interest in these problems from the 1920s until the 1940s, it is perhaps only to be expected that much of what Hayek said in his book of 1944, *The Road to Serfdom*,[35] is anticipated in these articles.

A central issue Hayek relentlessly addresses is the distinction between socialism and planning. He renames the Socialist Calculation Debate "the Collectivist Calculation Debate". He favours the term "collectivist" in order to make a distinction between the aims and methods of socialism. Socialism, in its simplest form, can be defined as an ethical belief that the position of property-less classes of society should be improved by a redistribution of income derived from property.[36] Hayek does not explicitly express any antipathy towards this stance. However, the collectivist brand of socialism involves a centralized structure of socio-economic planning, which coordinates the collective ownership of the means of production, and then the collectivist control of production itself. What Hayek criticizes are these centralized methods of planning rather than its goals. At one point he explains that there is a danger that these same methods might be used for quite different purposes, such as dictatorship by the aristocracy or by an ethnic or other élite. Furthermore, in a presentation made to Austrian industrialists in 1948, in which he offered a brief summary of his arguments against such forms of economic planning,[37] he announced that "a planned economy leads to loss of freedom with inexorable inevitability".[38] The methods of central planning would inevitability lead to a system that deprives people of freedom.

Hayek argues that this centralized economic planning gradually becomes an end in itself, that its only function is its own self-justification, as it invades every area of human freedom. He refutes the claims of the socio-political holism which views society as a homogeneous whole; while (with the merest hint of paradox)[39] he proposes that the economic conditions of a society cannot be independent of its other (for example, its political and cultural) aspects. On the former point, he believes that while individuals can productively plan their own economic activities, such planning is inappropriate to a nation or a state. He argues that the more the entire nation plans, the more difficult it becomes for each individual citizen to plan for his or her own economic life. He adds that this planning cannot be restricted to the economic area but also extends into other areas. He argues against the nineteenth-century notion that spiritual and cultural concerns are not influenced by economic conditions. Economic planning inevitably influences other areas. Both of these issues are closely connected with the problem of totalitarianism, and Hayek's criticism of central planning can be equated with a critique of totalitarianism. For Hayek, collectivism means totalitarianism, whose politically holistic strategies annihilate economic individualism and the social freedom of the individual.[40]

Hayek develops his political theories in opposition to virtually every collectivist, holist and planner of his time, as well as their immediate precursors, including Karl Mannheim,[41] Hegel and Marx.[42] He also names such German intellectuals as Sombart, Plenge or Schmitt in this connection, as antagonistic to the libertarian ideals of the French Revolution.[43] He further appears to number among his opponents such members of the German Historical School as Schmoller,[44] in that they focused their thoughts upon entire societies, nations and states. Hayek views these theoreticians as disciples of holism and totalitarianism. In a specifically Austrian context, however, it is basically towards Otto Neurath and Otto Bauer that he directs his criticisms.[45]

Hayek mentions Neurath's contribution as the most interesting of the early socialist theories, though some theoretical conflict can be seen between the two men.[46] Neurath committed himself to the socialization scheme from the end of the war until the middle of the 1920s, and consequently also to the Social Democratic Party. Hence his ideas have much in common with Bauer's. There is a contrast here between the Austro-Marxist and the Austrian School of Economics. (As for Bauer,[47] Hayek sees his ideas in terms of the creation of socialized industries within an otherwise competitive system, and seems to think rather more of his practical proposals than of his theoretical contributions.)

It seems valid to include, alongside Neurath, another important ideologue of the period, Othmar Spann. There is some historical evidence that Spann disliked Hayek,[48] and his name appears only once in *Serfdom*,[49] which quotes one of his followers,[50] an economist called Plenge.[51] However, Spann's increasing influence during the 1920s seems important in relation to Hayek's explicit criticism of corporatism.[52] Spann viewed his own theories in terms of a corporative system of planning, one whose structure would lie somewhere in between a system of free exchange and collectivism.[53] In fact, Neurath also drew upon a vision of a corporative system, in support of socialization.[54] The relationships between corporatism and ideas of collectivist central planning – and these theorists' attempts to justify this system – are therefore significant to the argument between Hayek and these two of his opponents.

## Why was Hayek against central planning?

In terms of the contrast between Hayek and such thinkers as Neurath and Spann, we may now examine these economists' different attitudes towards rationality and rationalization, their ideas about value systems and price systems, and their criticisms of dictatorship. (Both sides opposed dictatorship, in spite of their conflicting views on totalistic politics. Here we can therefore glimpse a distinction between their senses of dictatorship and totalitarianism.)

**Rationality and rationalization**

As I have already suggested, attitudes towards economic planning often boil down to problems of individual and collective modes of rationality, and questions as to whether these two can or should be the same. An equation of personal and social modes of rationality can be seen quite clearly in those arguments which Neurath based upon his experiences during the First World War. He often mentions rationalization (*Rationalisierung*)[55] in relation to socialization, and proposes that the ideal social system is founded on a quest for rationality and efficiency. He witnesses these concerns at the core of capitalism and he therefore commends capitalism's institutions and structures, such as the Taylor system and industrial and bank organizations.[56] He does not see any discrepancy between individual and collective modes of rationality.

Neurath supports this "rational" system not because of its ruthless, mechanical efficiency, but because of his belief that it offers the best way to build a humane society. He criticizes free competition in that it forces people into homogeneity,[57] and claims that a new system, derived from the Taylor system, would serve the plurality of national needs and individual life-styles, and would function equally well in relation to different kinds of labour.[58] He believes that the modern techniques of rationalization may enable different people to work in different ways. He criticizes the ways in which theorists and practitioners fail to address their contemporary situations.[59]

Neurath recommends a centralized planning strategy as a method by which a state might achieve his own socio-economic aims. He considers it the fault of the free competition system, the *Verkehrswirtschaft*, that the Taylor system met with such catastrophic results.[60] He advances a social strategy that could combine theories of labour, business and mechanization, and therefore proposed that the centralized hub of socio-economic planning would require all possible information to produce its productive and efficient schemes. He emphasizes the importance of statistical information,[61] which can provide invaluable data on economic values.

More broadly, Neurath implies that these contemporary techniques of social planning will define the very history of European nations, and that therefore the economy (*Wirtschaft*) and economists must race to keep pace with these developments. He hails the coming of the age of rationalism and utilitarianism, whose theories will determine the lives of all individuals and which will eventually become the orthodox economic tradition.[62] Here we recall that Neurath was an important member of the Vienna Circle which then espoused the ideals of logical positivism (scientific rationalism).[63]

The contrast between Neurath and Hayek is clear. For Hayek, the idea of social rationalization, for whatever reasons (however humane), remains dangerous: the ends cannot justify the means. He thinks it preferable that individuals, with their "bounded" or limited rationalities, should strive only for their own interests, and this struggle of (enlightened) self-interest might prove the best basis on which society's institutions may be formed.

A more concrete concern for Hayek is that rationality forces knowledge to fall into the hands of power, and that this process inevitably deprives people of their freedom. He says that the degree of political control is crucial,[64] especially in terms of freedom of (consumer) choice and of occupation. Hayek first believes it impossible for the centre of planning to take possession of all knowledge and information,[65] but then he eventually comes to see this as a dangerous possibility which would deny people their rights to freedom. For example, he argued that even something as simple as the political determination of national interest rates invites countless problems.[66] Hayek adds that this kind of political power can change the nature of politics itself and thus makes democracy impotent and meaningless.

Hayek warns of the dangers of the new notion of "collective freedom" in this connection. Such corporatists as Spann insisted upon the advantages of this new breed of freedom, which contradicted the individualistic ideals of the French Revolution, arguing that only a "collective freedom" which conformed to the requirements of society could be a true kind of freedom. Hayek feels that this tactic wears only the guise of freedom and would herald the death of truth, under a system in which knowledge and information would become the propagandist tools of state ideologies.[67] He opposes any such scheme to use human knowledge and beliefs as instruments of political purpose, on the grounds that this "instrumental" rationality is the first step on the road to totalitarianism.

### *Value, price and competition*

Hayek believes in the value and importance of social institutions created by individuals of limited rationality. In particular, he commends the working of the price mechanism within the institution of money, in so far as this mechanism mediates between almost every material exchange and acts as a cushion against the callous efficiency of extreme rationality.

The issue of value was of central importance to the Austrian School of Economics and to Hayek. Here again, Neurath presents an interesting contrast. Hayek criticizes Neurath's belief that considerations of value are not necessary to the supply of commodities and that the calculations of central planning authorities can be carried out in kind (without the mediation of money), a conclusion which Neurath draws from his experiences of the war-time economy. Hayek however believes that the price mechanisms of the free market can provide the only rational assessment of value. This, he says, is because the price mechanism works through the process of competition. For Hayek, competition is not so much a merciless struggle for existence, as an indispensable, developing process by which information may be revealed about the value systems dispersed through society. Without competition, the structures of value remain generally obscure or vague, and might therefore be exploited by any form of political power which has access to total information.

Hayek suggests the "moral or political"[68] implications of free competition and argues that it is a requirement of the game of this kind of competition that no economic transactions may be performed without pre-established rules: the

"Rule of Law" (as he calls it) which prevents any government from pursuing arbitrary, coercive (legal or illegal) courses of action. He insists that this is an important condition for liberty, and that centralized societal planning is not compatible with this Rule of Law.

Hayek gives the example of Nazi Germany as a collective state which is "moral" in the sense that the power of the state itself becomes "an institution which imposes its views on all moral questions, whether these views be moral or highly immoral",[69] while a liberal state is not in these terms totalistically "moral". He examines the specific example of the moral totalism of the Nazi regime. The general public acceptance and assumption of the Nazi creed or ideology[70] can focus upon children through sports, outdoor activities and social clubs, or upon any citizen through politically sanctioned modes of greeting and forms of address. He concludes that the prototype of a totalitarian party may be created through the organization of "cells" of political activists and devices for the permanent supervision of private life.[71] Hayek's sense of the word "moral" quite unusually does not imply individual moral activity or awareness; on the contrary, the imposition of national morality (or ideology) undermines the expression and the very existence of moral individualism.

It is often said that Hayek's concepts of liberty and freedom can be defined only passively, in terms of their distance from the reach of power;[72] but the same may be said of his ideas of value and morality. These concepts quite clearly seem to demonstrate the consistency between his economic theories and his philosophical or political writings.[73] The structure of his whole thought is founded upon a notion of a dispersed and heterogeneous constellation of human value systems, a dispersal of value, information and power which passively maintains individual morality and freedom, and upon the idea that the price mechanism is the only determining (but flexible and natural) structure which can be consistent with this system. Hayek considered these principles apt, consistent and true throughout every economic, political and social structure of a state.

### Criticism of dictatorship

The idea of dictatorship is often barely distinguished from the concept of totalitarianism, but we can perhaps see the difference between these two notions when we examine them closely. Both Neurath and Hayek are opposed to dictatorship, but not for the same reasons. Both see dictatorship as a mode of planning whose decisions may be taken by one or more individuals, but which allows no space for argument or debate. As such it is the antithesis of democracy; yet dictatorship can and did (in its most dangerous form) arise out of the heart of democracy.

This problem becomes all the more important when groups of people divided along political, cultural, religious, ethnic, social or economic lines, living in close proximity to one another, claim for themselves their rights as minorities. Neurath argues that democracy should not be defined as the domination of a dictatorial majority over society's minority groups, but rather as the acceptance of nonconformity within a chosen social order. He claims that the political or moral will of the majority may take the form of a dictatorial oppression of the minority.[74]

By contrast, Hayek seems rather too optimistic when he admits to the possibility of "good" dictatorship.[75] However, Hayek generally supports democracy for a number of reasons based on his notions of freedom.[76] Unlike his implicit and passive readings of freedom and morality, Hayek's definition of democracy is uncharacteristically active, explicit and therefore perhaps inappropriately prescriptive (even undemocratically so); but his argument fails to give any positive insight into the practical importance of democracy. Even though he is, conversely, apparently aware of the great danger of democracy being subsumed to the desires of a moral majority and consequently becoming the dictatorship of the many,[77] when he discusses the problems involved in any democracy which boasts absolute, plenary power.[78] (It may not, however, have been until 1951 that the paradoxical mechanism by which a relatively liberal and individualistic voting system might foster dictatorship was demonstrated, by Arrow.[79]) Hayek may well have been conscious of the problems faced by minority groups within a national democracy,[80] but he could not explain them within the framework of his theory. This appears to suggest the limitations of Hayek's liberalism, which, as Neurath points out, assumes and requires the homogeneity of individuals.

## Appraisal

### *The contribution of Hayek's* Serfdom

Hayek's contribution to the discussion of rationality and rationalization within the collectivist calculation debate which preoccupied the political intelligentsia of inter-war Vienna lies in the fact that he demonstrates the difference between a social order or an equilibrium achieved and maintained by the self-regulating mechanism of supply and demand, and one enforced by the coercive power of central planning. These differences may now seem obvious, but those who entered into more refined theoretical deliberations in the wake of the debate – socialists and general equilibrium theorists alike[81] – were not in fact alert to these particular ideas; essentially, they failed fully to recognize the importance of power. In these terms, we can hardly overstress the contemporary and continuing significance of Hayek's crucial recognition of the dangers posed by any authority that seeks to schematize and rationalize the structure of an economy or a society. His main point is that power cannot be transferred from the hands of individuals to any political centre without undergoing a treacherous change in its nature.[82] This transfer of power inevitably leads towards the politics of socio-economic interventionism, which undermines individual morality and freedom, and which wrecks democracy. He argues that only a competitive economic system founded upon natural mechanisms of price and value can safely mediate between individual and collective modes of rationality, in that it necessarily minimizes the power exercised by people over people through a process of politico-economic decentralization.

### *Hayek's consistency in economics and in political philosophy*

The consistency of Hayek's economic and political philosophies may result from the ways in which Hayek evolved and extended his own ideas through his investigations of inter-temporal equilibrium.[83] His clarification of the processes by which dispersed, private knowledge may be disseminated, demonstrates the weight of that kind of political power which attempts to posit itself at the centre of these structures of dissemination, and hence, by contrast, suggests the value of the free market as a site for the economic interaction of individuals of bounded rationality.[84] He goes on, along these same lines, to analyse the extreme case of a totalitarian society in which this latter process cannot take place.

In his *Serfdom*, Hayek warns Britain that he fears he might be forced there to revisit his experiences of the totalitarian tendencies of Germany and Austria. In doing so, Hayek seems to display a classic failing of liberalism. This liberalism (in its usual economic or political sense) may oblige its advocate to seek asylum in unfamiliar territory, when it is (as it so often is) threatened by oppressive nationalism in its own land. Although in exile this liberalism may never have to relinquish its grip upon its essential, defining characteristic, its creed of freedom, it cannot any longer advance any effective or credible response to the problems of nationalism and totalitarianism on which it has turned its tail and from which it has, for the sake of its own survival, fled.

### Notes

1  The author wishes to thank Mr Pierre Garrouste for very instructive comments.
2  März (1983/1991), p. 106.
3  We have a few pieces of evidence from Hayek's contemporaries: "It could not have been a surprise of five [*sic*] (Lachmann, Shenfield, Neumann, Andren, Seldon) that Hayek follows 'Collectivist Economic Planning' by [*sic*] *The Road to Serfdom*" (Seldon (1984)). "In a sense, in *The Road to Serfdom*, Hayek is merely stating the moral and political conclusions of that (collectivist calculation) debate" (Polanyi (1944), p. 293).
4  In the Introduction to *Serfdom*, Hayek wrote about his personal experiences and their influence upon this book.

> The author has spent about half of his adult life in his native Austria, in close touch with German intellectual life, and the other half in the United States and England. In the later period he has become increasingly convinced that at least some of the forces which have destroyed freedom in Germany are also at work here and that the character and the source of this danger are, if possible, even less understood than they were in Germany.
>
> (Hayek (1944/1994), p. 5)

By the way, I owe the term "rational liberalism" to Vanberg (1994), p. 181.
5  Hayek (1944/1994), p. 4.
6  "A community which entrusts final authority in the field of economic policy to a central agency would sooner or later be forced to transfer the formulation of its political will to a hierarchically organized team of leaders. Conversely, the free interplay of market forces would also guarantee the free interplay of political forces. Thus Hayek established a direct connection between a private enterprise economic system and a liberally organized society" (März (1983/1991), p. 108).

7 It is said that his thoughts were welcomed quite warmly in England in the 1980s and also in the countries of Eastern Europe in the first half of the 1990s, but not thereafter.

8 Hobsbawm (1990), p. 198 shows a map of the distribution of nations in 1910.

9 Namely, they could either (1) become independent and create a new nation-state for themselves, or (2) accept the connection (Anschluß) to Germany and become a part of it, or (3) ally themselves with Bela Kun who was leading Hungary's communist revolution, or (4) make a kind of new union (Donau Union) with several nations around them. It is said that the second and the third alternatives were welcomed by many people (Yada (1995), p. 29).

10 "The most passionately discussed topic was the 'viability' *Lebensfähigkeit* of the new Austria; most of the authors took a decidedly negative view" (März (1983/1991), p. 187).

11 Food and coal supplies were insufficient, the rate of unemployment was quite high, the currency was unstable and the lack of capital was a serious problem (Hoor (1966), p. 140).

12 Tschuppik (1923).

13 Braunthal (1961), Ch. 3, Kamijo (1994), Ch. 4.

14 This group included Karl Renner, Max Adler, Rudolf Hilferding, as well as Otto Bauer (Leser (1981), p. 9).

15 Ibid., pp. 11–12.

16 Janik and Toulmin (1973), Ch. 2. But I do not mean to say here that the Austrian School did not have the intention of "enlightenment through education".

17 März (1983/1991), pp. 99–100.

18 Böhm-Bawerk (1896/1962).

19 For example, Bauer, H. (1924).

20 "Die Wiener Schule bewies noch einmal ihre Fruchtbarkeit, als in den 1920er Jahren …, eine ungewöhnlich große Anzahl jüngerer und weithin bekannt gewordener Theoretiker aus ihr hervorgingen" (Hayek (1965), p. 70).

21 "Diese Jahre (die Jahrzehnt vor Ausbruch des ersten Weltkrieges), in denen·Wieser, Böhm-Bawerk und Philippovich gleichzeitig an der Wiener Universität wirkten, waren die des größten Ansehens der Wiener Schule" (ibid.). After this there came the period of "Red Vienna".

22 "The real surprise came with the next appointments when two of the most distinguished economists in Vienna at that time, Schumpeter and Mises, were passed over in favor of Othmar Spann and Hans Mayer" (Craver (1986), pp. 2–3).

23 From the latter half of the twenties, there had developed a movement within the Austrian School of Economics that aimed at the mathematization of economics and the refinement of economic theory. This movement was led by Karl Menger who began to organize mathematical colloquia and also partly by Oskar Morgenstern. This movement was to blossom in the 1930s, maintaining its connection with the mainstream of the Austrian School. It also boasted connections with another intellectual group, the Vienna Circle, of logical positivists. Cf. Nakayama (1998a).

24 Bauer was the chief member of the "socialization programme" of 1919 (Braunthal (1961), Introduction).

25 Bauer, D. (1919). This text was originally published as a series of newspaper articles in the *Arbeiterzeitung.*

26 Mises wrote the article in question in 1922, and it is included in the volume edited by Hayek (Mises (1922/1975) and (1922)).

27 There are others who apart from Bauer and Mises participated in this debate in the twenties, but I will deal with them on another occasion.

28 Schumpeter also discusses rationality and rationalization in this connection (Schumpeter (1921), (1947)).

29  I wrote this section with reference to Hayek's obituary in the German weekly-newspaper *Die Zeit* (Böhm (1992)). At the 1999 AHTEA conference in Paris, the influence of Friedrich von Wieser on Hayek was discussed. In addition, some historian also pointed out the influence of Othmar Spann on his early work. This issue offers much further scope for investigation.

30  More specifically, he studied state science (*Staatswissenschaft*) as the first major and law as well.

31  Browne (1981), p. 111. Also, Hayek (1928).

32  Browne (1981), p. 114.

33  Hayek (1933/1975a) and (1933/1975b), respectively.

34  Hayek (1948a).

35  Hayek himself remarks that "[they] may be regarded as an application of the same ideas to a particular problem" (ibid., p. v).

36  Hayek (1933/1975a), p. 14 and (1944/1994), p. 38. His later criticism of socialism in *The Fatal Conceit* is beyond the scope of this chapter.

37  Hayek (1948b). The subject of the report is "Politische Folgen der Planwirtschaft", that is, political consequences of the planned economy.

38  "Planwirtschaft führt zur Unfreiheit: Eine unerbittliche Zwangläufigkeit" (Hayek (1948b)).

39  Hayek's liberalism may be seen as a kind of descriptive holism which argues against the prescriptive and proscriptive holism of totalitarianism; a criticism of holism using another kind of holism.

40  We could see this issue as one of piecemeal social engineering, to use Karl Popper's term. In addition to their personal friendship, we can see some alliance between the theories of Popper and Hayek in terms of their criticisms of social engineering. They both praise the evolutionary formation of institutions in preference to rationalistic planning. But this is only the first approximation and needs further investigation.

41  We can find many quotations from Karl Mannheim that are criticized in *Serfdom*.

42  Hayek, ibid., p. 25.

43  Hayek (1944/1994), pp. 185–7.

44  Hayek (1933/1975a).

45  Hayek (1944/1994), pp. 29–31.

46  Hayek, ibid., p. 29. The argument between Neurath and Hayek on *Serfdom* can be seen in Neurath (1945). Neurath's theoretical reasoning against the free market system is shown in Neurath (1919a).

47  Hayek criticizes Bauer's *Der Weg zum Sozialismus* (1919).

48  Craver (1986), p. 16.

49  Ibid., p. 194.

50  On this relationship, see Lebovics (1969).

51  Plenge suggests a similarity between the war economy of Germany and the corporative constitution of economic life, which Hayek views critically (Hayek (1944/1994), p. 189).

52  Hayek says that corporatism would be worse than the centrally planned economy, as "a state of affairs which can satisfy neither planners nor liberals" (Hayek (1944/1994), p. 46). He also sees "organized capital and organized labour" as an element of corporatism ( ibid., p. 214). He states that "the impetus of the movement toward totalitarianism comes mainly from (these) two great vested interests" (p. 213).

53  Spann (1921/1972).

54  Neurath (1945), p. 980. In fact, Neurath does not entirely agree with Spann because of his stance as a socialist. Spann was, as is known, quite opposed to socialism and especially to Marxism.

55  Tribe (1995) argues that Neurath's direct opponent on the issue of rationalization was Max Weber.

56 Neurath speaks of the Taylor system in the following terms: "Das Taylorsystem, welches für die Verwaltungswirtschaft der Fabriken erfunden wurde, kann in erweitertem Maßstabe auch für die Verwaltungswirtschaft der Staaten herangezogen werden" (Neurath (1917/1919a), p. 150). However, Neurath goes on to voice some concerns on this subject ((1919b), p. 214).

57 Neurath (1918/1919), p. 216.

58 Neurath, ibid., p. 207.

59 "Das beharrliche Schweigen der Theoretiker und Praktiker diesem schwierigen Fragenkomplex gegenüber ist unwürdig und entspricht nicht dem Ernste der gegenwärtigen Situation" (Neurath, ibid., p. 203).

60 Neurath (1919c), p. 224. Also, "Innerhalb einer sozialisierten Wirtschaft kann eine weit größere Mannigfaltigkeit der Lebensweisen ermöglicht werden, als innerhalb der freien Verkehrswirtschaft" (Neurath (1919b), p. 214).

61 Neurath (1919c), p. 227.

62 Ibid.

63 I will not investigate this here, as it involves many and various issues. But we might remember the case of Karl Menger, who was a member of the Circle, but organized his own mathematical colloquia at the end of the 1920s, at a time when Neurath showed an explicit tendency towards "unified science". Menger and Neurath displayed rather different attitudes towards science; Hayek also disagreed with Menger on the grounds of the latter's excessive reliance upon abstract modelling. The position of Morgenstern, who supported Menger's ideas, is also important.

64 "What is relevant for us is essentially the degree to which the central control and direction of resources is carried in each of the different directions" (Hayek (1933/1975a), p. 18).

65 There is a very famous passage in which Hayek expresses the impossibility of getting all necessary information. "We need only to remember the difficulties experienced with the fixing of prices, even when applied to a few commodities only, and to contemplate further that, in such a system, price-fixing would have to be applied not to a few but to all commodities, finished and unfinished, and that it would have to bring about as frequent and as varied price-changes as those which occur in a capitalistic society every day and every hour, in order to see that this is not a way in which the solution provided by competition can even be approximately achieved" (ibid., p. 214).

66 In referring to Böhm-Bawerk's article "Macht oder Ökonomisches Gesetz" (Power or Economic Law)? (1914), Hayek says that "interest would have to form an important element in the rational calculation of economic activity" (Hayek (1933/1975a), p. 28).

67 Hayek (1944/1994), p. 173.

68 Ibid., p. 84.

69 Ibid., p. 85.

70 "It is not rational conviction but the acceptance of a creed which is required to justify a particular plan" (ibid., p. 126).

71 Ibid.

72 One commentator suggests that Hayek's concept of freedom is sovereign, but remains passive in the sense that he sees freedom in terms of keeping one's private realm untouched by external power (Shand (1990)). Another points out that it is because the concept of knowledge is much more relevant than that of power. But it should be emphasized that this passiveness does not have negative implications here.

73 I disagree with the idea that "apart from what he has to say on the socialist calculation issue, Hayek's main argument in favour of market competition is its role as a discovery process" (Vanberg (1994), p. 189), as Hayek seems to be quite consistent in this area.

74 Neurath (1945/1981), p. 980.

75 "There is nothing bad or dishonorable in approving a dictatorship of the good. Totalitarianism, we can already hear it argued, is a powerful system alike for good and evil, and the purpose for which it will be used depends entirely on the dictators" (Hayek (1944/1994), p. 148).

76 Firstly, as a better solution for the conflict of ideas than fighting, then as a safety net for individual freedom and thirdly as a valid method to educate the masses (Shand (1990)).

77 "The whole system will tend toward that plebiscitarian dictatorship in which the head of the government is from time to time confirmed in his position by popular vote, but where he has all the powers at his command to make certain that the vote will go in the direction he desires" (Hayek (1944/1994), pp. 76–7, and Chapter 5 in general).

78 "If democracy resolves on a task which necessarily involves the use of power which cannot be guided by fixed rules, it must become arbitrary power" (Hayek (1944/1994), p. 79 and p. 95).

79 Arrow (1951/1963) and also, Nakayama (1998b).

80 Hayek (1944/1994), p. 96.

81 Such as Lange, Taylor, Arrow, Debreu.

82 "By concentrating power so that it can be used in the service of a single plan, it is not merely transferred but infinitely heightened ... so much more far-reaching as almost to be different in kind" (Hayek (1944/1994), p. 159).

83 We recall that Hayek wrote an article about inter-temporal equilibrium in 1928 (Hayek (1928)).

84 Klausinger ((1989), p. 173) mentions this fact, pointing out that Hayek also noticed the importance of natural absorption of monetary shock. Here we can also see some connection between Hayek and Morgenstern in terms of their assumptions of bounded rationalities, which is asserted by both of them. I would like to investigate this connection on another occasion.

## Bibliography

Arrow, K. J. (1951/1963) *Social Choice and Individual Values*, 2nd edn, Yale University Press.

Barry, N. (1984) "Ideas Versus Interests: The Classical Liberal Dilemma", in Burton *et al.* (1984).

Bauer, H. (1924) "Bankerott der Grenzwerttheorie", *Der Kampf*, März, Jg. 17/3.

Bauer, O. (1919) *Der Weg zum Sozialismus*, Wien.

Böhm, S. (1992) "Die Verfassung der Freiheit", *Die Zeit* on 2 April.

Böhm-Bawerk, E. von (1896/1962) "Unresolved Contradictions in the Marxian Economic System", *Shorter Classics of Eugen von Böhm-Bawerk*, Vol. 1, South Holland: Libertarian Press.

Braunthal, J. (1961) *Ein Lebensbild, Otto Bauer. Eine Auswahl aus seinem Lebenswerk*, Wien.

Browne, M. S. (1981) "Erinnerungen an das Mises-Privatseminar", *Wirtschaftspolitische Blätter*, Jg. 28 (4), pp. 110–20.

Burton, J. (1984) "The Instability of the 'Middle Way'", in Burton *et al.* (1984).

Burton, J. *et al.* (eds) (1984) *Hayek's "Serfdom" Revisited: Essays by Economists, Philosophers and Political Scientists on "The Road to Serfdom" After 40 Years*, London: The Institute of Economic Affairs.

Craver, E. (1986) "The Emigration of the Austrian Economists", *History of Political Economy* 18: 1, pp. 1–32.

Finer, H. (1945/1977) *The Road to Reaction*, Westport: Greenwood Press.

Gissurarson, H. H. (1984) "The Only Truly Progressive Policy", in Burton *et al.* (1984).

Gray, J. (1984) "The Road to Serfdom: Forty Years On", in Burton *et al.* (1984).

Hayek, F. A. von (1928) "Das intertemporale Gleichgewichtssystem der Preise und die Bewegungen des 'Geldwertes'", *Weltwirtschaftliches Archiv* 28, pp. 33–76.

—— (ed.) (1933/1975) *Collectivist Economic Planning: Critical Studies on the Possibilities of Socialism*, Clifton: Augustus Kelley Publishers.

—— (1933/1975a) "The Nature and History of the Problem", in Hayek (1933/1975).

—— (1933/1975b) "The Present State of the Debate", in Hayek (1933/1975).

—— (1944/1994) *The Road to Serfdom*, Fiftieth Anniversary Edition, Chicago: The University of Chicago Press.

—— (1948a) *Individualism and Economic Order*, Chicago: The University of Chicago Press.

—— (1948b) "Planwirtschaft führt zur Unfreiheit", *Die Wirtschaft* 17 Jan., Dokumentation Arbeiterkammer für Wien.

—— (1965) "Wiener Schule", *Handwörterbuch der Sozialwissenschaften*, 12. Tübingen: Auflage.

Hobsbawm, E. (1990) *Nations and Nationalism Since 1780*, Cambridge: Cambridge University Press.

Hoor, E. (1966) *Österreich 1918 – 1938: Staat ohne Nation, Republik ohne Republikaner*, Wein/München: Österreichische Bundesverlag für Unterricht, Wissenschaft und Kunst.

Horwitz, S. (1998) "Monetary Calculation and Mises's Critique of Planning", *History of Political Economy*, no. 3, pp. 427–50.

Janik, A. and Toulmin, S. (1973) *Wittgenstein's Vienna*, New York: Simon & Schuster.

Kamijo, I. (1994) *History of Social Thought for Understanding the Nation and the National Problem* (in Japanese), Tokyo: Azusa Shuppan.

Klausinger, H. (1989) "Hayek and New Classical Economics on Equilibrium Analysis: Some Second Thoughts", *Jahrbuch für Sozialwissenschaften*, 40, pp. 171–86.

Lebovics, H. (1969) *Social Conservatism and the Middle Classes in Germany, 1914–1933*, Princeton: Princeton University Press.

Leser, N. (1981) "Austromarxistisches Geistes- und Kulturleben", in Leser (ed.) (1981) *Das geistige Leben Wiens in der Zwischenkriegszeit*, Wein: Österreichischer Bundesverlag.

—— (ed.) (1981) *Das geistige Leben Wiens in der Zwischenkriegszeit*, Wein: Österreichischer Bundesverlag.

März, E. (1983/1991) *Josef Schumpeter: Scholar, Teacher and Politician*, New Haven and London: Yale University Press, English translation of *Josef Alois Schumpeter: Forscher, Lehrer Und Politiker*, Wein: Verlag für Geschichte und Politik.

Mises, L. von (1922/1975) "Economic Calculation in the Socialist Commonwealth", in Hayek (ed.) (1933/1975).

—— (1922) *Die Gemeinwirtschaft: Untersuchungen über Sozialismus*, Jena.

Nakayama, C. (1998a) "The Place of K. Menger in Relation to his Contemporary Austrian School of Economics", Working paper for the 10th conference of SASE (International Conference on Socio-Economics), July, Vienna.

—— (1998b) "Arrow's Impossibility Theorem and the Paradox of Democracy", Working paper at the international conference "Transition in historical perspective: What can be learned from the history of economics", held 17–20 September 1998 in Krakow.

Neurath, O. (1919a) *Durch die Kriegswirtschaft zur Naturwirtschaft*, München: Verlag von Georg D. W. Callwey.

—— (1919b) "Wesen und Weg der Sozialisierung", originally in *Verlag von Georg D. W. Callwey in München* and reprinted in Neurath (1919a).

—— (1919c) "Technik und Wirtschaftsordnung", originally in *Verlag von Georg D. W. Callwey in München* and reprinted in Neurath (1919a).

—— (1917a/1919) "Kriegswirtschaft, Verwaltungswirtschaft, Naturalwirtschaft", originally in *Europäische Wirtschaftzeitung*, and reprinted in Neurath (1919a).

—— (1917b/1919) "Das umgekehrte Taylorsystem", originally in *Kunstwart und Kulturwart* and reprinted in Neurath (1919a).

—— (1918/1919) "Lebensmittelnot und Regierungsmacht", originally in *Die Volkswirtschaft*, Wien.

—— (1945/1981) "F. A. Hayek, 'The Road to Serfdom'", *Gesammelte philosophische und methodologische Schriften Bd. 2*, Wein: Verlag Hölder-Pichter-Tempsky.

Polanyi, M. (1944) "The Socialist Error: 'The Road to Serfdom' (Books of the Day)", *The Spectator*, 31 March.

Schumpeter, J. A. (1921) "Sozialistische Möglichkeit von Heute", *Archiv für Sozialwissenschaften*, Band 48.

—— (1947) *Capitalism, Socialism and Democracy*, New York: Harper Brothers.

Seldon, A. (1984) "Before and After '*The Road to Serfdom*'; Reflections on Hayek in 1935, 1944, 1960, 1982", in Burton *et al.* (1984).

Shand, A. H. (1990) *Free Market Morality: The Political Economy of the Austrian School*, London and New York: Routledge.

Shearmur, J. (1984) "Hayek and the Wisdom of the Age", in Burton *et al.* (1984).

Spann, O. (1921/1972) *Der wahre Staat, Vorlesungen über Abbruch und Neubau der Gesellschaft*, Leipzig/Graz. Nachwort von F. A. Westphalen, Gesamtausgabe, Vol. 5.

Tribe, K. (1995) *Strategies of Economic Order*, Cambridge: Cambridge University Press.

Tschuppik, K. (1923) "Wien und die Gesellschaft: Ein Beitrag zum Thema Staat und Gesellschaft", *Die Börse*, No. 51, 20 December (Arbeiterkammer für Wien, Dokumentation).

Vanberg, V. (1994) "Hayek's Legacy and the Future of Liberal Thought: Rational Liberalism Versus Evolutionary Agnosticism", *Cato Journal*, 14 (2), pp. 179–99.

Yada, T. (1995) *Die Lehren aus der Modernen*, (in Japanese), Tokyo: Tosui Shobo.

# 6 Hayek's borderless economy

## His escape from the household model

*Laurence S. Moss*

### Introduction

Friedrich A. Hayek's teacher, Friedrich A. von Wieser, taught that in important ways the economy was like a large household managed by a benevolent patriarch. Von Wieser wrote of a "natural economy." On the level of positive economics, this natural economy was presented as a thought experiment designed to help us understand the meaning of "inputing" marginal utility to the resources that helped produce the national output (von Wieser, 1956). On a normative level, von Wieser regretted that the modern economy, because of dishonesty, and monopoly power, did not behave like a natural economy and he advocated government intervention (von Wieser, 1967).

In the debate over economic calculation under socialism that took place during the 1930s and 1940s, several socialist writers set out to solve the problem of how a central planner could simulate the natural-economy solution after the resale market for the trading of capital goods (or the trading of equity shares) had been abolished. Hayek found the proposed solutions most unsatisfactory and far wide of the mark.

Apparently, these arguments pushed Hayek to confront the problem of economic organization from new angles. The socialist understanding of the economic problem was seriously misconceived even though his former teacher, von Wieser, also thought in these terms. A modern economy was not like a household writ large. Indeed, it was not centered about any geographic region of the world or coextensive with the political borders of any national state.

The large economy, as Hayek came to understand, would never function like a patriarchal household without unleashing awful totalitarian practices. These practices included the language of anger and hate. Instead, the extended order of the market was a nexus of communication linkages, authentication procedures, and shared meanings of understanding (Hayek, 1937a, 1945). In the last decades of his life, Hayek preferred to call this a "catallaxy" to sharply distinguish this arrangement from a mere household economy. Production, consumption, and exchange activity refer always to particular locations and addresses, but the substance of what is going on, the shared meanings of promises, commitments, and authentication verdicts would exist (or better consist of) common understandings shared by an increasingly globalized population participating in a borderless world.

The purpose of this chapter is to trace this development in Hayek's thinking about what is the real economic problem that the institution of the market system is supposed to solve. I shall demonstrate that Hayek's mature appreciation of the problem of economic organization involved a rejection of the long-standing and favorite approach of his teacher von Wieser which centered around thinking of the economy as geographically compact and coextensive with the local national economy. Instead, Hayek envisioned a borderless world in which coordination is brought about by language, the adherence to customs and rules, and shared meanings.

## The coordination problem

After many frustrating sorties with the socialists, a disappointed Hayek gradually and sadly came to realize that equilibrium theory, no matter how many improvements were stuck onto it, was incapable of solving "the coordination problem." The coordination problem had to do with the mobilization of information that is originally privately held or available to the vast multitude of private individuals in a disaggregated and particularized form. Some socialist writers, Oskar Lange and Fred Taylor may be examples, apparently believed that some information had to be centralized or else effective coordination would fail to take place (Lange and Taylor, 1964). Hayek's mission was to prove that exactly the opposite was true. Institutions such as the mechanisms that accompanied the price system could indirectly produce more coordination by mobilizing the information that was best left decentralized and always in the possession of private individuals (Hayek, 1945).

Hayek's seminal "Economics and Knowledge" (1937a) distinguished the use of the equilibrium construct in what he called the "Pure Logic of Choice," where a single individual tried to allocate something that was scarce in order to maximize some "single ultimate end" from the use of the equilibrium concept when analyzing society as a whole, where the problem involves a multiplicity of ends held by a multitude of private people and how they roughly brought these ends into some sort of coherence by following the customs of the marketplace (see Kirzner, 1976, p. 133). In the first case, where a single individual is calculating how best to allocate his budget over available goods and services in the market, the concept of equilibrium has a definite meaning linked up to the broader concept of embarking upon a plan to solve a problem of personal utility maximization. In the second case, when we analyze an equilibrium that pertains to a whole community of individuals, we have a multitude of individuals trying to pursue their privately held plans concurrently more or less over the same period of time. According to Hayek, "the problem which we [that is, economists] pretend to solve is how the spontaneous interaction of a number of people, each possessing only bits of knowledge, brings about a state of affairs in which prices correspond to costs, etc., and which could be brought about by deliberate action only by someone who possessed the combined knowledge of all those individuals" (Hayek, 1937a).

What is there about the world and the processes and mechanisms that it contains that can assure the mutual compatibility of the agents' plans? One agent may count on another individual selling his land to the developer of the suburban mall, but the seller of that land may in fact be planning to keep the land for a restful homestead. In order for all plans to be carried out together, the individual members of society must have "correct foresight" and this extraordinary concept itself becomes for Hayek "the defining characteristic of a state of equilibrium" (Caldwell, 1988, p. 526). At other places, Hayek hinted that the use of language and other mechanisms of communication played an important part in the solution of the coordination problem (Hayek, 1937a).

Hayek saw the problem of general equilibrium as involving some process necessarily involving a sequence of events in which the individual members of society learn about the facts adhering to the world around them. The facts include not only information about resources, commodities and their characteristics, but the perceptions that are held by other people in the market. It will not do to assume that individuals have perfect knowledge. This amounts to taking one of the most interesting problems in the social sciences and simply defining it away. Hayek insisted that the economic writers of his day ignored the important problem of how individuals can ever obtain the knowledge they need to realize their privately held plans concurrently. The challenge was "how to change economics so that it could reveal the coordinating function of markets in a world of subjectively-held and dispersed knowledge" (Caldwell, 1988, p. 530).[1] This required that Hayek shake off the influence of one of the pioneers of the Austrian School tradition and one who had without a doubt once served as Hayek's mentor.

## A teacher's influence

Hayek described von Wieser as his teacher and the one person who "originally had the greatest influence on me" (Hayek, 1994, p. 57).[2] The German version of von Wieser's *Social Economics* was published in 1924 a year or two after Hayek had graduated from the University of Vienna where von Wieser taught.[3] One of Hayek's earliest publications, "Some Remarks on the Problem of Imputation," was specifically devoted to von Wieser's work (Hayek, 1984). The structure of this book and other writings by von Wieser are critically important to Hayek's early thought because they argue for the patriarchal model in which coordination is self-contained in the mind of a single decision-maker who may or may not choose to communicate with another person. Let us summarize von Wieser's style of theoretical reasoning.

Von Wieser proposed that we start with the logical analysis of the "simple economy" (von Wieser, 1967, p. 9). The simple economy is not the economy of a single individual household but the economy of millions of active households – as many as can fit into a modern nation-state. All the same, this economy is under the control of a single valuing mind. This is the mind of the benevolent patriarch.

Also peculiar is that all the many households in von Wieser's nation-state are "ideal economic subject(s)" and follow their perceptions of utility maximization without making any errors, displaying any weaknesses, dishonesty, and avoiding moments of passion (von Wieser, 1967, p. 10). The imagined economy has the "breadth of a national economy with all its wealth, technical knowledge, and problems of economic calculus" (von Wieser, 1967, p. 19). The main difference between the von Wieser construct and the modern exchange economy, which we inhabit, is that the entire "broad economy is guided by a single mind" thereby eliminating the need for monetary exchange (von Wieser, 1967, pp. 19–20). The simple economy is "entirely detached from exchange [and] therefore lacks the connecting medium, money" (von Wieser, 1967, p. 49). The purpose of this construction is to solve the problem of imputation by showing how the subjective value of final consumer goods is "passed backwards" or "upstream," and affects the valuation of producer goods. In Hayek's words, "the solution of the problem of imputation has to be attempted without recourse to exchange. Any solution, therefore, has to be based on the assumption of an economy guided by a uniform will, which von Wieser has called the 'individual economy'" (Hayek, 1984, p. 34).

Von Wieser also believed that his construct removed "the influence of power" and permitted the study of the basic economic problems of how to produce, when to produce, and what to produce as it would be seen and solved by a benevolent patriarch (von Wieser, 1967, p. 142; Hayek, 1962, pp. 26–7). Von Wieser explains further that the central planner "foresees ends, weighs them without error or passion, and maintains a discipline that ensures that all directions are executed with the utmost precision and skill and without loss of energy. ... [This model of the economy] is embraced only to enable us to fasten our attention exclusively on the effects that emanate from economic purposes" (von Wieser, 1967, p. 20).

The device served at least two purposes for von Wieser. First, he could show that it is subjective marginal utility that determines value, including the value attached to producer goods. Value is imputed back and allocated among all the resources that helped produce the current consumable products. In his earlier book, *Natural Value*, von Wieser explained why a rational patriarch when allocating different types of land, land of varying quality, would have to implicitly attribute "Ricardian rent" to the best quality land in order to adequately account for all the value created and place limits on what land is cultivated and in what temporal sequence.[4] Furthermore, when deciding how many capital goods to produce allowance must be made for the interest rate to determine when the construction of one additional capital good (the marginal capital good) simply becomes too expensive to produce in terms of forgone consumption alternatives. The necessity of imputing value categories such as rent and interest derives from the manner in which a single human mind solves the problem of scarcity. Interest and rent are not arbitrary payments extorted from the market system by the special relationships of power that exist only in a capitalist society. Rather, rent and interest are fundamental value categories associated with rational calculation and not the particular accidental institutional arrangements of European history. Von Wieser concluded that "the theory of the simple economy is an essential prerequisite to the description of this social economic process" (von Wieser, 1967, p. 151).

Second, by showing that the same value phenomenon would emerge in a simple economy under the control of a single planner, von Wieser hoped to convince both socialists and "individualists" that there were certain fundamental economic phenomena that had nothing to do with power relationships in society, but adhere to the very understanding of a natural economy.

Now, the transition from the simple economy to a description of the social economy is quite difficult, as von Wieser readily admitted. Whereas "the simple economy ... explains the condition of an isolated and idealized individual economy that follows its laws of motion without restraint [in the social economy] these individual units meet from all directions. Indeed they clash with great force. We must, therefore, ascertain whether their conjunction does not alter their law of motion and whether in particular the amount of power does not exercise a decisive control" (von Wieser, 1967, p. 151). In his last writing, von Wieser proved himself one of the pioneers of the general theory of power in society (von Wieser, 1983).

In a social economy, commodity exchanges must occur through the medium of money. Now, different people will compete for existing goods and services and money prices will emerge. The prices will not equal the "common price" that could exist if industry were managed in the most efficient way and regrettable monopoly forces were not present (von Wieser, 1967, p. 237). Such machinations in the market will enable the large captains of industry to "obtain a resultant price which decreases the general utility and yields excessive profits to them personally" (von Wieser, 1967, p. 237). Von Wieser warned of the phenomenon of "price stratification" where broad classes of commodities are traded among the members of higher-income brackets and poor people cannot afford to participate in these price formations at all. A similar phenomenon applies to the labor market whereby stratification clusters workers into non-competing groups (von Wieser, 1967, pp. 317 and 370–1). According to von Wieser, "economic principle demands that, at all times, the highest attainable satisfaction of needs should be the aim of economic efforts" (von Wieser, 1967, p. 397). Under modern conditions, if the aim of economy were simply to distribute stores of goods then "no other distribution could be tolerated but one guided by 'the rational needs,' as the well known socialistic formula prescribes" (von Wieser, 1967, p. 398). But, von Wieser insisted, the aim of the economy includes both production and distribution. Modern conditions require that incentives be maintained so that individuals will exert themselves to obtain the goods and services that are then the subject of socialist speculations about the ideal distribution. And so it may turn out that "a system of rules, which distributes very unequally the enormous gains to which it is instrumental, is after all more beneficial to the mass of the citizens, than another [that winds up] doling out ... much smaller proceeds according to 'principles of right and reason'" (von Wieser, 1967, p. 398). In the end, the idea of use value is now replaced by "exchange value" with its effect that "price should lie between utility and power" (von Wieser, 1967, p. 237).[5] As the years wore on, von Wieser became more adamant about the importance of "natural economy" as an ideal ethical model against which the modern economy can be compared and shown to be inferior and in need of reform.

## Turning away from von Wieser

Treatises devoted to estate management date to the ancient Greek period of the fifth to the fourth century BC, and it was from the science of estate management that modern economics derives its name – the name of "economics."[6] And not only its name. The habit of thinking of the economics as a household writ large stuck for more than a thousand years (Moss, 1998). The image of a decision-maker, responsible for balancing scarce means among competing uses in order to achieve some "best" or "optimal" result, remained at the heart of the discipline of economics. Certainly, this approach informed von Wieser's theory of the natural economy. But Hayek was to escape from this pattern of thought.

In his later years, Hayek came to believe that the discipline studies a vast and deeply rooted communication network of some sort that sprouts up "spontaneously" and serves to reconcile private interest with the public interest in some ironic way. Hayek contrasted the notion of "economy" against what he preferred to call a "spontaneous order" or "catallaxy" as follows:

> An economy, in the strict sense of the word, is an organization or arrange-ment in which someone deliberately allocates resources to a unitary order of ends. Spontaneous order produced by the market is nothing of the kind; and in important respects it does not behave like an economy proper. In particular, such spontaneous order differs because it does *not* ensure that what general opinion regards as more important needs are always satisfied before the less important ones.
>
> (Hayek, 1978, p. 183)

In his later reflections on the economic calculation debate of the 1930s and 1940s, Hayek realized that many of his disagreements with his socialist oppo-nents stemmed from their intention to replicate and perpetuate a different understanding of "the economy" than the one that informed Hayek's thinking both during those debates and more explicitly later on. Von Wieser was wrong in thinking that the economy should be imaged as if it were a patrician estate. The (national) economy does not – in fact it cannot – behave like an economy proper and to try to force it to do so will result in a violation of the most sacred and cherished understanding of human liberty.

During the economic calculation debate, the so-called liberal socialists Oskar Lange and Fred M. Taylor explained how the benevolent central planner could establish simple rules and procedures that would steer the economy toward a final general equilibrium position that would be a "Pareto optimal" position (see Lange and Taylor, 1964). Hayek responded to these challenges with a variety of arguments over the space of many important articles during the 1930s and 1940s. Excellent summaries of the calculation controversy have appeared in many places (Caldwell, 1997a, 1997b; Vaughn, 1994). I shall not offer still another summary of the flow of arguments back and forth here. There is however one line of argument that I do wish to devote some space to here because it has not been emphasized in the large literature about Hayek.

In 1938, Hayek published an article entitled "Freedom and the Economic System" in *Contemporary Review* (Hayek, 1938). Six years later in his veritable best-seller *The Road to Serfdom*, Hayek stated that the "central argument of this book was first sketched in an article entitled 'Freedom and the Economic System,' which appeared in the *Contemporary Review* for April, 1938" (Hayek, 1961). Hayek explained that all versions of centralized economic planning presuppose

> a much more complete agreement on the relative importance of the different ends than actually exists, and that, in consequence, in order to be able to plan, the planning authority must impose upon the people that detailed code of values which is lacking. And imposing here means more than merely reading such a detailed code of values into the vague general formulae on which alone the people are able to agree. The people must be made to believe in this particular code of values, since the success or failure of the planning authority will, in two different ways, depend on whether it succeeds in creating that belief. On the one hand it will only secure the necessary enthusiastic support if the people believe in the ends which the plan serves; and on the other hand the outcome will only be regarded as successful if the ends served are generally regarded as the right ones.
>
> (Hayek, 1938, p. 183)

Whispers of this important idea can be found still earlier in Hayek's writings. Consider Hayek's lengthy summary of the debate about economic calculation that he included as the last chapter in his 1935 work, *Collectivist Economic Planning*. Hayek admitted that one choice that a central planner can make is to become a complete dictator who "himself ranges in order the different needs of the members of the society according to his views about their merits [and in this way] saved himself the trouble of finding out what the people really prefer and avoided the impossible task of combining the individual scales into an agreed common scale which expresses the general ideas of justice" (Hayek, 1963, pp. 216–17). If the central planner chooses to remain benevolent – and not become a dictator – then he must try to broker a complete agreement among the members of society about the ends or goals put forward under the plan. This is difficult, time consuming, and in the end not possible unless some simple end or goal is found to which all members of society can commit themselves.

In the 1944 *Road to Serfdom*, Hayek explained why central planning must inevitably lead to totalitarianism. The "worst features of the existing totalitarian systems are not accidental by-products but phenomena which a totalitarianism is certain sooner or later to produce" (Hayek, 1961, p. 135). The more highly populated the society and the more diverse the geographic region, the more the people will differ in both their tastes and views on any subject (Hayek, 1961, p. 138). Naturally, these same educated people will make the prospects of any central plan nearly impossible to steer into full force and effect. If the central planner wishes "to find a high degree of uniformity and similarity of outlook, [he must] descend to the regions of lower moral and intellectual standards where the more primitive and 'common' instincts and tastes prevail" (Hayek, 1961, p. 138). The central planner seeking to coalesce the community will seek to find "the lowest common denominator which unites the largest number of people" (Hayek, 1961, p. 139).

The lowest common denominator is the negative program of hating an enemy. The enemy can be within the region itself – an internal enemy – such as the "Jew" or the "kulak," or external. Raising a passionate hatred by way of fiery speeches and frenzied invective seems to be "an indispensable requisite in the armory of a totalitarian leader" (Hayek, 1961, p. 139). The worst leaders rise to the top because

> there is little that is likely to induce [highly moral men] to aspire to leading positions in the totalitarian machine, and much to deter them[;] there will be special opportunities for the ruthless and unscrupulous. [Indeed] the positions in as a totalitarian society in which it is necessary to practice cruelty and intimidation, deliberate deception and spying, are numerous. Neither the Gestapo nor the administration of a concentration camp, neither the Ministry of Propaganda nor the S.A. or S.S. (or their Italian or Russian counterparts), are suitable places for the exercise of humanitarian feelings.
>
> (Hayek, 1961, p. 151)

The von Wieser thought experiment started out as an innocent construct to show that spontaneous social formations can often produce price relationships and other economic outcomes that mirror those that would have been created had a wise and benevolent patriarch been in charge of the whole economy. But now Hayek took notice of an alleged fact about the political processes of the world. That fact was that a wise and benevolent central planner will not be able to accomplish very much unless he becomes the opposite of what he starts out – namely, as a clever and merciless dictator. The von Wieser thought experiment only worked because one of its premises was that all individuals and resource owners give zealously of themselves and cooperate fully with the central leader. But this is equivalent to positing a system that abstracts completely from the freedom cherished by citizens of a modern pluralistic society.

What is remarkable about the market system and the associated capitalist institutions is that it is totally unlike a household that needs to have all the goals and objectives of its members listed and prioritized. In a market system, no single hierarchical list of priorities needs to be drawn up. The market system produces a prosperity that is entirely different from the output of a farm or the output of a patriarchal household estate. In a modern market system, there is no balancing and comparison of utilities between and among the participants. Not only is there no benevolent patriarch involved at all whose job it is to make interpersonal comparisons of utility, nothing like this needs to take place in order for a catallaxy to emerge and take root. The impersonal mechanisms of the market, when operating through the price system and tempered by competition and shared customs and rules, do not produce the results sought by the modern patriarch. A catallaxy – or spontaneous order – does not operate to maximize some single measure of annual production or aggregate utility with a bordered area. It does something else entirely.

These insights took Hayek's thinking about the economy in new directions and sharply away from von Wieser's imputation theory and the older themes of the Austrian School.

## Hayek's style of economic reasoning

In his later years, Hayek moved away from the view that "the economy" is rooted in a particular geographical location mostly characterized by the local use of a single currency and protected on all sides by the armies of a single dominant political unit. In short, Hayek envisaged an economic community that was not rooted in geography at all, but in a shared collective understanding and acceptance of certain "end-independent" rules – an economy that is virtual and without borders. A person could join this economy not by having to physically move his person and things to a particular place, but rather by joining a conversation in which particular values, norms, and customs are shared and articulated.

Physical action and especially human action would take the form of carrying out certain "habitual modes of conduct" (Hayek, 1988, p. 16). Hayek offers only a precious few examples of what he means by these rules, but they include linguistic exhortations such as "Always keep a promise that you have solemnly made," "Save for a rainy day," and "Do not steal what belongs to someone else" (Hayek, 1988, pp. 14–17; p. 90; and p. 131). I think the direction of his thought is as important as the examples he actually presented.

The American philosopher John Searle has presented an interesting account of how linguistic conventions are at the heart of social institutions, that in some ways capture some of the themes present in Hayek's later work (although Searle does not specifically mention Hayek as a pioneer investigator). According to Searle, certain acts of speech are used to assign "status" and in many cases "power" to certain particular individuals, whose pronouncements thereafter create new structures of meaning and so on. Consider a clergyman duly authorized by some authenticating board to conduct a marriage. The speech utterance "I now pronounce you husband and wife" functions almost like magic words to change everything from the required support of children born to the union to the descent of property with the death of either (or both) of the married partners. Now, the status-changing apparatus of most societies has to do with authentication activities that affect the shared meaning we possess as a linguistic group regarding particular people or particular objects. The institutions themselves shape and reshape the plans and actions of acting man and therefore are themselves objects of purposeful behavior in market systems.

Consider a world economy that is constituted by language, norms, rules of behavior, and rules pertaining to the creation and replication of certain institutions. This is a somewhat wider understanding of "economy" than a geographical location where people live, wheat is grown, and steel mills operate and belch out dirty smoke. I do not think that a linguistically constituted virtual economy can detach itself entirely from the brute facts about those things that individuals need to consume and digest in order to keep on living another day; still a market order extended by language and shared meanings can be imagined. Such an economy would have no "center" at all. Images of a central planner would be entirely misleading. This economy would be a nexus of communication linkages, authentication procedures, and shared meanings. It would be a network of connections and function, something like a "world wide net", without a single central location or address. Production, consumption, and exchange activity would refer always to particular locations and addresses, but the substance of what is going on, the shared meanings of promises, commitments, and authentication verdicts would exist in the common understandings and shared meanings held by the market participants.

Elsewhere I argued that the trend of Hayek's thinking points us toward a "globalized notion of the economic system" (Moss, 1998, p. 85). I detected a steady evolution in Hayek's thinking away from the nation-state as the center of economic activity toward a more decentered global vision. Let me compare some of Hayek's early thinking in this direction with what came later. Consider the interesting set of lectures that Hayek delivered at the Institut Universitaire de Hautes Études Internationales in Geneva in 1937, on the subject of monetary nationalism and international stability (Hayek, 1937b/1971). In the preface to the published version of the lectures, Hayek professed a moral commitment to "the human race in general" and indicated a refusal to do what so many other economists do – discuss only those ideas that are politically feasible under present-day conditions. It is clear that the advocates of monetary nationalism – the "bad guys" in Hayek's account – are willing to take the internal wage level as established by trade union activity as "a given," and then adjust international economic policy so as to mitigate the harshest impact of the negotiated union wages on the employment levels, and so on (Hayek, 1937, p. 53).[7] Hayek's main point is that such a policy cannot long be sustained because the workers do not suffer from any systemic wage illusion. If the workers (presumably through trade union activity) were to raise wages above the level that would reveal areas of comparative advantage in one or another line of productive activity, the fall in living standards would occur regardless of whether the monetary authorities try to "cover up" the overvaluation of the local labor by a strategic cut in the exchange rate. In addition, the workers are not ignorant robots. They would immediately identify the depreciation of their currency with a loss in the purchasing power of their wages over imported goods, and agitate for higher wages all over again.

Hayek advocates the need for "an improvement of the rules of the game which were supposed to exist in the past" along the lines of a return to an international commodity standard. Hayek advocated open markets free of international tariff and quota, and a firm commitment on the part of the central banks to guarantee that "one form of money will always be readily exchangeable against other forms of money at a known rate" (Hayek, 1937b, p. 84). This meant that central banks would lose their freedom to alter the domestic supply of money to offset the pressures of local workers' groups advocating higher wages. Domestic monetary autonomy on behalf of national objectives was inconsistent with free trade and fixed change rates. In the end, Hayek called for an international monetary system in which domestic central banks would remain interdependent – not autonomous – and committed to world monetary stability and the maintenance of fixed currency rates of exchange (Hayek, 1937b). This was a vision directly opposed to the ideal of John Maynard Keynes and his students who argued for central bank independence.

In 1976, Hayek looked back and described his older *Monetary Nationalism and Economic Stability* as "hastily and badly written on a topic to which I had earlier committed myself but which I had to write when I was pre-occupied with other problems" (Hayek, 1976a, p. 81). The main thesis of the 1937 work was the importance of fixed currency rates in a world bent on freeing up local central banks from international commitments. Hayek described his 1976 book *Denationalisation of Money: An Analysis of the Theory and Practice of Concurrent Currencies* as a "further development of the considerations which determined [his earlier 1937] position" (Hayek, 1976a, p. 81). The idea is that by allowing private money creation, a productive competition would develop which promotes economic prosperity and preserves economic freedom.

According to Hayek, regions with stable money would prosper and become the envy of other regions of the world. In the end, the areas in the world where "one currency predominates would ... not have sharp or fixed boundaries" and certainly need not line up even approximately with the borders of any particular nation-state (Hayek, 1976a, p. 88). In addition, there could be geographical areas where more than one single currency compete for domination – what Hayek calls "overlap" – and with the "dividing lines" fluctuating constantly (Hayek, 1976a, p. 88). Stable money would allow all people who adopt it to pursue their private plans with a greater opportunity for success.

The 1976 currency-reform proposal is still further evidence that the trend of Hayek's thinking over at least forty years of his life was away from any economy rooted in the mental heuristic of a patriarchal household writ large. By denationalizing money and still retaining the idea of a monetary order under which economic calculation is both viable and useful, Hayek implicitly adopted the view that the economic order exists or at least adheres in the mental images and sustained interconnections of the world community.

In his last and perhaps most controversial book, *The Fatal Conceit*, written one half-century after his 1937 lectures, Hayek repeated many of his earlier statements that the discipline of economics needs to be renamed (Hayek, 1988). He insisted again on the name "catallactics" because the focus would no longer be about the rules pertaining to household management, but the steady and orderly intercommunication between economic units that has proved so valuable in raising living standards. Economic units would communicate about those issues and matters that help them align their expectations and coordinate their separate behaviors, so that each separate economic unit experiences a decided advantage in achieving its intended goals. The economist would embrace a discipline that no longer pretended to advise consumers or managers about how best to make decisions. The subject matter of economics would be descriptive rather than prescriptive and include "the theories people have developed to explain how most effectively to discover and use different means for diverse purposes" (Hayek, 1988, p. 98).

## Conclusion

My purpose here has been to offer a thematic component in the careful investigation and study of Hayek's life and scientific work. I maintain that his journey from a von Wieser-like economics based on household management – the simple economy – to an economics based on the evolution and replication of shared images and meanings that serve to align private incentives and offer the greatest prospects for personal success is very evident in his writings. If there were a single moment when Hayek "turned" from one way of thinking to the next, I think that moment occurred during the economic calculation debate with the socialists during the 1930s and 1940s. I have argued here that Hayek realized both (1) that the market order does not require any single planner to draw up a commensurable list of goals or priorities among the individual members of the community, and that (2) the market order works best and is most sustainable if no attempt were made to engineer the economy into patterns resembling von Wieser's ideal "simple economy." Now the first point was an obvious one which his teacher, von Wieser, would have readily accepted. It was the economic calculation debate that drove Hayek to the second point and von Wieser's idea that the simple economy could serve as an ethical template for contemporary society. Hayek appreciated that even mild central planning would end up unleashing the worst totalitarian abuses on the members of society by appealing through the language of hatred and innuendo to the basest and most wicked prejudices held by men and women.

Perhaps an ideal centrally planned economy would be like a household in which all members of the community are treated "as if" they belonged to a single household carrying out its activities at a particular geographic location. But if this were so then an ideal centrally planned economy really has nothing to do with the market order as it performs and currently exists. The rules, norms, and customs that are adopted by the community "do not preserve *particular* lives but rather increase the *chances* (or prospects or probabilities) of more rapid propagation of the *group*" (emphasis in original, Hayek, 1988, p. 131). This means that it may not be individually rational for an individual to perform a certain act but when he does so (perhaps out of habit, or perhaps out of religious conviction, or perhaps out of an emotional drive) he promotes the survival and propagation of his group.

But why does a complex market system work best when no attempt is made to describe or even record a hierarchical list of preferred ends? Although Hayek never answered this question completely, the trend of his thinking is away from the image of an economy that needs to be managed to optimize some measure of output or aggregate utility within a definite region. What emerges to take the place of the nation-state economy is the idea of the market as a self-organizing system constantly recreating the conditions for its replication. Such an economy is profoundly borderless and Hayek must be credited with moving economics in this new and bold direction.

I suspect that by pointing to the early influence of von Wieser's ideas on Hayek's writings and how that influence was purged completely in his mature writings, I have succeeded in attaching a thematic quality to his entire lifework, that may have been somewhat overlooked in the recent literature on Hayek's scientific work.

## Acknowledgements

I am especially indebted to Professor Jack Birner who made several especially valuable suggestions that have greatly improved this chapter and given it greater focus. I also wish to thank Professor S. Ioannides for his helpful comments.

## Notes

1  Caldwell complains that Hayek seems somewhat unaware of the fact that "actions based on subjective expectations of the state of the world will cause external reality to change" (Caldwell, 1988, pp. 529–30).
2  Hayek goes on to remark that "I only met [Ludwig von] Mises really after I had taken my degree. But now I realize – I wouldn't have known it at the time – that the decisive influence was just reading Menger's *Grundsaetze*. I probably derived more from not only the *Grundsaetze* but also the Methodenbuch, not for what it says on methodology but for what it says on general sociology. This conception of the spontaneous generation of institutions is worked out more beautifully there than in any other book I know" (Hayek, 1994, p. 57).
3  I shall cite from the English translation of *Social Economics* that was published in 1927 (von Wieser, 1967). There is always some danger that the English translation omits some subtle word or thought that may indeed distort von Wieser's considered meaning. I shall assume the risk in this chapter of relying on the English text as representing the "sort of thing" that Hayek must have heard in the classroom when he studied under von Wieser only a few years earlier than the publication of this most important contribution.

4    "In the inventory of the communistic state the lands of better quality will be entered at an amount corresponding to the capitalization of their rents. The agricultural officials will require to be made responsible for the return of a rent from these better lands corresponding to their quality. In fact, in all those connections it will be impossible for the communistic state to act differently from any large landowner of the present day, who tries to manage his property economically, and to have an effectual control over his servants" (von Wieser, 1956, p. 116).

5    From this von Wieser went on to advocate a repudiation of the supposedly "classical" theory of non-intervention in favor of the modern welfare state (von Wieser, 1967, p. 409). For example, interferences with the labor contract were a much discussed topic both in America and central Europe during the first part of the twentieth century, especially with regard to compulsory accident insurance. Von Wieser evidently endorsed these interventions (von Wieser, 1967, p. 409; Fishback and Kantor, 1998).

6    "The first Western writer to equate the household with its property and its management with the undivided authority of the household head, was the Greek writer Xenophon. ... He coined the word 'economicus' to mean estate management. But it was the Roman Columella ... who in the first century AD, wrote the most systematic of all treatises about the art of managing an agricultural estate ..." (Moss, 1998, p. 76).

7    I assume that Hayek's short list of advocates of monetary nationalism includes John Maynard Keynes. Hayek does name R. F. Harrod as an "ardent advocate of Monetary Nationalism" but the context makes it clear that there are many other monetary nationalists out there as well (Hayek, 1937, p. 48).

## Bibliography

Bator, Francis M. (1957) "The Simple Analytics of Welfare Maximization," *American Economic Review* 17 (March): 22–59.

Boettke, Peter J. (1997) "Where Did Economics Go Wrong? Modern Economics As A Flight From Reality," *Critical Review* 11 (Winter): 11–64.

Boettke, Peter J. and D. L. Prychitko (1994) "The Future of Austrian Economics," *The Market Process: Essays in Contemporary Austrian Economics*. Aldershot, England: Edward Elgar.

Butos, William N. (1985) "Hayek and General Equilibrium Analysis," *Southern Economic Journal* 52 (October): 332–42.

Caldwell, Bruce (1988) "Hayek's Transformation," *History of Political Economy* 20 (Winter): 513–41.

—— (1997a) "Hayek and Socialism," *Journal of Economic Literature* 35 (December): 1,856–90.

—— (1997b) "Introduction," in F. A. Hayek, *Socialism and War: Essays, Documents, Reviews* in Hayek, *The Collected Works of Friedrich A. Hayek*, 19 vols. Chicago: University of Chicago Press, 10: 1–50.

Fishback, P. V. and S. E. Kantor (1998) "The Adoption of Workers' Compensation in the United States, 1900–1930," *Journal of Law and Economics* 41 (October): 305–41.

Hayek, Friedrich A. (1932) *Prices and Production*, 2nd rev. edn. London: George Routledge & Sons.

—— (1933) *Monetary Theory and the Trade Cycle*. London: Jonathan Cape.

—— (1937a) "Economics and Knowledge," *Economica* 4: 33–54. In Hayek (1952) *Individualism and Economic Order*. London: Routledge & Kegan Paul.

—— (1937b) [1971] *Monetary Nationalism and Economic Stability*. New York: Augustus M. Kelley.

—— (1938) "Freedom and the Economic System," *Contemporary Review*, pp. 434–42. Reprinted in F. A. Hayek, *Socialism and War: Essays, Documents, Reviews*. Bruce Caldwell, ed. In Hayek, *The Collected Works of F. A. Hayek*, 19 vols, 10: 181–8.

(1945) "The Use of Knowledge in Society," *American Economic Review* 35 (September): 77–91.

—— (1960) *The Constitution of Liberty*. Chicago: University of Chicago Press.

—— (1961) [1944] *The Road to Serfdom*. Chicago: University of Chicago Press.

—— (1962) [1941] *The Pure Theory of Capital*. London: Routledge & Kegan Paul.

—— (1963) [1935] *Collectivist Economic Planning: Critical Studies on the Possibilities of Socialism by N.G. Pierson, Ludwig von Mises, Georg Halm, and Enrico Barone*. London: Routledge & Kegan Paul.

—— (1967) "The Results of Human Action but Not of Human Design," in Hayek, *Studies in Philosophy, Politics, and Economics*. New York: Clarion Book, pp. 96–105.

—— (1969) "Three Elucidations of the Ricardo Effect," *Journal of Political Economy* 10 (April), pp. 483–5.

—— (1973) *Rules and Order*. In Hayek, *Law, Legislation and Liberty*, Vol. 1. Chicago: University of Chicago Press.

—— (1976a) *Denationalisation of Money: An Analysis of the Theory and Practice of Concurrent Currencies*. London: Institute of Economic Affairs.

—— (1976b) *The Mirage of Social Justice*. In Hayek, *Law, Legislation and Liberty*, Vol. 2. Chicago: University of Chicago Press.

—— (1978) "Competition as a Discovery Process," in *New Studies in Philosophy, Politics, Economics and the History of Ideas*. Chicago: University of Chicago Press.

—— (1979) *The Political Order of a Free People*. In Hayek, *Law, Legislation and Liberty*, Vol. 3. Chicago: University of Chicago Press.

—— (1984) [1926] "Some Remarks on the Problem of Imputation," in Hayek, R. McCloughry, ed., *Money Capital and Fluctuation. Early Essays*. Chicago: University of Chicago Press.

—— (1988) *The Fatal Conceit: The Errors of Socialism*. In Hayek, *The Collected Works of F. A. Hayek*, 19 vols, I.

—— (1994) *Hayek on Hayek: An Autobiographical Dialogue*. S. Kresge and L. Wenar, eds, Chicago: University. of Chicago Press.

Keynes, John Maynard (1971) [1930] *A Treatise on Money*, 2 vols. In Keynes, *The Collected Economic Writings of John Maynard Keynes*. London: St. Martin's Press. Vols 5 and 6.

—— (1973) [1936] *The General Theory of Employment, Interest, and Money*. In Keynes, *The Collected Economic Writings of John Maynard Keynes*. London: St. Martin's Press. Vol. 7.

Kirzner, Israel M. (1976) [1960] *The Economic Point of View: An Essay in the History of Economic Thought*. Kansas City: Sheed & Ward.

Lange, Oskar and Fred M. Taylor (1964) [1938] *On the Economic Theory of Socialism*. New York: McGraw-Hill.

Menger, Carl (1950) [1871] *Principles of Economics*. J. Dingwall and B. F. Hoselitz, trans. Glencoe, Illinois: The Free Press.

Moss, Laurence S. (1994) "Hayek and the Several Faces of Socialism," in M. Colonna, H. Hagemann, and O. F. Hamouda, eds, *Capitalism, Socialism and Knowledge: The Economics of F. A. Hayek*, 2 vols. Aldershot, England: Edward Elgar, II: 94–113.

—— (1997) "Austrian Economics and the Abandonment of the Classic Thought Experiment," in W. Keizer, B. Tieben, and R. van Zijp, eds, *Austrian Economics in Debate*. London: Routledge, pp. 151–71.

—— (1998) "Friedrich A. Hayek: Super-Dissenter," in R. P. F. Holt and S. Pressman, eds, *Economics and its Discontents: Twentieth Century Dissenting Economists*. Cheltenham, UK: Edward Elgar.

Searle, John R. (1995) *The Construction of Social Reality*. New York: Free Press.

—— (1998) *Mind, Language and Society: Philosophy in the Real World*. New York: Basic Books.

Vaughn, Karen (1994) *Austrian Economics in America: The Migration of a Tradition*. New York: Cambridge University Press.

von Wieser, Friedrich (1956) [1988] *Natural Value*. New York: Kelley & Millman.

—— (1967) [1927] *Social Economics*. A. F. Hinrichs, trans. New York: Kelley Publishers.

—— (1983) [1926] *The Law of Power: Das Gesetz der Macht*. W. E. Kuhn, trans. Bureau of Business Research at the University of Nebraska–Lincoln.

# 7 Mind, market and institutions

## The knowledge problem in Hayek's thought

*William N. Butos and Thomas J. McQuade*

## Introduction

The "knowledge problem" – the thesis that knowledge is constrained by both absolute and practical considerations to be incomplete – provides cohesion and continuity in Hayek's work across several domains of inquiry,[1] including his cognitive and market theories. It also is a central explanatory element in Hayek's attempts to come to grips with the nature of general social order, and is his bridge for bringing insights worked out in the economic domain to bear on this wider social domain. As Hayek expanded his field of vision, insights from the catallactic domain proved to be of profound significance in studying social arrangements, including why some forms of social order may be more conducive to the realization of liberal ideals than others. As his analysis, however, turned increasingly toward broader social theory, his defense of classical liberalism became more normatively based and further distanced from the basic scientific thrust of his approach. Clearly, Hayek's work comprises a research program of significant scope and promising fecundity, yet the insights he gained through analysis of economic phenomena were not sufficient to enable definitive conclusions to be derived analytically in the wider social domain. This is not altogether unexpected – there are good reasons, which we shall detail, why a shift of domain from the relatively narrow and well-defined area of economics to that of the broader social arena would of necessity introduce complexities and difficulties.

We propose that one way to proceed around these difficulties is to introduce the idea of orders as active structures in which knowledge is generated – the other side of the coin to the knowledge-constraining aspects of orders. In effect, we suggest that insights about the nature of knowledge and order from Hayek's analysis of mind be applied not only to the market order but also to social orders in general. In beginning to explore this idea, we note that it gives us the basis for treating sensibly some controversial issues that have arisen at the borderline between economic and social theory. And, looking beyond particular issues, we can speculate on the potential of this idea for studying social theory from a perspective based on the general scientific study of knowledge-generating orders and their institutional components.

To summarize, we make a four-point argument in the sections that follow. First, that the concept of constrained knowledge is central to Hayek's theories of both mind and market. Second, that this concept is also a central element in Hayek's attempt to build a social theory that he hoped would validate liberal ideals, but, third, this attempt foundered on the complexities of the social domain. Last, we suggest that a possible way forward is to recognize the knowledge-generating aspect of orders along with the knowledge-constraining aspect and to conceive of social theory as the scientific study of orders.

## Knowledge, mind, and market

Hayek's study of what knowledge is and how it is distributed, and in particular his theme of "constraints on knowledge," is the key to identifying significant elements of continuity between his cognitive psychology (1952b)[2] and his general market theory (1937, 1945).[3] In the former, Hayek proposes a theory in which the mind is seen to construct an interpretation of reality by classifying sensory inputs using a "system of rules" (Hayek, 1978, p. 41) that arranges sensory qualities within a connected, latticed and preexisting (but mutable) network of pathways and categories. Because "perception," Hayek (1952b, p. 142) says, is "always interpretation, the placing of something into one of several classes of objects," the knowledge the sensory order produces is an abstract representation of reality, a representation created by an instrument of classification – the mind, itself organized as an hierarchical order governed by classificatory rules (Hayek, 1952b, ch. 6). Hayek's theory holds that sensory inputs only become meaningful to the individual if they can be classified into preexisting categories. Since the generation of knowledge, according to Hayek, is necessarily subject to binding (yet unspecifiable) constraints determined by the classificatory rules and structure of the mind, knowledge of external reality is constitutionally constrained. This idea, which emerges foundationally from Hayek's cognitive psychology, also permeates Hayek's work in other areas, including his methodological work (Birner, 1999b)[4] and, as we shall now argue in greater detail, in his market theory as well. The fundamental similarities in his explanatory schemata for cognitive and market theories can be identified as follows:

*No central locus of control*[5]    At the cognitive level, the sensory order is constituted by and is a byproduct of the relationships and interactions of the entire classificatory apparatus, a system without a single locus of control. As Hayek says in *The Sensory Order*:

> [T]he whole of these [sensory] qualities is determined by the system of connexions by which the impulses can be transmitted from neuron to neuron; that it is thus the position of the individual impulse or group of impulses in the whole system of connexions which gives it its distinctive quality.
>
> (1952b, p. 53)

He describes neural functioning in terms of an information network by which impulses are classified, organized, and linked together. The transmission and interpretation of such impulses within the resulting structure enables the individual to form conjectures about external reality and to engage in behaviors adaptive to new circumstances. Hayek's theory of mind articulates an order that is decentralized, that engages in the conveyance of relational qualities within itself, and that is self-regulative via feedback, learning, and adjustment.[6]

For the catallaxy, the relevant units of analysis are individuals who pursue their own ends and interact with each other according to certain rules or routines concerning trading and property. There are sufficient overlapping routines among individuals that allow all to benefit from dispersed practical knowledge, and this is largely achieved through a self-regulating price system. Prices are disequilibrium phenomena that signify to market participants opportunities for action and establish, in effect, a context for entrepreneurial discovery and thus for the ongoing remediation of plan discoordination.[7] In the catallaxy – a "spontaneous order produced by the market through people acting within the rules of the law of property, tort and contract" (Hayek, 1976, p. 109) – the patterns of interaction produced by agents following these rules cease to be explainable by the pure logic of choice as if the system were simply a single mind. Once the division of knowledge is introduced, we pass from the economics of a "household" into an entirely different realm of investigation in which adaptation, innovative capability, and unintended consequences take on decisive importance.

*Processing of "divided knowledge"* In both cases there is a sense in which distributed knowledge is made generally accessible. In Hayek's cognitive theory, sensory impulses are perceived because they have been classified or distributed within a multilayered and mutable latticework of connected preexisting categories. Knowledge of the events or objects antecedent to these impulses "will always be a description in terms of the relation of the quality in question to other sensory qualities" (1952b, p. 31). The individual's interpretation of some external object is not made on the basis of a single attribute, but on the basis of several different classification rules that have been used to sort and relate various qualities of the object or to classify the same quality with qualities of other objects. In short, knowledge does not exist as a datum, but as a decentralized relational structure of qualities that are linked together in ways that are meaningful for the individual.

In his "knowledge papers" (1937, 1945) and elsewhere, Hayek identifies the use of decentralized knowledge as the central problem of economics, referring specifically to knowledge of "particular circumstances of time and place" (in contrast to scientific or codifiable knowledge) that each individual possesses. Because practical knowledge is decentralized, it simultaneously implies a constraint on what any individual can know. Hayek's identification of the division of knowledge relocates the economic problem away from the use of given (i.e. known) knowledge and toward the discovery of knowledge and mechanisms that enable the transmission and use of dispersed knowledge. His solution is well known: the price system of the market economy is a particular institutional arrangement that provides opportunities for individuals to discover knowledge and engage in activities in which they are able to economize on what they need to know.

*Knowledge embedded in tacit rules*[8]    At the level of the individual, Hayek's cognitive theory suggests that tacit rules – and the complex adaptive mechanisms they drive for achieving a closer fit with the external environment – establish strictures against a conception of rationality based on simple maximization or "rational expectations." And in his market theory, Hayek argues against a conception of economic rationality based on Pareto optimality and favors one that sees the market process as a discovery process without conscious direction and not based on a hierarchy of ends (the only ends being those of the individual participants).

For Hayek, the essential activity of the mind is its classificatory functioning, not whether classification is conscious or unconscious. He holds that the processes governing conscious activity are the same as those that govern nonconscious activity, and, further, suggests (1952b, pp. 23, 24) that there is a kind of knowledge that refers to classificatory rules about which we are unavoidably and necessarily unaware. These are rules determined by the experiential history of the individual and the evolutionary history of the species, a history that provides the individual with a range of dispositions to action conducive to survival. His view (p. 39) is that "knowledge that" is explicit and derives from a reservoir of "knowledge how" that can never be made fully articulate. He says "we are not in fact able to state all the rules which govern our perceptions and actions" (1967, p. 60) and that "we *always* know not only more than we can deliberately state but also more than we can be aware of ... and that much that we successfully do depends on presuppositions which are outside the range of what we can either state or reflect upon" (p. 61, emphasis added).[9]

One of Hayek's major claims is that the tacit knowledge each individual possesses will be used by the price system through each individual's participation, and thereby can be used by individuals to adjust their activities to remove less satisfactory states of affairs. The self-regulative character of this system depends on what Hayek refers to as "abstract rules of conduct," essentially negative – and largely tacit – rules that not only help to guide activities in most circumstances, but which also allow for broad latitude in their application. Integral to this error-removing and self-correcting process (as has been pointed out and developed by Kirzner and others) is the role of entrepreneurial discovery in its arbitrage dimension operating through the filter of a profit and loss in promoting greater dovetailing of individual plans.

To summarize: in both domains of mind and market, Hayek shows that knowledge is "constrained" in that it is the contingent product of a decentralized process, one which is not subject to conscious, centralized control and which depends for its operation on particular interacting elements and their interaction routines.

## Knowledge and social theory

Hayek's interest in broader social theory and normative issues becomes more prominent by the 1940s. This expansion beyond technical economics (which he never fully left) may have been hastened by the eclipse of Austrian economics in the aftermath of the Keynesian "avalanche" and the socialist calculation debate's lesson that Austrians were perhaps not really in the (new) mainstream. But this expansion also arose from Hayek's conviction that the understanding and appreciation of the liberal order had substantially eroded. He believed liberalism was "the abandoned road" and that it was his "duty" to write "social philosophy" to explain the errors of planning and the value of freedom (1944, pp. vi–viii). We see his broader social theory as having been built upon his scientific work, including his study of the knowledge problem, in an attempt to generate normative insights from an antecedent analytical framework. There are, however, difficulties that his normative analysis poses for his broader social theory. We suggest that the temptation to promote strong normative results in social theory is premature in the absence of a more fully worked out theory and study of social orders as "natural phenomena."

Hayek's two most comprehensive studies in broader social theory are *The Constitution of Liberty* (*CL*, 1960) and *Law, Legislation and Liberty* (*LLL*, 1973, 1976, 1979). Hayek himself recognized that their differences reflected real changes in the way he saw the world. Although in both works[10] his aim was to "restate the 'ideal of freedom'" (1960, p. 1) or, similarly, to argue that "the preservation of a society of free men" depends on expounding "fundamental insights" (1973, p. 2),[11] *CL* is more traditionalist in its belief that the existing institutional framework could be reformed to produce those conditions that would promote liberal society. In *LLL*, by contrast, Hayek concluded that the "traditional doctrine of liberal constitutionalism" (1973, p. 2) had failed to secure liberty and that it was the failure of liberal democratic institutions which accounted for the erosion of freedom. As Buchanan might put it, Hayek moved from questions about changes within a set of rules to questions about changes in the rules. In *LLL* Hayek referred to this as a "problem of constitutional design" (1973, p. 4).

Despite such important differences in the two treatises, there are elements common to both. One of these is Hayek's interest and willingness to engage broad issues in social theory and to do so from a distinctly normative perspective. For Hayek, however, this perspective was usually informed by and defended on the basis of scientific analysis. Even though his normative analysis itself raises certain questions, we are inclined to take Hayek at his word when he claims the demise of liberalism and the drifting away from liberal principles was primarily a result of intellectual mistakes, not the wrong values. This point was made repeatedly by Hayek and is found in *The Road to Serfdom* (1944), *CL*, *The Fatal Conceit*

(1988),[12] and also in *LLL*, where he claimed the crucial argument was between "evolutionary [critical] rationalism" and the core philosophical error of "rational constructivism," an error that Hayek believed science could unmask and resolve. Demonstrating that, Hayek asserted, would produce the knock-down punch to a "whole family of schools of scientific as well as political thought" (1973, p. 6). Thus, while *CL* deals to an important extent with certain kinds of details concerning policy issues and the opportunities for attaining a liberal society within a given institutional framework of rules, *LLL* identifies the central problems more abstractly in terms of competing philosophical positions and the implications they hold for understanding the emergence, nature, and evolution of social orders.

However, notwithstanding Hayek's reorientation toward more constitutional issues, in these later writings the theme of knowledge still figures prominently in the arguments upon which liberalism is defended. For Hayek, understanding the creative powers of a free society begins with recognizing that "our ignorance is the beginning of wisdom" (1973, p. 22), for only then can "we learn to understand what role [reason] does in fact play and can play in the working of any society based on the co-operation of many separate minds" (p. 69). Hayek's anti-rationalist stance is an argument in "defense of reason against its abuse" so that a fuller understanding may be gained of the conditions necessary for "its effective functioning and continuous growth." In turn, this requires that we accept the undesigned and uncontrollable aspects of a society based on liberal principles such as the rule of law, property, and limited government. But recognizing the existence of constraints on individual knowledge concerning "particular facts which are or will become known by somebody" (p. 13) also provides a key to understanding the mechanisms and structures that arise spontaneously and through collective choice. It is in response to "our irremediable ignorance" that "most social institutions have taken the form they actually have" (p. 13). As Hayek (1960) puts it:

> Most of the advantages of social life ... rest on the fact that the individual benefits from more knowledge than he is aware of. ... Civilization begins when the individual in the pursuit of his ends can make use of more knowledge than he has himself acquired and when he can transcend the boundaries of his ignorance by profiting from knowledge he does not himself possess (p. 22). ... Though we are usually not aware of it, all institutions of freedom are adaptations to this fundamental fact of ignorance (p. 30).[13]

His emphasis on the role of spontaneously formed orders, such as the catallaxy or "grown law" for just conduct, in promoting liberal society is explicitly founded on the epistemic advantages that such orders confer to individuals in adjusting to unknown circumstances. Such advantages, he observes, cannot be attained by an "organization" or a central planning agency because they direct the actions of individuals through specific commands aimed toward specific ends based solely on the knowledge available to a single mind or agency. In contrast, a society based on rules that are general, end-independent, and apply to all individuals provides the conditions conducive for the formation of a spontaneous order in which individuals are free to use "knowledge which nobody possesses as a whole" (1973, p. 49). The consequence of this is that under liberal principles "a spontaneous order of human activities of much greater complexity will form itself than could ever be produced by deliberate arrangement" (1967, p. 162).

Hayek describes the transmission of rules guiding conduct as occurring through a selection and retention process involving the imitation and weeding out of rules of conduct, habits, and traditions. He maintains that the process is undesigned and the rules themselves are "observed in action without being known to the acting person in articulated … form" (1973, p. 19).[14] He shows his antipathy for "rational constructivism" by disputing the primary role of reason in guiding the evolution of society. He claims that "better rules of conduct" confer advantages to those using them and thus are imitated by successive generations.[15] His selection mechanism occurs at the societal group level: those groups who practiced better rules would achieve greater success than other groups who used inferior rules in that they might not only displace such groups but also sustain larger populations.[16] Despite the tautological ring to this claim, Hayek seems here to offer what may be described as a "rational theory of tradition," in that he identifies a Lamarckian evolutionary process in which "Our habits and skills, our emotional attitudes, our tools, and our institutions – all are in this sense adaptations to past experience which have grown up by selective elimination of less suitable conduct" (1960, p. 26).[17]

The epistemic consequence of alternative social arrangements and institutions is a central theme in Hayek's broader social theory.[18] But Hayek also wanted to defend the liberal order as a normative ideal and to show how it could be achieved.[19] These two agendas are combined in his broader social theory. He believed that by adhering to liberal principles, the resulting social order would generate outcomes more beneficial than the available alternatives. He approached the evaluation of such outcomes in two different ways: (1) for the catallaxy, the absence of any particular ends of the overall order and the impossibility of interpersonal utility comparisons required him to reject standard welfare economics in favor of a conception focusing on the "conditions under which the chances for any individual taken at random to achieve his ends as effectively as possible will be very high" (1978, p. 184),[20] and (2) as noted above, the quasi-criterion for group selection in terms of sustaining large populations (1988, ch. 8). However, he attempted to maintain his normative claims on the basis of scientific argument. And this argument, as we have indicated, centered on demonstrating the superior epistemic properties of spontaneous orders. His central thrust was to conceive of the social realm in terms of relating progress to the formation of increasingly complex orders (and suborders) and to analyze these according to their epistemic properties. The liberal goal of freedom, typically defined to refer to limited government, the rule of law, property rights, and a domain of individual autonomy protected from arbitrary interference, was deemed essential for promoting the emergence and growth of spontaneous orders and thereby deriving from such orders the epistemic advantages necessary for progress.

In making this argument, Hayek drew substantially upon epistemic themes from his work in catallactics, and in so doing elevated the problem of constraints on knowledge to the status of a generalizable social principle.[21] Thus, in *CL* Hayek's discussion of the "Creative Powers of a Free Civilization" (the title of Chapter 2) is couched in terms of what Hayek calls "the great problem" of the division of knowledge that is resolved "because civilization enables us constantly to profit from knowledge which we individually do not possess" (p. 25).[22] And in the first volume of *LLL* (1973), Hayek's central argument, which he uses against rational constructivism, is based on the observation that "man's actions are largely successful … because they are adapted both to the particular facts which he knows and to a great many other facts he does not and cannot know" (pp. 11–12) and that "the fact of our irremediable ignorance of most of the facts which determine the processes of society is, however, the reason why most social institutions have taken the form they actually have" (p. 13). He goes on to note that it was his 1937 and 1945 "knowledge articles" which were the "starting point for those ideas which in the present book are systematically applied to a much wider field" (p. 13).[23]

But in carrying forward insights from economics, Hayek also realized that his scientific analysis of spontaneous orders would not necessarily generate the requisite conditions or support fully the kinds of outcomes necessary to sustain the "Great Society." For example, Hayek (1973) observes that just because the evolution of "grown law" has "certain desirable properties does not prove that it will always be good law or even that some of the rules may not be very bad" (p. 88). This most frequently occurs, Hayek claims, when evolved law legitimates a view of justice applicable for certain individuals that "could not meet the more general requirements of justice" (p. 89). The fact that the spontaneous emergence and development of law may lead the legal system into an "impasse from which it cannot extricate itself" implies for Hayek that we cannot "altogether dispense with legislation" (p. 88). A direct consequence of this acknowledgement was that it prompted Hayek to consider the kinds of meta-arrangements which the orders of the catallaxy, law, and social interaction might require for their maintenance. This, however, committed Hayek to an analysis containing more normative elements. It also pushed the discussion toward problems increasingly distanced from those kinds of spontaneous orders, especially the catallaxy, that had received the most detailed and rigorous analytical treatment. And finally, the level of abstraction ultimately required for Hayek's broader social theory seems to be less clearly definitive in demonstrating exactly how such arrangements, over other possible ones, were in fact consistent with or essential to the liberal order. As Hayek moved into broader social theory, the sort of clarity associated with catallactic theory seemed more difficult to obtain; his analysis becomes, in a sense, more "fuzzy."

## Problems in social theory

It is not surprising that Hayek's social theory would bump up against certain rather formidable problems, as others have also suggested.[24] As Hayek moved into questions of broader social theory, the less relevant were the insights of catallactic theory for addressing those questions – a point that may be gleaned from Hayek (1960, pp. 3–4) when he says "though I still regard myself as mainly an economist, I have come to feel that more and more that the answers to many of the pressing social questions are to be found ultimately in … principles that lie outside the scope of technical economics." Although the various orders of the social realm have features in common, it certainly does not follow that they function similarly or even generate normatively comparable outcomes. We can identify the kinds of problems that are encountered in moving from the spontaneous order of the catallaxy to that of the broader social order as follows:

*The problem of complexity* Broader social theory seeks to understand an overall order having a degree of complexity exceeding that of "sub-orders," such as the catallaxy, that operate within or as part of it. This means that the analysis of the broader social order involves not just the social order alone but also understanding the ways the various sub-orders interact with each other. Understanding the operation of a broader social order, let alone how it might change or evolve, is a daunting undertaking. Further, Hayek has claimed that the kind of knowledge we may hope to gain as we move into increasingly more complex phenomena becomes itself more abstract or general. In "The Theory of Complex Phenomena" he says:

> The advance of science will thus have to proceed in two different directions: while it is certainly desirable to make our theories as falsifiable as possible, we must also push forward into fields where, as we advance, the degree of falsifiability necessarily decreases. This is the price we have to pay for an advance into the field of complex phenomena.
>
> (1967, p. 29)

If this is true, then our knowledge will refer to less particular aspects of phenomena as we proceed into the investigation of the broader and more complex social domain.[25]

*The problem of mechanisms* The fact that two complex orders are spontaneous does not imply that the same or even similar mechanisms explain their operation. Any similarity would need to be demonstrated. Using mechanisms from economics to explain, for example, how or why one set of specific arrangements regarding rules of property might be weeded out in favor of another is really the application of theories from one context where their use makes sense (the catallaxy) to another where their relevance is not self-evident. Similarly, Kirznerian entrepreneurship makes sense as a catallactic mechanism, but applying it to questions about extra-economic behavior may not be legitimate. Similar reservations apply to the spontaneous order of scientific activity: science is not a market order and consequently we cannot routinely presume that the functioning of the order of science is describable using catallactic concepts.

*The problem of abstraction*   The kinds of *ceteris paribus* assumptions invoked in social theory often depend on the level at which the analysis is being conducted. Within the broader domain of social theory, the sub-domain of catallactic theory, for example, may use a general conception of property to analyze various questions without loss of explanatory power for many, if not the majority, of problems relevant for catallactic analysis. Given the economist's problem situation, there may be no compelling reason to dwell on the full legal complexities and particularities associated with property rights; rather, in many cases, the economist can simply take as given an institutional framework of property rights of a complexity assumed suitable for the analysis of the particular economic question at hand.

At the level of broader social theory, however, taking such arrangements among the givens is likely to involve certain difficulties because the specification of different kinds of rules may imply significant differences in the kinds and functioning of social institutions consistent with those rules; consequently, it is often the case for broader social theory, in contrast to economics, that one of its central tasks will be to more fully specify the details of property rights. While the economist may appropriately take certain institutional arrangements as exogenous and to treat them as part of the *ceteris paribus* conditions, the theorist operating at the broader social level would appear to have the more difficult job of explaining in adequate detail the social institutions upon which the catallaxy is based.

*The problem of criteria*   Catallactic theory is non-normative. However, some economists have found it useful to theorize about the outcomes generated by a hypothetical catallaxy using various conceptions of equilibrium. Hayek's (1937) notion of "plan coordination" requires that individuals' plans dovetail so that each plan may be executed without disappointment. We might even extend this conception empirically, as Hayek suggested (1937, p. 44), and speak of equilibrium as an actual tendency. In doing so, we come a step closer to identifying a kind of normative status to this notion of equilibrium on the grounds that it is not unreasonable to imagine that individuals would prefer to achieve their plans than not – see Kirzner (1992). Only within the catallactic context does the identification of such a normative criterion serve a useful (although limited) purpose. And using a single metric for evaluative purposes is not *per se* illegitimate within that specific context; but neither is it necessarily complete since it is possible to specify other conceptions of equilibrium that could be made to carry normative implications. At the broader social level, however, it seems that we often are dealing with outcomes where normative criteria are considerably more difficult to specify, let alone compelling enough to elicit broad acceptance. This probably has something to do with the broader purview of social, as opposed to catallactic, theory. Consequently, individuals' preferences in the social domain are likely to refer to many different classes of possible outcomes, some of which are highly abstract and impalpable, that are likely to reflect abiding incompatibilities among individuals for which no simple adjustment, such as would occur in the market by price changes, is likely to resolve. The added difficulty in identifying evaluative criteria at the broader social level casts doubt on the usefulness of normative propositions. Although Hayek's "population quasi-criterion" for cultural evolution is coherent and has empirical content, it does not answer the question of whether a randomly selected individual, even one with strong liberal convictions, would want to live in such a society.

The central message from these above considerations is that the kinds of relatively well-defined questions and analyses that catallactic theory is suited to address are not so easily achieved in the area of broader social theory. Even as Hayek ventured further into social theory, he continued to rely on catallactics to provide important elements of the conceptual framework for elucidating the liberal order, a very natural disposition – for it was in the catallaxy that he was able to most plainly identify the functioning of a spontaneous order. However, as Hayek delved deeper into social theory it became more problematic to transfer over the sorts of analytical and even normative assurances sustained and suggested by catallactic theory and its empirical application. An evolutionary perspective, though probably nascent in much of his work, took on considerably greater significance by the 1970s, even though in doing so it seemed to stir into the mix elements some commentators find questionable.[26]

## Orders as knowledge-generating objects

In the final analysis, Hayek's program, with its consistent stress on the limits of knowledge, has yet to give rise to a fully analytical theory of social order. In seeking a possible path for continuing Hayek's work, we note that, while the problem of order presents us with the realization that there are inevitable constraints on knowledge, there is another side of the coin – the importance of the knowledge-generating characteristics of orders.

In considering the problems raised by Hayek's attempt to move from catallactics to the more complicated cases of social orders, we claim that, while Hayek clearly saw individual knowledge as order-dependent (i.e. dependent on the structure of the sensory order), he never *fully* generalized this idea to the market order or to other social orders. When talking about knowledge in the context of the market he seems always to refer to the potential within the market order for *communication* of dispersed and tacit individual knowledge, not to the *generation* of completely new knowledge.

Ironically, the idea of order-dependent knowledge and of its generation as referring to a different classification is brought out very clearly in Hayek's sensory order work, where he emphasizes the contingency of individual knowledge with respect to the structure in which it is generated. He says explicitly that "a question like 'what is X?' has meaning only within a given order" (1952b, p. 4). Later, in "The Primacy of the Abstract," he is equally clear in saying that "it is meaningless to speak of perceiving or thinking except as a function of an acting organism in which the differentiation of stimuli manifests itself in the differences of the dispositions to act which they evoke" (1978, p. 40). Again, in the same article, he characterizes human knowledge as "primarily a system of rules of action" (p. 41) in which appropriate action patterns are invoked by sensed combinations of stimuli – an effective classification of the stimuli, but one very much tied to the actual structure of the classificatory apparatus.

But, in applying this idea to orders other than the sensory order, he becomes much less clear. He does clearly distinguish between scientific knowledge and individual knowledge of "the particular circumstances of time and place" (1945, p. 521), but does so without referring to the distinct contexts in which these different sorts of knowledge are generated. When he speaks of the function of the market system as enabling "the utilization of knowledge not given to anyone in its totality" (p. 520), he fosters the notion that there actually is such a thing as that totality independent of the circumstances of its generation, and that the problem is how best to accumulate it. Of course, he strenuously denies that direct accumulation is even possible, and clearly represents the price system as communicating "by a kind of symbol, only the most essential information" (p. 527). But, although the idea seems to be just below the surface, he never explicitly identifies the price symbols as knowledge generated by the market order.[27] And in speaking, somewhat loosely, of the price system as "a mechanism for communicating information" (p. 527) he exposes himself to the sort of out-of-context readings, evident in the work of Grossman (1989) and other modern "theory of information" economists, who construe the issue simply in terms of dispersed information being directly communicated between individuals by means of the price system.

In his later social theory, Hayek seems to cast his problem in terms of understanding the nature of social order in general, as opposed to understanding, as at least conceptually separate things, the various orders that have formed or could be formed in a social context. His orientation comes through fairly clearly in his specific definition of order:

> By "order" we shall throughout describe a state of affairs in which a multiplicity of elements of various kinds are so related to each other that we may learn from our acquaintance with some spatial or temporal part of the whole to form correct expectations concerning the rest, or at least expectations which have a good chance of being correct.
>
> (1973, p. 36, emphasis omitted)

This is a concept of "order" in a *very* general sense, encompassing as it does simple physical orders such as inorganic crystals. It is also a surprisingly passive view of orders in that it abstracts completely away from any idea of orders as active, knowledge-generating objects. Absent is any hint of the function of orders as being characterized by forms of knowledge specific to them, dependent on the particular structure of the order and on the properties of its elements and their connections. Bianchi (1994) has perceptively taken issue with the character-ization of "order" as simply an orderly state – in particular, with the fact that it abstracts away from the procedures of discovery going on within social orders. She points out that order "is not a state of affairs, but a process; not a correct state, but a corrigible one" (p. 245). We suggest that Bianchi's insight can be captured by conceptualizing social orders, like the sensory order, as knowledge-generating objects, as complex and dynamic objects in a state of continual adaptation to their environment, capable of generating classifications of events in that environment.

We would expect on the basis of such a perspective that not all social orders will have the same knowledge-generating capacities, a point we can develop in connection with the socialist calculation debate. A system of central planning is an order constructed (in the idealized limit) as a single locus of control, a "sensory order" assisted by some data-gathering organization that can communi-cate some of the articulable aspects of the particular circumstances of time and place back to the center. There are two major problems with this arrangement. First, a significant amount of the potential input data is in the form of tacit indi-vidual knowledge and is not directly communicable in this way. Second, even allowing that the arrangement is capable of capturing at least some of the dispersed knowledge, there is nothing in the structure of the order to enhance its classificatory possibilities or its feedback ability, and so there is no capability for generating higher-level knowledge, i.e. knowledge beyond that which a single sensory order is capable of generating.

The order of the market system, by contrast, not only involves structures which react to input data in the form of tacit knowledge, but also processes its input data through an elaborate classificatory process, out of which are gener-ated classification results in the form of prices and other abstract attributes of goods which feed back to augment individual knowledge. This is a classification process of quite a different nature and scope to that of a sensory order, and it is no surprise that a system of central planning, lacking it either in whole or in part, is significantly less agile in an adaptive sense than a market system. This does not imply the "impossibility of socialism," as some suggest,[28] but rather that a socialist society, in the absence of pricing data from outside of itself, could not continue to support the level of population, let alone civilization, that its proponents assume.[29] Casting the analysis in terms of the actual knowledge-generating capacities of possible alternate arrangements is in essence an elaboration of the idea of "comparative institutional analysis" cogently put forward by Coase (1960) and Demsetz (1969).

We may also use the idea of knowledge-generating orders to understand from a different angle the implications of how a market order functions under different institutional arrangements. Accordingly, it is possible to frame the effects of "Big Players" – market participants such as finance ministers and central bankers who, as described by Koppl and Yeager (1996), are immune to the discipline of the market[30] – in terms of the different learning responses of a market order in two different environments. In ordinary markets, the input data is in the form of the knowledge of local circumstances held individually by the many market participants. The market order classifies this input to produce market knowledge in the form of the prices, qualities, and reputations, which reflect the order's adaptation to the external phenomena. In contrast, if Big Players are active, the input data includes strong components emanating from them, and so the resulting classification (prices, etc.) is an adaptation not only to the distributed individual knowledge but to the Big Player's input. If this is very strong it can, to some extent, drown out the other inputs, so that the market's adaptation is, in large part, to the input from the Big Player and much less so to the inputs from the other market participants.

In these circumstances, market participants correctly attach special significance to future inputs from the Big Player compared to the "underlying fundamentals" (the inputs from everyone else). If Big Players engage in discretionary policy, market participants are not likely to learn the new (and ever-changing) environment quickly enough to adapt fully and the market classifications will be only poor representations of the actual circumstances. Although the market order produces knowledge as well attuned to its inputs as its reaction time permits, the epistemic quality of the market signals is lower in a Big Player market. In these circumstances, market participants are likely to form expectations heavily based on what others think the Big Player is going to do, thereby providing a rationale for "herding" behaviors. The epistemic effect of discretionary Big Players, in short, carries implications for market orderliness and the coordination of individuals' plans.

We also note that a sensory order-inspired perspective directs attention toward the structural characteristic of orders as multilayered objects with classification and reclassification taking place at successive layers. This bears upon the recent discussion, beginning with Vanberg (1986), questioning Hayek's consistent use of methodological individualism in his analysis of the selection of "appropriate" social rules. Vanberg argues that "the notion of cultural group selection [of such rules] is theoretically vague, inconsistent with the basic thrust of Hayek's individualistic approach, and faulty on its own grounds" (p. 97). The problem centers on the explanation of how it can be that behavior patterns beneficial to the group, but seemingly not directly beneficial to a particular individual implementing them, could emerge and survive.

There is, however, a way that the behavior patterns of self-interested individuals, taken together with the institutional context in which that behavior takes place, can appear to have been the result of selection by the group. Behavior that would certainly be seen as individually disadvantageous if all options were open to the individual can be quite consistent with self-interest in an institutional context that constrains the possible options and presents specific directions of opportunity to the individual. Soldiers who risk death in the attempt to capture a strategic hill would not appear to be behaving rationally to anyone who ignored the very particular context of those actions in terms of the norms and conventions those individuals rely upon. Once particular and multilayered institutions are established, knowledge is generated by that order that does not require "group selection" to account for the adoption of rules seemingly disadvantageous to the individual. Attention to the layered institutional structure of the order in which the behavior is played out diffuses the problem in a manner completely consistent with methodological individualism.[31]

These applications of the idea of order-dependent knowledge hint at the potential fruitfulness of a conception of social theory as a science whose objects of interest are orders and their institutional components. In economics it has usually been tacitly assumed that it is unproblematic to apply the pure logic of choice to market-level phenomena by the simple expedient of aggregation. But if we view the market order as a complex object whose structure and properties are the central focus of investigation, this modeling tactic of summing the elements to describe the whole appears as a staggeringly severe simplification, and it is certainly a tribute to the ingenuity and insight of economists that so much can be said from such a sparse platform. At a minimum, it assumes away most of the adaptive and innovative capability of the market order. If, on the other hand, we propose to pursue a study of the actual structure of the market order, then representing the elements of that order as (in general and on average) self-interested utility-seekers is unproblematic as far as it goes, but it would need to be supplemented with an understanding of exactly how and on what levels these elements interact and interconnect to form an overall order. As Hayek put it, we can only understand the market order if we are able "mentally to reconstruct it by tracing the relations that exist between the elements" (1973, p. 38). Only then can we lay out the general process through which the classification of the input data, the "distributed knowledge" of the circumstances of time and place, takes place.

People, the elements of the market order in the structural sense, tend to interact with each other by engaging in action sequences of expectable form, i.e. routines.[32] Such a view is entirely consistent with Hayek's characterization of the sort of classification performed by the sensory order – a classification resulting in the generation of propensities for action, appropriate combinations of which are instantiated in response to specific configurations of stimuli. Actual sequences of observed behavior can thus be understood as conforming to particular abstract routines with free parameters chosen and fixed according to the situation at hand. While the term "institution" is subject to a bewildering variety of competing meanings and connotations, we hope that it is integrating rather than confusing to define as an institution any abstract routine deducible from commonly observed interpersonal interactions.[33] Such routines are general in that they do not determine specific outcomes, but they do constrain the set of possible outcomes by structuring the interaction. And since it is the cumulative effects of numerous interactions at various levels that result in the formation of the order, the nature of these institutions, their structure and properties as abstract objects in their own right, is an issue of obvious concern. Indeed, according to Hayek himself, "the question which is of central importance as much for social theory as for social policy is thus what properties the rules [which govern action] must possess so that the separate actions of the individuals will produce an overall order" (1973, p. 45). These institutions are to be understood as forming the interconnections between the elements in a social order and so, by determining the structure of the order, determining its classification capability. This classification capability determines the knowledge the order is capable of generating.

We have argued that the fundamental continuity in Hayek's work derives from his ongoing concern with what are as much problems in epistemology as problems in economics or social science. In following the idea that there may well be some explanatory potential in pushing forward the notion of orders as knowledge-generating objects, it is possible to characterize Hayek's project as the scientific study of various aspects of such objects. These are structures, with both tangible and intangible components, that have the effect of generating the attribute we call "knowledge" in that they form abstract representations of phenomena external to them by a process of classification. Such an inquiry would be a science in the same way that biology is the study of various aspects of living objects – it would be epistemology treated as a natural science, not as a branch of philosophy. In this sense, it quite literally follows that the Hayekian research program should be viewed as a scientific project about knowledge.

To define exactly what we mean by "knowledge" presents much the same problem as trying to define "life" – it is not a thing in itself, but a characterization of an emergent attribute of a complex object organized in a particular way. To describe life structurally, you can only describe the various elements of the living object – what they are, how they are arranged, how they interact, how they are changed by the interaction. To describe it functionally, you can only describe the other attributes of living objects – what they enable the object to do, how they interact with the environment, and how they change. And to describe it historically or phylogenetically, you can note that living objects reproduce in certain ways with particular sorts of variations and are subject to selection, so that an evolutionary story can be pieced together. Describing knowledge requires the same sorts of understanding of the complex objects in which it is generated.

If knowledge is defined with reference to the order in which it was generated, then it is strictly incorrect to say that the market gathers up "divided" individual knowledge, accumulating separate pieces of knowledge or information into one, generally accessible bundle. Instead, the market takes, as input, knowledge in the individual sense, i.e., individual knowledge with respect to potentially useful goods and services, and classifies this, producing a totally *different* kind of knowledge. This is vital for human survival because the classifications produced by the market can be perceived by individuals and interpreted by them as enhancements to their individual knowledge, hence increasing their adaptive ability and furthering their pursuit of happiness.[34]

This sensory order-inspired view of knowledge-generating objects might provide us with a new gestalt, a new way of investigating social phenomena in general, for if it can be applied to the further understanding of markets it can also be applied to other social orders such as science, law, and politics. There is some irony in the thought that a major impediment to Hayek's attempts to understand social phenomena by applying insights gained from economic theory might have been the fact that he did not draw out the full implications of his own work on sensory orders.

## Conclusion

Hayek's overall research program is a coherent, innovative, and path-breaking body of work, underlying which is a basic concern with the problems and difficulties inherent in the generation and use of knowledge. It has provided deep insights into the nature and functioning of market activity, and it has been deployed by Hayek and others with the aim of better understanding non-market social processes. It is our contention, however, that this attempted extension of the application of the Hayekian insights to more complex social arrangements has not been an unambiguous success, and that attempts to use them to justify societal arrangements of a classical liberal sort introduce normative presuppositions outside the basic scientific thrust of Hayek's work.

But the inability of Hayek's promising program to give rise to a fully analytical theory of social order cannot be ascribed solely to an inadvisable introduction of normative elements and certainly not to any obvious slips in the analysis itself. What is needed, as Coase so famously remarked (1960, p. 42), is a change of approach. And it is a change of approach that we think is fully consistent with the main thrust of Hayek's work – the furtherance of the understanding of the nature of knowledge and order. Hayek has left us with the basis for a social science research program that focuses on the investigation of the structure, function, and evolution of a particular class of knowledge-generating objects called "orders." The scientific study of orders arising in society, and the types of order-dependent knowledge they generate, could form the heart of a distinctively Hayekian approach to social science. This research program contains within it a strong hint that perhaps "the knowledge problem" and "constraints on knowledge" have been stressed to the exclusion of the other side of the coin – the positive possibilities for the generation of knowledge.

## Acknowledgements

We would like to thank Stephan Böhm, Mario Rizzo, Roger Koppl, Jack Birner, Israel Kirzner, Peter Boettke, Karen Vaughn, and members of the NYU Austrian Economics Colloquium and the George Mason University Economics Workshop for helpful comments on earlier drafts of this chapter.

## Notes

1  See Weimer (1982), Gray (1984), and Loasby (1999).
2  When Hayek was still a student he produced a manuscript in 1920 that was the basis of *The Sensory Order*.
3  This connection has been alluded to before (see Butos, 1997), and has been developed by Birner (1999a).
4  For Hayek, "explanation" occurs through the formation of a model – an abstract construction that "will always refer to classes of events" (1952b, p. 182) in which "our conclusions and predictions will also refer only to ... a *kind* of phenomena, rather than to a particular event" (1967, p. 15). Our knowledge of complex phenomena, he claims, largely derives from models that describe patterns in the phenomena or explanations of the principles at work.
5  Our "decentralization" arguments, including their link to *The Sensory Order*, have been made independently, and in more detail, by Birner (1996).
6  See Butos and Koppl (1993).
7  See Böhm (1989).
8  See Polanyi (1966), Agonito (1975), and Lavoie (1985).
9  Hayek's initial statement of this point appears in the 1942 essay "Scientism and the Study of Society," where he argues it is contradictory to say we can "'explain' our own knowledge" because claiming so "would require that we should know more than we actually do" (1952a, p. 49).
10  Also in *The Fatal Conceit*: "This book argues that our civilization depends, not only for its origin but also for its preservation, on what can be precisely described only as the extended order of human cooperation, an order more commonly ... known as capitalism" (Hayek, 1988, p. 6).
11  There is a duality in the way Hayek fits "freedom" into his social theory. In some instances, such as the quotes in the text, freedom appears as a criterion of the Great Society, while in others, freedom is defended as a necessary condition for individuals to use dispersed knowledge.
12  In describing "the main point of my argument," Hayek claims the central conflict between "advocates of the spontaneous extended order created by a competitive market, and on the other hand those who demand a deliberate arrangement of human interaction by central authority based on the collective command over available resources is due to a factual error by the latter about how knowledge of these resources is and can be generated and utilized" (1988, p. 7).
13  Similar statements are also found in Hayek's last book, *The Fatal Conceit* (1988). For example, "Modern economics explains how such an extended order can come into being, and how it itself constitutes an information-gathering process, able to call up, and to put to use, widely dispersed information that no central planning agency, let alone any individual, could know as a whole, possess, or control" (p. 14) or "the extended order *circumvents* individual ignorance" thereby adapting us "to the unknown" (p. 81, his italics).
14  "It is this submission to undesigned rules and conventions whose significance and importance we largely do not understand, this reverence for the traditional, that ... is indispensable for the working of a free society" (1960, p. 63).
15  Hayek, it seems, recognizes that the evolution of rules consistent with freedom requires "the existence of individuals and groups simultaneously observing partially different rules" for "the selection of the most effective ones" (1960, p. 63).
16  For Hayek (1988) "the close connection between population size and the presence of, and benefits of, certain evolved practices, institutions, and forms of human interaction" (p. 120) carried a significant implication: "I have been contending that socialism constitutes a threat to the present and future welfare of the human race, in the sense

that neither socialism nor any other known substitute for the market order could sustain the current population of the world" (p. 121).

17 See also Hayek (1988, ch. 1).

18 For a development of this theme based on institutions as repositories of knowledge, see, for example, Vaughn (1999).

19 In *CL* Hayek says "This book is not concerned mainly with what science teaches us. Though I could not have written it if I had not devoted the greater part of my life to the study of economics. ... I am not concerned here exclusively with facts, nor do I confine myself to statements of cause and effect. My aim is to picture an ideal, to show how it can be achieved" (1960, p. vii).

20 Also see volume 2 of *LLL*, pp. 126–32 (Hayek, 1976).

21 Gray (1984) observes that "the view of knowledge [Hayek] defends can be shown to be presupposed by many of the positions [he] has adopted in economic theory and social philosophy" (p. 3) and that his oeuvre "has throughout exemplified a distinctive conception of the powers of the mind and of the character of human knowledge" (p. 116).

22 Hayek maintains that the problem of knowledge becomes more acute with the progress of civilization: "The more civilized we become, the more relatively ignorant must each individual be of the facts on which the working of his civilization depends. The very division of knowledge increases the necessary ignorance of the individual of most of this knowledge" (1960, p. 26).

23 Also see Hayek (1973, pp. 14–17) and (1988, pp. 6–10, 14–15).

24 See Miller (1976), Gray (1984), Kukathas (1989), Barry (1994), Shearmur (1996), and Witt (1994).

25 See also Hayek (1952b, pp. 169–72).

26 Doing justice to these issues would take us far afield, but see, for example, Gray (1984, chs. 2, 6), Vanberg (1986), Kukathas (1989, ch. 6), and Shearmur (1996, chs. 3, 5).

27 At least one commentator, however, does attribute such an identification to Hayek – Böhm (1994, p. 169) says that "knowledge yielded by market prices is knowledge generated through the operation of the market order – that is, it cannot be generated in any other way ... ."

28 See, for example, Salerno (1990).

29 See Mises (1920, p. 18). We thank Israel Kirzner for clarifying this point.

30 Also see Machlup's (1936) suggestive essay.

31 See also Whitman (1998) for a thorough discussion of this issue including a defense of Hayek from an evolutionary point of view.

32 This is not intended to imply that the behavior patterns are rigid – such an algorithmic metaphor is intended only as a model – and one with free parameters that can be instantiated (by individual choice) in any specific circumstance. Whether such behavior patterns are characterized in terms of "routines" or "rules" is a matter of modeling preference.

33 Such a definition is quite capable of encompassing elaborate institutional arrangements. Just as a software system can be a complex arrangement of nested programs and subroutines, so an institutional system can be a complex arrangement of nested institutions, with the lower-level institutions (such as property-respecting procedures) acting as resources on which the higher-level ones (such as demander or supplier routines) depend. It is consistent with the discussion of the meaning of "institution" in Langlois (1986, p. 19).

34 It is to be emphasized that we are not characterizing social orders as "group minds" which can generate knowledge that is somehow superior to individual knowledge. The sorts of knowledge generated by different types of order are different in type and scope, arising from different classifications performed on different inputs. Knowledge generated in social orders can, indeed, feed back to augment individual knowledge,

and thus at least partially solve the problem of "division of knowledge," as Hayek (1937) asserts for the case of the market order – not by replacing individual knowledge but by supplementing it. And neither are we characterizing orders as "social collectivities" to be understood as unanalyzed wholes. We agree with Hayek (1943, p. 69) that to regard such social phenomena "as in any sense more objective than the intelligible actions of the individuals is sheer illusion."

## Bibliography

Agonito, R. (1975) "Hayek Revisited: Mind as a Process of Classification," *Behaviorism* 3 (Fall), pp. 162–71.

Barry, N.P. (1994) "The Road to Freedom: Hayek's Social and Economic Philosophy" in *Hayek, Co-ordination and Evolution*, eds J. Birner and R. van Zijp, London and New York: Routledge, pp. 141–63.

Bianchi, M. (1994) "Hayek's Spontaneous Order: The 'Correct' versus the 'Corrigible' Society" in *Hayek, Co-ordination and Evolution*, eds J. Birner and R. van Zijp, London and New York: Routledge, pp. 232–51.

Birner, J. (1996) "Decentralization as Ability to Adapt" in *Economic Institutions, Markets and Competition*, eds B. Dallago and L. Mittone, Aldershot, Hants: Edward Elgar.

—— (1999a) "Making Markets" in *Economic Organizations and Economic Knowledge: Essays in Honor of Brian J. Loasby*, eds S. Dow and P. Earl, Aldershot, Hants: Edward Elgar.

—— (1999b) "The Surprising Place of Psychology in the Work of F.A. Hayek," *History of Economic Ideas* 7, pp. 1–2.

Böhm, S. (1989) "Hayek on Knowledge, Equilibrium, and Prices: Context and Impact," *Wirtschaftspolitische Blätter* 2, pp. 201–13.

—— (1994) "Hayek and Knowledge: Some Question Marks" in *Capitalism, Socialism and Knowledge: The Economics of F.A. Hayek, Vol. II*, eds M. Colonna, H. Hagemann, and O.F. Hamouda, Aldershot, Hants: Edward Elgar, pp. 160–77.

Butos, W.N. (1997) "Hayek and Rational Expectations" in *Austrians in Debate*, eds W. Keizer, B. Tieben, and R. van Zijp, London and New York: Routledge, pp. 220–43.

Butos, W.N. and R. Koppl (1993) "Hayekian Expectations: Theory and Empirical Applications," *Constitutional Political Economy* 4:3, pp. 303–29.

Coase, R.H. (1960) "The Problem of Social Cost," *Journal of Law and Economics* 3, pp. 1–44.

Demsetz, H. (1969) "Information and Efficiency: Another Viewpoint," *Journal of Law and Economics* 12 (April), pp. 1–22.

Gray, J. (1984) *Hayek on Liberty*, London and New York: Routledge & Kegan Paul.

Grossman, S. (1989) *The Informational Role of Prices*, Cambridge: MIT Press.

Hayek, F.A. (1937) "Economics and Knowledge," *Economica* 4 (n.s.), pp. 33–54.

—— (1943) "The Facts of the Social Sciences," *Ethics* 54:1 (Oct.), pp. 1–13, reprinted in *Individualism and Economic Order* (Henry Regnery, 1948).

—— (1944) *The Road to Serfdom*, Chicago: University of Chicago Press.

—— (1945) "The Use of Knowledge in Society," *American Economic Review* 35:4 (Sept.), pp. 519–30.

—— (1952a) *The Counter-Revolution of Science*, Chicago: Free Press (1955).

—— (1952b) *The Sensory Order*, London: Routledge & Kegan Paul.

—— (1960) *The Constitution of Liberty*, Chicago: University of Chicago Press.

—— (1967) *Studies in Philosophy, Politics and Economics*, Chicago: University of Chicago Press.

—— (1973) *Law, Legislation and Liberty*, vol. 1 "Rules and Order," Chicago: University of Chicago Press.

—— (1976) *Law, Legislation and Liberty*, vol. 2 "The Mirage of Social Justice," Chicago: University of Chicago Press.

—— (1978) *New Studies*, London: Routledge & Kegan Paul.

—— (1979) *Law, Legislation and Liberty*, vol. 3 "The Political Order of a Free People," Chicago: University of Chicago Press.

—— (1988) *The Fatal Conceit*, Chicago: University of Chicago Press.

Kirzner, I.M. (1992) *The Meaning of Market Process*, London: Routledge.

Koppl, R. and L.B. Yeager (1996) "Big Players and Herding in Asset Markets: the Case of the Russian Ruble," *Explorations in Economic History* 33, pp. 367–83.

Kukathas, C. (1989) *Hayek and Modern Liberalism*, Oxford: Oxford University Press.

Langlois, R.N. (1986) "The New Institutional Economics: An Introductory Essay" in *Economics as a Process*, ed. R.N. Langlois, Cambridge: Cambridge University Press, pp. 1–25.

Lavoie, D. (1985) *National Economic Planning: What is Left?*, Cambridge, MA: Ballinger.

Loasby, B.J. (1999) *Knowledge, Institutions and Evolution in Economics*. London: Routledge.

Machlup, F. (1936) "Why Bother With Methodology?" in *Methodology of Economics and Other Social Sciences*, New York: Academic Press.

Miller, E.F. (1976) "Hayek's Critique of Reason," *Modern Age* 20:4, pp. 383–94.

Mises, L. (1920) *Economic Calculation in the Socialist Commonwealth*, Ludwig von Mises Institute (1990).

Polanyi, M. (1966) *The Tacit Dimension*, New York: Doubleday.

Salerno, J. (1990) "Why a Socialist Economy is 'Impossible,'" postscript to L. Mises, *Economic Calculation in the Socialist Commonwealth*, Ludwig von Mises Institute.

Shearmur, J. (1996) *Hayek and After*, London: Routledge.

Vanberg, V. (1986) "Spontaneous Market Order and Social Rules: A Critique of F.A. Hayek's Theory of Cultural Evolution," *Economics and Philosophy* 2 (June), pp. 75–100.

Vaughn, Karen I. (1999) "Hayek's Implicit Economics: Rules and the Problem of Order," *Review of Austrian Economics* 11:1–2, pp. 129–44.

Weimer, W.B. (1982) "Hayek's Approach to the Problems of Complex Phenomena: An Introduction to the Psychology of the Sensory Order" in *Cognition and the Symbolic Processes*, vol. II, eds W.B. Weimer and D. Palermo, Millsdale, NJ: Lawrence Erblaum, pp. 241–85.

Whitman, D.G. (1998) "Hayek Contra Pangloss on Evolutionary Systems," *Constitutional Political Economy* 9, pp. 45–66.

Witt, U. (1994) "The Theory of Societal Evolution: Hayek's Unfinished Legacy" in *Hayek, Co-ordination and Evolution*, eds J. Birner and R. van Zijp, London and New York: Routledge, pp. 178–89.

# 8 Uncertainty, institutions and order in Hayek

*Raimondo Cubeddu*

## Introduction

Friedrich A. von Hayek's scientific program can be interpreted as a *theory of order*,[1] which enquires into the method of conception, development, and classification by the human mind of sensory events in the outside world as well as the means and methods for exchange of information on the latter. Furthermore, his program seeks to indicate the approach that will *allow* a social order to be achieved after starting from a plurality and diversity of individual sensory orders. For this reason it is based on the realization both of the inadequacies and fallibility of individual knowledge and of the social dispersion of knowledge, attributing a primary role to these flawed aspects. Yet equally important in Hayek's theory is the fact that in the process of value attribution and therefore within the cognitive process, individual action is conditioned by what may be termed *subjective temporal expectations*. That is to say, individual action is affected by the problematic situation the individual finds himself facing (i.e. the issues and problems with which he is concerned), and by the amount of time he allocates (or which he estimates he will have at his disposal) to satisfy his needs, likewise subjectively perceived.

From this perspective, Hayek sees the free market process and catallactics as embodying the most favorable means (from the perspective of reducing *transaction costs*) through which individuals can exchange information (of varying degrees of correctness) on the likelihood of realizing subjective expectations. Order, rules and social institutions thus become tools capable of conceiving expectations and credible calculations with regard to the final realization of individual and social expectations and their costs.

More generally, it can be argued that Hayek's ideas ushered in a considerable change of perspective in the social sciences. The aim is no longer to establish criteria to distinguish right from wrong, true from false, good from bad in order to arrive at a definition or an application of a *common good*. Rather, efforts are directed toward studying what will produce social consequences – consequences that are sometimes unexpected, unforeseen, involuntary, etc. Hayek, however, does not exclude the possibility of comparing or evaluating social institutions. In brief, one can say that in his view the best political and social institutions are those which allow the individual to realize, in the shortest possible time, and from within a prescribed, certain and universalizable framework, the largest number of individual expectations and to reduce the extent of coercion.

In the area of the philosophy of social science and politics, Hayek's merit is therefore to have drawn attention to those actions which, good or bad, rational or illogical, result in social consequences. In other words, he confirmed the need to start from what individuals think, and not from what it might be more desirable for them to do.

My impression, nevertheless, is that the theoretical issues addressed by Carl Menger and Hayek, although expressed in different terms, scarcely diverge from those of Ronald H. Coase[2] or Douglass C. North.[3] Hayek is attempting to ascertain how a reduction of "transaction costs" can be achieved within a rather specific cultural context, one that is strongly characterized by the confidence that the role of institutions is not to reduce transaction costs and uncertainty, but instead to reach ethical goals thought to be superior to the processes of the free market economy. The latter, on the other hand, in Hayek's framework, leads to minimization of the social costs for the fulfillment of individual expectations, by granting a wider range of fluctuation than is the case for teleocratic institutions – although such institutions may well indeed be justified – without recourse to criteria of normative rationality.

The relationship between cultural beliefs – whether well founded or motivated or otherwise – and the development of individual expectations, including selection among these, is thus a central theme in Hayek's approach.

## The concept of order

For Hayek, the problem of order essentially consists in examining how order *can be engendered* by a socially dispersed, limited and fallible knowledge possessed by individuals who are characterized by the fact that they nurture different (sometimes irreconcilable) subjective expectations, and are often resistant to attempts made by other individuals seeking to appropriate themselves of their own time that can be transmuted into goods, money, services, knowledge, etc.

Social order, in Hayek's perspective, arises with varying degree of intentionality, from exchange of individual orders; or to use the terminology of *The Sensory Order*, from exchange and critique of individual patterns, which may be true or false representations of the phenomenological world and of the final fulfillment of individual expectations.

This process, although never made explicit by Hayek, presents a close affinity with what we might call the process of value attribution in the economic sphere, as formulated by Menger and additionally by other representatives of the Austrian School, whose fundamental theses are equally defined, not without reason, by the expressions theory of subjective value (*Theorie des subjectiven Wertes*) and subjective economics. In the *Grundsätze*, Menger studies the way in which we pass from the subjective attribution of value with regard to goods, needs, and services to a theory of the market order; in the *Untersuchungen* he aims to show that the process of formation of this order resembles that of social institutions. In both cases, in effect, economic institutions as well as social institutions are the partly unintended result of the way in which individuals endowed with limited and fallible knowledge (or, as Hayek would say, dispersed knowledge)[4] seek to minimize uncertainty about the achievement of those individual expectations that are likely to be affected by knowledge, by "exact natural laws" (*exacte Naturgesetze*) and by the circumstances in which the action is performed, while at the same time – and here is the real problem – such individuals also find themselves grappling with the problem of scarcity of goods, knowledge, and time set against the backdrop of the vastness of needs and objectives.

The question which Hayek seeks to answer is analogous to the one which Menger poses in the following terms: how is it that the main social institutions, language, religion, law, the state, the markets, money, prices etc. which clearly "serve the common welfare and are extremely significant for its development come into being without a common will directed towards establishing them."[5] The central point of the argument is thus the claim that there exist some social institutions endowed with normativity and efficiency which are the result of non-goal-oriented individual actions, whose expansion has surpassed the realm of the State, and yet has occurred independently of all political power.

The philosophy of social science and Hayekian political philosophy agree in envisaging the same political implications: it is in effect possible to draw up a theory of the social institutions, of their nature and functions – but also a political philosophy – based on the demonstration that the existence of a political power, government or state is not indispensable in the setting up of normative systems endowed with efficiency and sanctions.

As revealed implicitly through the position accorded to the term "cultural" – placed by Hayek between evolutionary and spontaneous in the expression "spontaneous cultural evolutionism" which he used to define his own theory of social institutions – it is not a question of passively accepting situations or individual values as an acquired fact. Nor should one cherish the idea of looking back at a reassuringly optimistic vision of the opportunities afforded by a mechanism for harmonizing individual values, delegating the power of intangible spontaneous evolution to the process of history.[6] Menger, who had supported this same thesis, concluded the *Untersuchungen* by stating that

> never, and this is the essential point under review, may science dispense with testing for their suitability those institutions which have come about "organically." It must, when careful investigation so requires, change and better them according to the measure of scientific insight and the practical experience at hand. No era may renounce this "calling."[7]

The merit of the Mengerian–Hayekian program on the birth and evolution of social institutions is not only to have associated this process with a more sustainable theory of human action than the concepts previously put forward by classical liberalism, but also to have confronted a problem which classical liberalism had always evaded. In fact, the mainstream approach of such a tradition had constantly oscillated between a utilitarian-contractual explication and a historical-evolutionary interpretation of social institutions, the latter sometimes assuming excessively conservative connotations as if all that exists were to be justified simply by being.

The originality of Hayekian theory of social institutions also consists in the importance he ascribes to the emergence of novelties or new circumstances, seen as the expression, hitherto unrevealed, of modified individual expectations, capable of indicating any failings, and thus calling into question the system of rules and even the institutions themselves.

For Hayek, the social institutions, like the "negative, universal and abstract codes of conduct," must constitute the means by which individuals may satisfy their changing expectations and reduce uncertainty. The better such institutions are, the more stable they will be (for their precariousness would invalidate the Rule of Law which is based on durability and universality), and the more they will manage even in the future, and in a predictable manner, to regulate the very expectations that are destined to be in a perpetual state of flux. As a consequence, if needs (conceived abstractly and subjectively) and uncertainty remain constant, the institutions and the rules are by their very nature subject to change and will continually require perfecting. Their function, however, is to allow the greatest possible number of individual expectations to be satisfied in the minimum amount of time, with the least costs and a minimum of unwanted consequences.

On this subject it is clear that even the Austrians, well before the studies that have appeared over the last ten years on the function of social institutions, believed – to use a definition given by North – that "the institutions are created to reduce uncertainty in relations between men."[8]

However, institutions, like rules, are not all created in the same way. Although Menger by no means ignores the existence of pragmatic institutions while Hayek is evidently aware of teleocratic institutions, their preference is for spontaneous or un-designed institutions such as catallaxies. They value the ductility of such institutions (due to the fact that their functioning requires the least use of coercive instruments) and appreciate their efficiency in comparison to teleocratic institutions, because spontaneous institutions have the benefit of reducing the costs of information transmission. Which is to say that they minimize transaction costs without increasing the concentration of political power, thereby avoiding the adverse consequences that would be implied by increased political power. For a growth of political power would translate into increased costs for safeguarding property rights and uncertainty of the law resulting from having empowered a third party – through elections – to produce rules (even if this does not always occur under a monopolistic regime and is carried out within the framework of a Constitution). Recourse to this same function with a view to increasing lawmakers' property rights was well known to the Austrians. Hayek, for example, freely uses this line of thinking to criticize, firstly, political theory concerning collectivist economic planning, secondly, the theory of social justice, and finally and in a more general manner the teleocratic, political-economic models.

## Sensory order and the philosophy of social science

Hayek suggests that the problem of order is analogous and must, for this very reason, be approached in the same way in the area of politics, economics, ethics, and psychology. The primacy accorded to the theory of order indicates therefore that these sciences are not based on any particular anthropology or on any special theory of human action. From this angle, the work *The Sensory Order* can be considered as the theoretical link between Hayek's different interests within the social sciences. It is thus fundamental in understanding the evolution of his ideas and his critique of scientism, of constructive rationalism and also of the numerous historicist social philosophers as well as the theories of dualism that postulate the existence of "a distinct mind substance."[9]

The theory that Hayek describes exhaustively in this work had already been sketched at the end of the twenties.[10] One may equally argue that his critique of the theory of general economic equilibrium, in the version given by the collectivist economic planning theorists, is in agreement with his theory on order.[11] In defending the possibility of rationalizing subjective expectations, theorists of collectivist economies seem to rely on the following (implicit) argument: subjective expectations are manually compatible to the extent that they are based on identical reactions to sensory stimuli "filtered" through a common rationality (even if, at times, such expectations may take on a pathological aspect in certain individuals). In contrast, Hayek shows that subjective temporal expectations as well as the identification and classification of sensory phenomena all bear a relation to subjective states of knowledge, experience, and time, so that it would cost dear and indeed would be well-nigh impossible to endeavor to render these expectations homogenous in all individuals, for expectations can be selected only if a deliberate attempt is made to have them trained toward a specific goal, or if there is intensive use of coercion, which of course tends to nullify any type of individuality.

Additionally, as already emphasized,[12] Hayek stresses that neither knowledge nor information can be seen as given or concentrated; and that these operations would in any case involve an individual and social cost, as would their transmission and dissemination. In effect, these factors have a bearing on the process of the production of goods as well as production of rules.

The conclusion to be drawn from *The Sensory Order* is that if classification of sensory data begins from subjective methods which vary according to the particular situation and cluster of issues (milieu, culture, time) each individual is facing, then these methods will tend to multiply for a collection of individuals, independently of the type of *civil association*[13] in force at the time. Additionally, at different times one and the same individual may take a different stance to his own particular situation, adopting different methods of identification and classification of his sensory data. Moreover, the way in which an individual addresses his situation is substantially affected by the amount of time each individual spends acquiring the elements and experience he needs to classify and order his sensations in a stable manner.

This inevitably carries a price, as does, likewise, the transmission of information (and experience) that enables a group of individuals to organize their sensations in an exchangeable way so that cooperation on foreseeable situations can be undertaken.

If we compare the theory of human action as stated in *The Sensory Order* with that expounded in essays on social science methodology, we can see that Hayek's problem is to understand the relationship between, the phenomena of the outside world, their interpretation, communication, and exchange by the individual and the genesis of order. This explains his interest in economic science, since it sought in a more satisfactory manner than any other discipline to provide an

> answer to the central question of all social sciences. How can the combination of fragments of knowledge existing in different minds bring about results, which, if they were to be brought about deliberately, would require knowledge on the part of the directing mind, which no single person can possess?[14]

The theme of social distribution of knowledge must be considered from this viewpoint. The problem of theoretical social sciences is not, in effect, of a logical nature. If it were so, then it would be sufficient to decide on the best possible use of the means available, taking for granted that these would include all the relevant information, a given system of preferences, and the power to totally control all necessary resources. This, however, represents an ideal situation, which has never been realized. Social science specialists find themselves confronted with data which relate only to individuals or groups of individuals. Consequently, knowledge which should be the basis on which to further one's plans, far from existing in a concentrated or integrated form, exists only in a fragmented form of partial and contradictory knowledge possessed separately and sometimes unwittingly by different individuals. Therefore the question facing economics and more generally the social sciences is not that of elaborating universally valid plans grounded on the rationality or ethical code of individuals and social groups: rather, it endeavors to determine how best to use a complex of knowledge which no individual possesses in its entirety.[15] In other words, the question is how to find "the best way of utilizing knowledge initially dispersed among all the people."[16]

The procedure consisting of the individualist and composite method of the social sciences thus has a direct link to the way in which the human mind classifies impulses arising from the phenomenal world. Methodological individualism likewise starts out from gnoseological considerations of relations between the human mind and data, ultimately reaching the conclusion that in this area of science one must avoid provisional theories, popular abstractions; since methodological individualism "refrains from treating these pseudo-entities as 'facts' [it] systematically starts from the concepts which guide individuals in their actions, and not from the results of their theorizing about their actions."[17] For this reason Hayek is not concerned "to explain the thought but merely to distinguish the possible types of elements with which we shall have to reckon in the construction of different patterns of social relationships." His interest thus focuses on the actions that give rise to unforeseen results and engender spontaneous regularities. As a result,

> if social phenomena showed no order except insofar as they were consciously designed, there would indeed be no room for theoretical sciences of society and there would be, as is often argued, only problems of psychology. It is only insofar as some sort of order arises as a result of individual action but without being designed by any individual that a problem is raised which demands theoretical explanation.[18]

It is in this framework, in direct relation to the emergence of a mental order, that one must consider Hayek's critique of methodological collectivism, which he accused of considering as facts "what are no more than provisional theories, models constructed by the popular mind to explain the connection between some of the individual phenomena which we observe." These "social wholes" are not "natural units" but "different complexes of individual events, by themselves perhaps quite dissimilar, but believed by us to be related to each other in a similar manner; they are selections of certain elements of a complex picture on the basis of a theory about their coherence."[19] It is therefore clearly the human mind which selects, on the basis of rational, coherent, or logical criteria, those elements which aid in construing the causal chain.

For Hayek it is not therefore a question of revealing the essence of phenomena, the "exact natural laws" of the succession of phenomena (as Menger endeavored to do). These "social wholes," in effect, "exist only if, and to the extent to which, the theory is correct which we have formed about the connection of the parts which they imply, and which we can explicitly state only in the form of a model built from those relationships."[20]

Although the impact of the arguments put forward in *The Sensory Order* on social science philosophy are evident, one cannot fail to note that they do not explicitly confront the principal problem of social science, namely the consequences that an action can have on the acts and expectations of others. This issue can also be expressed as the problem concerning the way conscious or unconscious human actions compete to produce a social order. In actual fact, this set of themes, which bears witness to the systematic character of Hayek's thought, is treated in the previously quoted methodological essays. This confirms the appropriateness, if not the necessity, of considering all Hayekian themes and works as a whole.

The strongest link can be identified in the essay *The Use of Knowledge in Society*,[21] where Hayek explores the impact ... of the unequal distribution of knowledge on economic planning among members of a society noting that planning requires concentration of theoretical and practical knowledge rather than dispersed knowledge. Here Hayek seeks to understand how the different classifications of social phenomena attained by individual minds can participate spontaneously in the creation of a hierarchy of expectations. The problem of unexpected consequences can likewise be regarded as the outcome of this diversity of classifications: for individual and collective actions deriving from these classifications produce effects (sensory stimuli) which, although abstractly alike, can be evaluated differently on the basis of the knowledge held by those who come into contact with them. It is in this way that new and unexpected situations are created which incite those who create the consequences – but also those who are subjected to them – to change their initial plans and redefine their expectations.

There follows a dynamic order where the tendency to balance between reciprocal expectations must be continuously reformulated in the light of the changing situation. But a further outcome is the impossibility of considering individual preferences as a given set from which to start out as a basis for proposals of economic, social, or political change. The purpose of social science is no longer to elaborate plans or evaluate human action on the grounds of ethical rules, but rather to find "the best way of utilizing knowledge initially dispersed among all the people."[22]

This argument can be divided into two complementary parts. The first concerns the order that is created between the subjective expectations of a plurality of individuals in relation to actions or events that impinge on them (whether foreseen or not): an order that can, but need not necessarily be fulfilled. The second concerns order as a possible outcome of a social trend (for instance different spheres of social life and interest, including conflicts) within a statist entity. All this might lead one to believe that in such circumstances individual liberty is under threat, although one may also take up the opposite point of view and question whether it is just that that individual liberty should have priority over order. In effect, if needs, ends, and individual knowledge are not only different but may be evaluated differently by different subjects, the result will be that each of them can make use in their own way of the opportunities offered in different forms by rules and by institutions. Unless one can foresee constant intervention by a body situated above the process of catallactics, which would intervene in order to restore balance, then the only way to guard against this inconvenience is to intervene in knowledge distribution, by resorting to a type of operation similar to that prescribed for the distribution of goods by the theorists of social justice, so severely criticized by Hayek. However, in order to be effective, such an intervention would have to be unlimited, endowed with centralized knowledge of the dynamics of social phenomena, and would have to be superior to the dispersed knowledge that characterizes the process of catallactics.

*The Sensory Order* sets out a framework in which models of social phenomena can be elaborated by the human mind. If one wishes to make a comparative assessment, it should be noted that such models could only be compared with other alternative models that are designed to solve the same problem in a different way, or with interpretations of the same phenomenon. Comparison becomes impossible if the term of assessment is a phenomenal world that leads us to reformulate our classifications in the wake of conjectures as to its actual place in the world. In the case of social phenomena, the success of an interpretation or a solution therefore has less to do with the objective reality of phenomena than with a particular distribution of knowledge. However, this distribution can lead to a failure to recognize the virtues of a theory (or of a solution). As a result, achieving an order based on a spontaneous balance between subjective expectations appears problematical, particularly if one considers that this order has no genetic-natural foundation – as in the Mengerian approach – but is instead founded on an evolutionary-cultural approach. Thus, in the final analysis, the liberal model of order requires the concomitance of exogenous circumstances. For example, although this may be a limit case, the fortuitous distribution of the effects of human action, their interpretation on the basis of social distribution of knowledge in which – by manipulation of the media and other sources of information – false theories could be circulated or unfulfillable expectations aroused, could wipe out this "genetic tendency" toward the formation of a system of reciprocal selection and could totally thwart the satisfaction of subjective expectations, thereby shattering this system of dynamic balance that is the social order.

Political order is therefore an undesigned entity related to the natural inequality of human beings. It is something that does not exist in nature, but exists only as a more or less unintentional by-product of individual relationships that do not necessarily have to occur. The liberal order, therefore, is not a natural necessity, but only a cultural potentiality.

These problems and more specifically those which concern relations between universal norms of human action and subjective expectations, and between catallactics and politics, are, we know, addressed by Hayek in *The Political Order of a Free People*, the third volume of *Law, Legislation and Liberty* and in *The Fatal Conceit*, works in which, however, references to the themes of *The Sensory Order* are relatively rare.

## Knowledge and politics

The Hayekian philosophy of social science is therefore based on a theory of knowledge and human action that is inextricably linked to the different ways in which different individual minds seek to give order to sensory perceptions. Order, in this framework, is achieved by inserting perceptions in models which are at one and the same time environmental, cultural, and genetic and are moreover subject to a constant evolutionary process.

The passage from individual order as described in *The Sensory Order* to extended order is conceived by Hayek as an essentially cultural phenomenon linked to the possibility of exchanging information and knowledge among multiple individual orders. The genetic-natural aspect of the encounter between several individuals, although essential, does not on its own explain the transition from individual order to extended order, for such a transition is dependent on the – perhaps chance – occurrence of circumstances deemed cultural. Now, the cultural character of these circumstances may make them subject to evaluation and selection. And it is this which allows us to determine whether one instance of an extended order is preferable to any other.

Hayek, like Menger, believes that social teleocratic institutions and nomo-cratic social institutions can cohabit within an extended order. However, Hayek concedes that nomocratic social institutions have a much wider possible range of applications; furthermore, and most importantly, if an extended order is taken as a teleocratic order, this would result in a less flexible system and would impose a greater rate of coercion. This, in turn – as is clearly revealed by studies on the gnoseological premises and political implications of collectivist economic planning – would have a heavy effect on transaction costs and reduce efficiency. This is without mentioning the effects it could have on indi-vidual freedom, the latter understood as the opportunity to fulfill one's own individual expectations and subjective aims irrespective of consent granted by the political power.

Hayek's distinction of types of order into artificial, natural, and the result of human action but not of human design[23] is analogous to that which Menger draws between social institutions which are pragmatic, organic-natural, and organic non-reflected. Both thinkers tend to prefer institutions of the third type but they do not rule out that the pragmatic institutions themselves might have a temporary advantage, albeit subject to temporal limitations. Naturally, if a unan-imous consensus is required in order to create them (and one can scarcely imagine anything different), then their lifespan will be shorter; on the other hand, they will be more flexible and they will adapt more rapidly and more successfully to new and unforeseen situations. Customarily, such orders or institu-tions arise to achieve specific ends, and their lifetime lasts only long enough to attain the purpose for which they came into existence.

Hayek, therefore, does not deny the existence of such institutions: he merely denies that they can be generalized. In fact, they are only conceivable if other institutions such as language, the law, or exchange precede them, none of which are the direct and consequential product of a collection of individual free wills. Accordingly, the superiority of nomocratic institutions or orders over teleocratic institutions or orders consists not merely in their greater flexibility but also in their genetic antecedence.

This having been said, if – as Hayek states – "there is hardly any action that may not conceivably affect others,"[24] then whenever a nomocratic system appears to be slow in reaching a balance following the emergence of some novelty that has sent shock waves through the knowledge distribution system, it is appropriate to intervene rapidly, on the basis of the actual presupposition of the system itself, in order to facilitate resolution of the problem. This can be done through legislation or by enacting policy measures aimed at maintaining and strengthening the efficiency of the nomocratic system. In this case, taking experience into account, intervention acts above all on the process of spontaneous formation of rules, in order to encourage attainment of a desirable state of knowledge distribution that will ensure exchange of expectations in conditions of reciprocal freedom.

As a result, Hayek, like most of the thinkers of *classical liberalism,* is not, in principle, against the legislative production of rules (as long as they are provided with certain characteristics). He even holds that in certain circumstances the speed of the process renders this operation preferable to an uncertain wait for spontaneous restoration of balance. Thus he brings together the concept of evolution and that of "expected time." Nevertheless, given that we cannot exclude a contrast between "the time of rules" and "individual time," it remains to be seen how to choose the most suitable persons to acquit themselves of such a function. A novel situation would not have the same impact, positive or negative, on all. Does whoever adapts the rules to the new situation do so in the interest of the rules or in his interest? And as for the rules themselves, do they have any interests?

These ideas are restated by Hayek in his criticism of Bruno Leoni's *Freedom and the Law,* in which he believes that "the case for relying even in modern times for the development of law on the gradual process of judicial precedent and scholarly interpretation has been persuasively argued." Although Leoni's thesis "is an effective antidote to the prevailing orthodoxy which believes that only legislation can or ought to alter the law," Hayek declares himself not persuaded by the idea that "we can dispense with legislation even in the field of private law." In this case, Hayek has a series of quite justified reservations, prompted by the fact that "for a variety of reasons the spontaneous process of growth may lead into an impasse from which it cannot extricate itself by its own forces or which it will at least not correct quickly enough"; his reservations are therefore linked to the desire for a "rapid adaptation of the law to wholly new circumstances" and to the realization that "the new law can properly fulfil the proper function of all law, namely that of guiding expectations, only if it becomes known before it is applied." In this context, it is worth pointing out that Hayek's reservations are dependent on the observation that between the moment of arrival of the "new circumstances" into a catallactic order and the moment when all the participants cannot foresee the consequences, those who create these new circumstances might be tempted to transform a temporary power into a more permanent power.[25]

In such a situation they would end up by possessing and managing knowledge that would allow them to direct the process of catallactics, off-loading onto others the potential adverse consequences arising from the creation of the new situation. In other words, and *opportunely,* Hayek reminds his readers that a situation may come about whereby certain individuals will act and will be able to choose, bolstered by their confidence in predicting the outcome of the process, while others might not be in a position to do so. In this case, Hayek argues, the desired adaptation of the rules of catallactics to the new circumstances might be more rapidly accomplished by limited legislative intervention, rather than through the generalization of jurisprudential decisions. Like the classical liberals, Hayek thus believes that appropriate intervention by the state may reduce individual and social uncertainty.

## From individual order to extended order

We have seen that Hayekian political philosophy, interpreted as a theory of the best political order, proceeds from a theory of freedom as the right to diversity: indeed, the *extended order* of the liberal state does not set itself the task of attaining ethical goals or natural goodness. Rather, by an "evolutionary selection of rules of conduct" and of individual and social expectations, it aims "*to adapt, through* [...] *partial and fragmentary signals, to conditions foreseen by and known to no individual,* even if this adaptation is never perfect."[26]

Naturally market choices may be devoid of moral motivation. But if the market is the place where, through exchange, reciprocal subjective expectations can be fulfilled, then the absence of moral motivation need not mean that the actions through which individuals seek to fulfill such expectations are not required to observe any rules. Those who defect (if recognized as transgressors) will sooner or later have to pay the costs. In this sense Hayek sees the moral rules as also having a negative aspect: they concern actions which must not be undertaken if one wishes to avoid the known or unknown consequences. These consequences are of different types, although interlinked by their own uncertainty; that is to say by their power to bring with them unwanted and unforeseen consequences, which experience tells us can result from the application of certain forms of behavior.

What has been said so far by no means implies that the individual need not feel responsible for the consequences of his own actions, although the above-described condition of uncertainty must clearly be taken into account. In other words, a moral imperative requires an individual to attempt to foresee (or seek to attempt to foresee) the consequences each action might have. This imperative is ultimately identified with another moral obligation that requires every individual, in seeking his own subjective goals, to observe universalizable norms of behavior, or the natural rights of others. The moral problem to which theoretical and practical social science must provide an answer can henceforth be formulated as follows: is it just, given the aim of improving one's own situation, to carry out actions whose possible negative consequences on other individuals are unknown?

Let us then reflect on what may happen if we start out from the trivial assumption that all human knowledge is limited and fallible (including therefore ethical knowledge) and that each living being seeks to improve his own condition with the aid of the knowledge he possesses. Let us further assume that he may proceed by analyzing his own situation – perhaps in an erroneous manner – and will in any case seek to improve it in the light both of the ideas he has formed concerning the external environment in which the attempt is to be undertaken and of the laws, which, in his view, regulate the environment. Then not only the

way in which the individual moves toward his goal but also the unforeseen consequences (which he may elect to disregard) will depend on the degree of exactness
with which he has imagined the outcome, the environmental situation and the
most suitable rules for achieving his goal (but also the validity of the rules he has
followed).

From this perspective, Hayek's problem is to show that ethical rules can also
be submitted to an evaluation whose reference point consists of the unintentional consequences that might occur if the rules were observed, or if the
outcome they prescribe were put into practice. One might even go as far as to
say that a large part of Hayek's effort is devoted to showing how neither the
goals nor the ethical rules can be exempted from this type of calculation. Hayek
also sets out to show that there is no reason to believe that in confronting these
economic problems from an ethical point of view one can obtain both a better
knowledge of the latter and better results from the point of view of economic
efficiency.

Building on these considerations, one could argue that for Hayek the best
political order is that in which the greatest number of individual expectations are
fulfilled without impeding the achievement of the greatest number of goals of
others. This amounts to claiming that the best political order is that which
succeeds in reducing the social costs of fulfillment of the largest number of individual ends. Hayek, of course, like Menger, who stated that total achievement of
individual ends was dependent on complete knowledge of the exact natural laws
– a totally impossible situation – does not deny that such an objective is beyond
the reach of individuals and institutions, since both must act in situations of
imperfect knowledge. Hayek's problem is therefore to minimize the cost of transmission and distribution of information. And among all human institutions,
catallactics is, to his mind, the best. Nevertheless, he is aware that such a result
presupposes extended communicability of information. This can be obtained,
albeit imperfectly, by methods which emulate solutions and rules that experience
has shown to be the best, i.e. rules that have been selected by competition in the
area of the market process whose aim is to make the most of resources (goods,
time, knowledge) that will, however, always be irremediably inadequate.

From this point of view the problem of the lack of time, linked to social
dispersion of knowledge, appears to have extreme importance. In effect, while
in the market process the time required for production of norms is greater than
in politics, in the latter one finds much greater time requirements and far
higher costs for the distribution of knowledge, associated with a higher presence
of norms.

From this point of departure, Hayek tries to identify the most efficient means
of information transmission that will facilitate cooperative behavior. In other
words, he aims to highlight the best method of rule production and the best
method of conciliation of different temporally subjective expectations.

Otherwise stated, the weaker effectiveness of collective choice is the result of
the fact that the homogenization of expectations and therefore of individual
times is a process which brings with it the imposition of a social (or public) time,

and this limits individual availability of time, and consequently individual freedom as well. This is because it grants a group of individuals the power to establish certain objectives, which, owing to the diverse individual classifications of phenomenal data, may not always be perceived by all individuals in such a way as to allow them to attain the objectives within the given time.

Basically, then, collective choices would be possible if there truly existed this common scale of values that Hayek sees as the focal point of the socialist and interventionist quest, and if it were unanimously shared. But even if it existed, or were to be discovered, it would be unable to solve the issue of how to optimize its utilization, given the enduring problem of diversity of times and individual knowledge.

It therefore appears justifiable to question whether the existence of social and political associations is helpful in addressing the above-described problems, or whether it does not simply complicate the picture even further. For such associations, which are increasingly differentiated in their cultural traits, refer to ethical, catallactic, and ethnic behavioral codes which are also becoming increasingly diversified. This presents us with a problem of political philosophy that leads us to query the validity of the current framework of the democratic nation-state, characteristic of the modern western tradition. It is a fact that the proper functioning of the democratic state effectively depends on the assumption that individual expectations lie within a narrow range of oscillation, one that is characterized by homogeneous or fungible values. Certainly, within the Hayekian perspective, the diversity of individual cultural approaches within a political association does lead to complications in communication and transmission of individual classifications of sensory stimuli. It also influences critical debate, and this in turn has negative repercussions on the possibility of adopting collective choices.

In this regard, the solution offered by democratic theory to the formation of order differs from that proposed by Hayek. Democratic theory advocates the establishment of rules that favor cooperative action by maximizing efficiency on the one hand, and the predictability of undesirable consequences on the other. This solution does not presuppose a code (of whatever nature) that antedates individual exchanges: instead, it presents itself as their outcome.

In fact, for Hayek both individual and social order represent possibilities that cannot be improved by limiting individual freedom to the detriment of collective choices, unless it be for brief periods, voluntarily, and for limited ends or in exceptional cases.[27] In a democratic regime public choices can never be the best possible choices, except by pure chance, precisely because of the social dispersal of knowledge.

In a system of this kind, political and juridical obligation succeed in achieving the expected results as long as the economic and the political sphere overlap in such a manner as to make it possible for the sovereign exercise of power to be devoted to ensuring the outcome of one or more specified ends. But when they do not overlap, the achievement of expected results is affected by the appearance and attempted inclusion of extraneous elements in a previously coherent normative system; consequently, a successful outcome is likely to be far more doubtful. Otherwise stated, the effectiveness of political-juridical obligation is a necessary condition for the proper functioning of a democratic system, once the public choices made within the system are no longer capable of obtaining the desired results, especially since the scope of such choices or the sphere in which they are designed to take effect is in any case subject to short-sighted electoral fluctuations. Alternatively, the system finds itself compelled to pursue achievement of the desired results at the cost of an increase in political production of rules, which decreases the space available for individual freedom and increases the cost of collective decisions: in a word, politics.

## From the philosophy of social science to political philosophy

If we were to express Hayek's thought using a different terminology from that adopted in *Law, Legislation and Liberty*, we could say that in democratic systems, taking into account the fragmentary distribution of knowledge, the cost of rule production (I refer here to his critique of legal positivism) is very high since it is carried out in a regime of monopoly and coercion.

However, the emergence of novelties and the ensuing effects both on the possibility of fulfilling individual expectations and on normative contexts raise a series of problems which will be all the more difficult to solve the greater and the more frequent are the novelties themselves. Since, to use a phrase from Keynes, "in the long run we will all be dead," one may legitimately ask what benefits accrue to individuals from obedience to long-term rules and behavioral codes. Certainly they are – abstractly at least – conscious that obedience to the rules produces optimal results not only for individuals but also for society, but they inevitably have only limited time at their disposal (or they have a restricted subjective temporal expectation); moreover, the effectiveness of long-term behavioral codes and rules will be verifiable only if they are observed universally and over indefinitely long periods. And this is not all, for the codes do not take into account that individual expectations may have changed in the meantime, and application of the rules in question may actually, through lack of time, imply failure to achieve their expectations.

One may readily agree that such complexities increase the difficulties faced by institutional teleocratic systems, but this does not authorize us to assume that the functioning and effectiveness of nomocratic systems are exempt from repercussions of this kind. Although abstractly rational or desirable, the famous scale in the first case, or the set of rules that prescribe not goals but behavior in the second case, could, given the unequal distribution of knowledge, fail to be perceived as suitable tools for achieving expectations within the time frame expected by individuals.

Consequently, the same rule does not have equal value for all individuals, since they have different amounts of time available and would in any case make different use of available time in obeying the rule. The institutions transform information-expectations into universalizable rules according to time frames, which, although they may be brief (and this is the essence of their effectiveness and their ability to function as tools to reduce transaction costs), are usable by individuals as a function of their own specific knowledge and their own available time. The moment at which an individual or a society becomes aware of the need for a rule that can inform them on the consequences and costs of fulfilling their expectations, or on the appropriate solution to a new problem, is separated from the moment of emergence or production of a rule by an undefined period of time, and this period can be modified by the fortuitous presence (or absence) of circumstances or by the effectiveness of the political system into which the rule is introduced. Meanwhile, the problem may have been resolved independently by the individual concerned, without political intervention, and may thus no longer exist. There may also be a general advancement of knowledge, leading to resolution of the problem without any need to resort to formulation of universal rules designed to prevent any negative consequences from affecting non-consenting individuals. It appears, then, that rules tend to act outside the bounds of time, whereas individuals need to make their calculations within tight time limitations. Furthermore, there is nothing to prove that since the rule previously functioned according to calculated costs, it automatically represents a decrease in transaction costs. The fact is that solving new cases with old rules may actually increase rather than decrease transaction costs, and may produce undesired consequences or negative externalities.

If the aim of political institutions is thus to reduce transaction costs in order to produce certainty, it becomes possible to compare nomocratic and teleocratic institutions. The former can be seen as having the disadvantage of requiring a more prolonged period of time to produce norms, while the latter are handicapped by taking longer to disseminate information on the norms. Nomocratic institutions can thus be regarded as the result of a process of spontaneous cultural selection and evolution, which tend to reduce coercion. Teleological institutions, on the other hand, cannot dispense with coercive tools. Furthermore, if the expected result is to be achieved within the expected time frame, teleological institutions will also involve the drawback of intensifying the concentration of knowledge. Therefore, they will concentrate power as well. In contrast, the major benefit of nomocratic systems, in Hayek's view, is that once the market is conceived as a system of information transmission, the acceleration of the process disseminating information leads to a reduction in transaction costs.

On the other hand, the defect inherent in this type of solution lies in what may be termed the paradox of induction: that is to say, the cost of transforming information into knowledge. For it is by no means certain that a greater quantity of available information will be matched by a shorter time requirement for knowledge transformation. Furthermore, in this case additional difficulties would arise, linked to the possibility of transforming sensory data (even if these have been elaborated into theoretical statements, which would nevertheless still be subjective) into theoretical statements. This is because the various lengths of time required for individual elaborations, taking into account the unequal initial distribution of knowledge, might not be reciprocally compatible, in the sense that the best solution might not automatically be recognized as such. If we imagine a situation of disequilibrium in social distribution of knowledge, linked to the emergence of earth-shaking novelties that shatter the system of order and seriously impair the possibility of making predictions as to the possibility of achieving individual actions and the costs and consequences of action, then this eventuality becomes a realistic hypothesis.

One of the problems Hayek left unresolved was precisely that of determining how information can be transformed into knowledge. Information broadens the range of individual expectations (which may or may not be rational: whether they are indeed rational or otherwise is of little importance). Knowledge, in the form of selection of information, places constraints on the range of expectations. Order is a particular arrangement of knowledge that has proved to be capable of fulfilling expectations and predicting their costs. It is clear that in this case there exists a close relation between expectations and order, and that the latter, which changes as a function of changing expectations, also succeeds in selecting among expectations and by indicating the possibility of fulfilling them their associated costs.

## Notes

1 Elster (1989) rightly points out that "Hayek's programme" answers the question "How is spontaneous order possible?" The Hayekian definition order is: "a state of affairs in which a multiplicity of elements of various kinds are so related to each other that we may learn from our acquaintance with some spatial or temporal part of the whole to form correct expectations concerning the rest, or at least expectations which have a good chance of proving correct" (Hayek (1973–79), I, p. 36).

2 Coase (1999) contains a revealing reference to the importance of Hayek's developing the idea of the economy as a system that "could be coordinated by a system of prices without the need for the existence of a plan. As Hayek has said, it mobilises that diffuses knowledge that exists throughout the world" (Coase (1999), p. 3). And on p. 6, where he discusses the problem of the coordination of knowledge in a complex society, Coase writes: "My answer to these questions is essentially Hayekian. I do not think that as a society we should attempt to plan what members should do."

3 In his (1994), p. 364, North agrees with the importance of Hayek's idea of the "transmission in time of our accumulated stock of knowledge." He refers to Hayek (1960), p. 27. However, Hayek (1952a) contains much that could also have a bearing on the institutional-cognitive approach that North discusses on subsequent pages and which are characteristic of his entire work. For an Austrian evaluation of Coase's ideas, cf., for example, Kirzner (1973), pp. 225–7 ("the possibility of costlessly acquiring information concerning available desirable opportunities is by no means sufficient to ensure that these opportunities will ever be grasped"), Kirzner (1992), pp. 161–2; O'Driscoll and Rizzo (1985), pp. 123–5 ("Coase's approach is an excellent static conceptualization of the problem [of competitive markets]"), pp. 138–9; O'Driscoll and Rizzo (1986), pp. 259–65; Thomsen (1992), pp. 109–11; Rothbard (1997), I, pp. 260–2, 275–6, 406–7; II, pp. 123–6.

4 Kirzner, even though he does not dwell on the relation between *The Sensory Order* and the Hayekian theory of knowledge (on which, however, he produced extremely

insightful reflections), rightly stated, in (1992), p. 163, that "A central role in Hayek's thought has been played by his insights into the problem posed by the phenomenon of dispersed knowledge."

5  Menger (1883), p. 163 (Engl. transl. p. 146).

6  The very definition of the Austrian theory of human action as a "theory of subjective value" (*Theorie des subjectiven Wertes*) implies that it is possible to elaborate a theory (even if it is *strong*) of subjective value and therefore (as Menger did in (1871) to elaborate criteria suitable for evaluating the ways in which individuals classify their goods and satisfy their needs (and their nature).

7  Menger (1883), p. 287 (Engl. transl. p. 234).

8  North (1990), p. 51.

9  Hayek (1952a), pp.177 ff.

10  Cf. Birner (1999a), but also Cubeddu (1994).

11  The change that came about in Hayek's overall approach to these issues in these years is, I would suggest, due to the fact that in 1933 (cf. Hayek (1933)) he began to take a greater interest in Menger than he had done previously. Indeed one might go as far as to say that up to 1933, and in contrast to his later attitude, Hayek's writings paid only scant attention to Mengerian issues.

12  Cf., for example, Gray (1984), Kirzner (1992), Cubeddu (1993), Lachmann (1994).

13  In this case I also use the terminology of Oakeshott (1975).

14  Hayek (1937), p. 54.

15  Hayek (1945), pp. 77–8.

16  Hayek (1945), pp. 78–9.

17  Hayek (1952b), pp. 37–8.

18  Cf. Hayek (1952b), pp. 39–40.

19  Cf. Hayek (1952b), pp. 54–6.

20  Hayek (1942–44), pp. 55–6.

21  On this subject cf. Kirzner (1992), pp. 163–79.

22  Hayek (1945), pp. 78–9.

23  Cf. Hayek (1973–79), I, p. 20.

24  Cf. Hayek (1960), p. 145.

25  Cf. Hayek (1973–79), I, pp. 88–9, 168n.

26  Cf. Hayek (1989), p. 76.

27  Cf. Hayek (1973–79), III, pp. 43–9.

## Bibliography

Birner, J. (1999a) "The Surprising Place of Cognitive Psychology in the work of F.A. Hayek," *History of Economic Ideas*, 7, 1–2, pp. 43–83.

—— (1999b) "Nascita e sviluppo del programma di ricerca economico di F.A. Hayek," in Clerici, G. and Rizzello, S. (eds), *Organizzazione, informazione e conoscenza. Saggi su Hayek, volume 1*, Turin: UTET 2000.

Coase, R. (1999) "The Task of the Society," in *ISNIE Newsletter*, Fall.

Cubeddu, R. (1993) *The Philosophy of the Austrian School*, London and New York: Routledge.

—— (1994) "From *The Sensory Order* to the Political Order," *Philosophy Politics Economics, PPE – Lectures, 12*, Department of Economics, University of Vienna.

Elster, J. (1989) *The Cement of Society. A Study of Social Order*, Cambridge: Cambridge University Press.

Gray, J. (ed.) (1984) *Hayek on Liberty*, London: Routledge, 1998.

Hayek, F.A. (1933) *Carl Menger (1840–1921), Introduction to Menger* (1933–36), now also in Hayek (1992).

—— (1937) *Economics and Knowledge*, now in (1949).
—— (1942–44) *Scientism and the Study of Society*, now in (1952b).
—— (1945) *The Use of Knowledge in Society*, now in (1949).
—— (1949) *Individualism and Economic Order*, London: Routledge & Kegan Paul.
—— (1952a) *The Sensory Order*, London: Routledge & Kegan Paul.
—— (1952b) *The Counter-Revolution of Science. Studies on the Abuse of Reason*, Glencoe, Ill.: Free Press.
—— (1960) *The Constitution of Liberty*, London: Routledge & Kegan Paul.
—— (1963) *Recht, Gesetz und Wirtschaftsfreiheit*, now in (1969).
—— (1969) *Freiburger Studien. Gesammelte Aufsätze*, Tübingen: J.C.B. Mohr [Paul Siebeck].
—— (1973–79) *Law, Legislation and Liberty*, London–New York: Routledge & Kegan Paul, quotation from 1982 edn.
—— (1989) *The Fatal Conceit: The Errors of Socialism*, Bartley III, W.W. (ed.), *The Collected Works of F.A. Hayek*, I, London–Chicago: Routledge, University of Chicago Press.
—— (1992) *The Fortunes of Liberalism – The Collected Works of F.A. Hayek*, IV, London–Chicago: Routledge, University of Chicago Press.
Kirzner, I.M. (1973) *Competition and Entrepreneurship*, Chicago: University of Chicago Press.
—— (1985) *Discovery and the Capitalist Process*, Chicago: University of Chicago Press.
—— (ed.) (1986) *Subjectivism, Intelligibility and Economic Understanding*, New York: New York University Press.
—— (1992) *The Meaning of Market Process. Essays in the Development of Modern Austrian Economics*, London and New York: Routledge.
Lachmann, L. (1994) *Expectations and the Meaning of Institutions. Essays in Economics by Ludwig Lachmann*, Lavoie, D. (ed.), London and New York: Routledge.
Menger, C. (1871) *Grundsätze der Volkswirthschaftslehre*, Wien: Wilhelm Braumüller; Engl. trans. *Principles of Economics*, reprinted New York: New York University Press, 1981.
—— (1883) *Untersuchungen über die Methode der Socialwissenschaften und der politische Oekonomie insbesondere*, Leipzig: Duncker & Humblot; Engl. trans. *Investigations into the Method of the Social Sciences with Special Reference to Economics*, reprinted New York: New York University Press, 1985.
—— (1933–36) *The Collected Works of Carl Menger*, 4 vols, with an Introduction by F.A. von Hayek, London: The London School of Economics and Political Science (Series of Reprints of Scarce Tracts in Economic and Political Science No. 17–20).
North, D.C. (1990) *Institutions, Institutional Change and Economic Performance*, Cambridge: Cambridge University Press.
—— (1994) "Economic Performance Through Time," in *American Economic Review*, June.
Oakeshott, M. (1975) *On Human Conduct*, Oxford: Clarendon Press.
O'Driscoll, G.P., Jr and Rizzo, M.J. (1985) *The Economics of Time and Ignorance*, London–New York: Routledge, 1996.
—— (1986) *Subjectivism, Uncertainty, and Rules*, in Kirzner (ed.) .
Rosenberg, A. (1988) *Philosophy of Social Science*, Oxford: Clarendon Press.
Rothbard, M.N. (1997) *The Logic of Action*, 2 vols, Cheltenham: E. Elgar.
Thomsen, E.F. (1992) *Price and Knowledge. A Market-Process Perspective*, London and New York: Routledge.

# 9 The organizational indetermination of spontaneous order in Hayek

*Mohammed Bensaïd*

## Introduction

Despite the great diversity of subjects Hayek dealt with in his long career, all of his work is inspired by a single unifying objective: to reconstruct the theory of liberalism on new foundations. The criticism of socialism is so prominent in this project that it is appropriate to ask whether Hayek's brand of liberalism is not just the opposite of socialism. In Hayek's thought, socialism is closely connected with consciously planned and created social institutions or organizations, whereas the institution that is the basis of a liberal society is the market. Hayek discusses markets mostly in terms of what they are capable of achieving whereas his analysis of organizations almost exclusively points to their limitations. This treatment seems rather uneven, and even though the critique of socialism constitutes one of Hayek's major theoretical contributions in its own right, both his "positive" and his "negative" defense of liberalism leave us wondering whether it is based on scientific or on normative arguments.

To examine this question, we will discuss Hayek's conception of organizations as part of his "negative" defense of liberalism, and not, as is more usual, as a challenge to established theories of the firm, or as a building block of an "Austrian" theory of the firm.[1] Our goal in this chapter is to try and evaluate, through Hayek's theory of organizations, the internal consistency and strength of his defense of liberalism.

The first brief section addresses Hayek's idea of what constitutes the economic problem. Second, we will analyze the central critique that he voices against socialist views of the organization. Finally, we will present our argument regarding Hayek's ambivalent thesis on organizations and its consequences for his theory of the spontaneous order of the market.

## Hayek's view of the central economic problem

Hayek defines the central problem of economics in several ways. One is to focus on the cognitive limits of economic actors and the main consequences of these limits: the dispersion and coordination of knowledge in society.

## Subjectivism: the nature of human cognition and human action

The *homo hayekiensis* is very different from the *homo oeconomicus*, particularly regarding the question of rationality. For Hayek, human knowledge is largely contextual and local, often tacit, personal, practical, changing, and specific to social context. One may characterize all of these features as "radical subjectivism" (O'Driscoll and Rizzo, 1985). Radical subjectivism really comes into its own in uncertain environments.[2] *Homo hayekiensis* is not a perfect, objective and optimizing rationalizer; instead, he relies on rules and institutions (Hayek, 1960, 1973). The particular characteristics of individual cognition have important effects on the social or collective level. This is particularly true for complex economic systems with a highly developed division of labor and knowledge.

Hayek distinguishes between two aspects of the same issue: the problem of dispersion of knowledge and the problem of adaptation to change. The fact that individuals possess knowledge that is personal, tacit, and local, leads to the dispersion of knowledge, a main factor of complex, modern economic systems.[3] Recognizing the division of knowledge in society takes us to the central problem in economics, that is the coordination of the whole economic system. Hayek has examined and developed this idea throughout his career, in his economics, social philosophy, and political philosophy. The second relevant aspect is the continuous changes that affect the internal and external environments of each economic actor.[4] Since "economic problems arise always and only in consequence of change," the solution is to take into consideration the crucial role of "rapid adaptation to changes in the particular circumstances of time and place" (Hayek, 1948, pp. 82–3). We must therefore examine adaptation on the institutional and organizational levels.

## Adaptation and coordination by decentralization

At the microeconomic level, adaptation by decentralization includes both the adaptation to "particular circumstances of time and place," and to changes that happen continually. At the macroeconomic level, adaptation is the coordination of dispersed knowledge. For Hayek, an effective decentralization is the most satisfying procedure. As a consequence, "the ultimate decisions must be left to the people who are familiar with these circumstances, who know directly of the relevant changes and of the resources immediately available to meet them" (ibid., pp. 83–4). We will not examine this notion of adaptation here.[5] Instead, we will illustrate its importance by discussing its role in three different theoretical contexts: the inter-systemic debate concerning the comparative merits of economic systems, i.e. socialism and capitalism; the intra-systemic debate concerning the relations between markets and organizations within the same economic system; and the intra-organizational debate concerning the merits of different organizational structures within the same organization. In the following sections we will discuss Hayek's contributions to these debates.

# Criticism of the utopian socialist organization

Could a socialist theory solve the problem of dynamic coordination of dispersed knowledge? According to Hayek, this is definitely not feasible for the simple reason that the principle of socialist organization requires an *ex-ante* coordination of the individual agents' actions structuring the economic system. In order to illustrate this argument, we will discuss three different models of socialism with their different organizational principles.

## *The centralist organization of Marx*

For Marx, the bourgeoisie has, in the course of the historical process, brought about progress by the introduction of capitalist separation (workers have been separated from the means of production). Separation operated through the institution of the private ownership of means of production. However, over time, insurmountable intra-systemic contradictions between productive forces and production relations would make it impossible for this progress to continue indefinitely. Reunification is thus a necessity and it cannot occur without the collective appropriation of the means of production and without the rational organization of the whole economic system.

In his theory of capitalism, Marx distinguishes between two types of division of labor, the technical division and the social division, differentiated by the corresponding modes of coordination. An *ex-ante* and intentional coordination governs technical division. As for social division, it is unintentional, *ex-post* and determined by the law of value. Hayek also distinguished between organized and spontaneous orders. These two orders correspond to those defined by Marx, except that Marx has a pessimistic vision of the viability of the capitalist system. For Marx, the development of capitalism entails increasing contradictions between the two modes of coordination, due to the increasing chaos created by the spontaneous coordination of the market. In Hayekian terms, this means that, for Marx, the more complex the system, the more insufficient is spontaneous coordination. Thus, only an organization in the form of a global plan, that is, systemic generalization of the organization, can go beyond the limits of capitalism.

Although Hayek shares several ideas with Marx, profound differences between the two theorists' perspectives remain. Hayek agrees that coordination by the market is not and cannot be optimal, but unlike Marx, he does not envision any alternative that is capable of maintaining an extensive division of knowledge and labor.[6] For Hayek, global reunification, as conceptualized and predicted by Marx, could not take place mainly for cognitive reasons. The ever-present constructivist rationalism in the organizational ideal of communism is mistaken according to Hayek. As he teaches us, how is it possible to believe that the global organization of a complex economic system could, in essence, be the simple extension of the technical and rational organization of labor within a firm? Indeed, the more complex an economic system, the more problems of coordination are left unnoticed or unsolved by a deliberate, centralized organization. Such a coordination is only possible in the case of a central agency capable of gathering and dealing with all the necessary knowledge and information regarding the different needs and production techniques. However, this task is impossible since subjective knowledge is distributed throughout the economic system.

### Organization as a device for calculating the general equilibrium

Planification can be conceived of as the elaboration and resolution of an equation system describing a general economic equilibrium. Dickinson proposed this solution in 1933; it consists of finding a practical solution to the theory of the formal similitude between socialism and capitalism (Lavoie, 1985). Dickinson's intuition is simple: it consists of turning a system of equations that model a general equilibrium into an effective planning process.

To construct this system of equations, the planning center must have sufficient information and knowledge about (1) the production functions of the different enterprises; (2) the utility functions of consumers; and (3) the resources in terms of primary factors. Dickinson thought that these three types of information were easy to gather and analyze. According to him, socialism differs from capitalism in the transparency of information about techniques and production costs. Socialism has a fundamental advantage over capitalism since in it "there is fullest publication of output, costs, sales, stocks, and other relevant statistical data." Consequently, in socialism "all enterprises work as it were within glass walls" (Dickinson, 1933, p. 239).

Dickinson recognizes that the effective organization of the planning activities may run into problems. Thus, it is impossible for practical reasons to collect detailed information on all the production functions and commodities. Nevertheless, Dickinson considers aggregation to be a pragmatic solution and a satisfactory method (ibid., p. 240).

The reason why Dickinson favors planification is fundamentally the same as Marx's: "only a global organization of the activities of production and redistribution seems reasonable in order to surpass anarchy and capitalist crises" (ibid., p. 240). From the center, organization means the total organization of the Walrasian system: the imposition of marginal rules which structure it; the organization of procedures for transmission; and the calculation of the general equilibrium. From the periphery, the organization is a technical subdivision of the whole planned system, which is cut down to a simple production or cost function, meeting the requirements of perfect competition. This allows us to see, *a contrario*, the "affinity" between general equilibrium theory (GET), and the centralist vision of organizations and economic systems.

In his discussion of Dickinson's model, Hayek develops two types of critical arguments: the computation argument and the knowledge argument. The computation argument shows that solving the system of equations is an enormous task. Given the limits of human computational capacities (and techniques), this task seems impossible on the practical level, particularly in the case of rapid change (Hayek, 1948, p. 156). The fact that much effort went toward finding a solution to this first critique brought about numerous planning procedures (Heal, 1973). These aim at minimizing the computational load at the center, by dividing and directing this load toward the peripheral entities. However, this technical problem remains secondary to Hayek.

The knowledge problem concerns the non-accessibility of factual knowledge. It shows that any attempt to equate economic planification with a large-scale equilibrium model entails, at the very least, that the center knows the production function of each local organization. Yet this knowledge cannot be considered as accessible or easy to transfer and analyze. Two arguments, which naturally reinforce each other, are found in Hayek's critique: tacit knowledge and the static nature of the general equilibrium model. As far as tacit knowledge is concerned, Hayek was conscious of this theme even in his first contribution to the socialist debate in 1935:[7]

> [M]uch of the knowledge that is actually utilized is by no means "in existence" in this readymade form. Most of it consists in a technique of thought which enables the individual engineer to find new solutions rapidly as soon as he is confronted with new constellations of circumstances.
>
> (Hayek, 1948, p. 155)

Hayek also criticized the unrealistic and static dimension of the GET. It is obvious that he attached a fundamental importance to the local level and to small, continuous changes, for practical reasons. According to him this constitutes the core of market dynamics:

> It is clear that we never come near the state of equilibrium described by the solution of such a system of equations. … We should not expect equilibrium to be reached unless all external change had ceased. The essential thing about the present economic system is that it does react to some extent to all those small changes and differences which would have to be deliberately disregarded under the system we are discussing if the calculations were to be manageable. In this way rational decisions would be impossible in all these questions of detail, which in the aggregate decide the success of productive effort.
>
> (ibid., pp. 156–7)

If centralized planning cannot be realized, could a decentralized planning model be the solution? That was the goal of Lange's model.

### *Organized Walrasian* tâtonnement *as decentralized planification*

Lange was not unaware of the limits of Dickinson's model and proposed to overcome them by creating a model of decentralized planning. For Lange, making

GET functional did not require, as Dickinson believed, a centralized organization. The application of GET requires neither more nor less information, nor calculations, as compared to the competitive market. The Bureau of Central Planning (BCP), in the course of its primary function of determining prices, does not need to know the individual production functions. The BCP only has to know the anonymous reactions of socialist managers[8] to the provisional prices it communicates to them. The BCP's role is limited to "crying out" these prices in order to elicit responses from managers, evaluate the net demand for each commodity, and to make prices vary until convergence reaches equilibrium (Lange, 1967, p. 88).[9] The managers need only to know their own production function at their own local level, and they only need to optimize the costs of production and the quantities of production.

Lange's solution presents itself as more realistic and economical in terms of cognitive resources than does Dickinson's model. But his point is also to demonstrate that socialism is superior to real capitalism (in this case, monopolistic capitalism). Lange gives several reasons for this.

The fact that a trial-and-error method would yield results more rapidly and efficiently than under a capitalist regime due to the center's possession of global and general information. In addition, it is not in the interest of monopolistic organizations, under capitalism, to innovate. Only the reintroduction of marginalist conditions of perfect competition could boost the economy. At this level, socialism is supposed to have a major advantage: the center can simulate competition without having to demonopolize productive structures. It can do so by disconnecting production from distribution, by establishing collective ownership of the means of production, and by imposing rules of marginalist calculation on socialist managers.

Lange seems to have tried to take into consideration the argument of dispersed knowledge. However, his solution is far from satisfactory and his view of decentralization is erroneous. We can illustrate this point by examining Hayek's critique of the functionality of the rule of marginal cost. Hayek questions the cognitive hypothesis underlying the neoclassical model proposed by Lange. For Hayek, it is not appropriate to compare economic actors to robots who would first receive objective information from the external world, then objectively analyze it, and finally objectively communicate their response. Even more alarmingly, Langean economic actors are supposed to be capable of "virtual" calculations of marginal costs without getting involved in action and without belonging to an appropriate institutional framework (Hayek, 1948, pp. 196–9). Everything that Lange takes for granted and considers as objective, easily accessible and transmissible, is seen by Hayek as the result of an active quest, of the competition or cooperation between businesses. For Hayek, one of the principal functions of a firm is the organization of productive and strategic knowledge. This is a logical consequence of subjectivism and heterogeneity being introduced into the theory of the firm.

Langean managers cannot play an entrepreneurial role; the BCP must take all responsibilities. Yet the BCP, being far away from local technological and economic realities, does not have feasible methods for knowing whether a certain method is effective or not:

> Since the man [the socialist manager] with the new idea will have no possibility of establishing himself by undercutting, the new idea cannot be proved by experiment until he has convinced the S.E.C. [Socialist Economic Council]. Or, in other words, every calculation by an outsider who believes that he can do better has to be examined and approved by the authority, which in this connection will have to take over all the functions of the entrepreneur.
>
> (ibid., pp. 196–7)

Hayek levels another critique against the center's control of managers' actions. The first task of the center is not to verify if the actions carried out comply with the plan, but to determine whether the chosen plan (or the one proposed in the iterative procedure) is an optimal one:[10]

> All [the manager's] calculations will have to be examined and approved by the authority. This will not be a perfunctory auditing, directed to find out whether his costs have actually been what he says they have been. It will have to ascertain whether they have been the lowest possible ones. This means that the control will have to consider not only what he actually did but what he might have done and ought to have done.
>
> (ibid., p. 198)

According to Hayek, there is no possible means to do this, or to encourage this unless the planner's knowledge is unlimited, in which case decentralization would be unnecessary. If we consider the BCP as the center and the actor as being the manager, this criticism might seem to be similar to that of modern principal–agency theory. The appropriate question to ask here is how to find the incentive mechanisms likely to motivate actors to give real information.[11] Yet for Hayek the problem is completely different: each entity carrying out verification should previously possess a criterion for comparing a manager's action (or proposal) with what needs to be done. This, however, presupposes the possibility of access to the production functions of different enterprises, which is impossible for cognitive reasons.

Lange only analyzed the problems caused by the *technical* difficulties of central calculations. His theory of decentralization does not take into account dispersed and subjective *knowledge*, that is, the necessity for a real separation. This is not surprising since collective property of the means of production is the institutional condition – necessary though insufficient – on which his socialism is based. His individualistic and objective conception of knowledge gives him a limited view of coordination and prevents him from going beyond the contributions of Marx and Dickinson.

### Summary of the debate on socialism

Can we speak of a socialist firm? The answer to this question is far from clear. Certainly, socialist firms or organizations exist on the level of the entire socialist system. But peripheral organizations – the local production units – are not autonomous economic firms because they depend on the global organization of the center. They lack real autonomy, a fundamental condition for efficient local adaptation. It is also necessary to scrutinize the links between forms of property and forms of organization (and coordination). For Hayek, there is a strong affinity between the collective ownership of the means of production, planning, and centralized organization. In contrast, there is no affinity between this same form of property and decentralization as in the case of market socialism.[12] The reconstruction of a coherent economic system is only possible if it is carried out in two completely different ways: through recentralization, or through the establishment of private ownership. According to Hayek, though recentralization seems coherent, it is not viable. The only coherent and at the same time viable system for him is capitalism. It is a system where private ownership and true decentralization are closely linked together. Private ownership is then a necessary condition for the effective decentralization of economic systems and will allow firms to be truly autonomous and efficient.

The coordination of dispersed knowledge is not only constrained by individual cognitive limits; it also depends on the institutional framework. The GET ignored these factors, and this leads to equating perfect planification with a perfect market. Therefore, the cognitive argument proving that socialism is not viable also justifies the need for local planning, that is, the existence of firms. In that case the division of labor and knowledge is not only the mere result of economic development, but it is also (and mainly) a necessary condition for it, and one of its most dynamic driving factors.

One of the main lessons to be drawn from the debate on socialism is the rejection of the dichotomy between markets and organizations. Hayek is against the drastic opposition between planning and *laissez-faire*. Such a limited view of the comparative analysis of systems has a negative consequence: it leads to the belief that opponents of socialism are against *any* idea of planning or organization. Yet, planning and organization are necessary even in decentralized market systems. This leads to two questions that are of more interest than the dichotomous vision of planning *versus* market: in what area would planning have a greater chance of yielding successful results? Should it be applied to individuals or to the entire economic system? Whether we choose one system over the other depends on how each makes the best use of the available and dispersed knowledge, and on its capacity to facilitate adaptation and innovation (Hayek, 1948, pp. 79–80). The second question is: what is the most appropriate institutional and legal framework for such a type of planning? It is the question as to "which is the most appropriate permanent framework which will secure the smoothest and most efficient working of competition" (ibid., p. 135). With this second question, the focus is on the relationship between types of planification or economic organization and types of institutions (legal and political).

## Organizations in the spontaneous order of the market

Hayek elaborated the theory of spontaneous order in opposition to socialism and as an attempt to go beyond the insufficiencies of the GET. His concept of spontaneous orders is based on a contrast with organized orders. The problem confronting Hayekian spontaneous order is that it is organizationally undetermined: Hayek does not distinguish between what we call atomistic and non-atomistic orders. This confusion reveals the ambiguities and limitations of his theory of organization and hence of his theory of spontaneous order.

### *The dichotomy between organized and spontaneous orders*

For Hayek, spontaneous order is, by definition, invested with the capacity to coordinate knowledge dispersed in a complex economic system. Organized orders do not have this capacity. The concept of order is central to Hayek's theory: it allows the study of the coordination processes of various individual expectations and actions. Hayek differentiates between organized and spontaneous orders. The degree of intentionality of the respective orders, their type of governing rules, their degree of complexity and the control over them are all characteristics which distinguish one type of order from the other.

*Degree of intendedness* By definition, organizations are intentional or consciously created orders whereas spontaneous orders are not, even though they are the results of human action. This aspect is certainly the most fundamental and its importance goes beyond the question of the origin of orders.[13]

*Degree of complexity* Organized orders are "relatively simple," or they remain confined to limited degrees of complexity, so that they are accessible to the director of this order. By contrast, spontaneous orders have degrees of complexity which are "not limited to what a human mind can master" (Hayek, 1973, p. 38).

*Types of rules* Organizations are, by definition, governed by direct commands and concrete rules issued by a center. On the other hand, in spontaneous orders, abstract rules compensate for the absence of the managing center. Abstract rules delimit the field of action of the various elements that compose the order, and therefore facilitate their global coordination.

*Control* The possibility of mastering the elements and relations within an organization justifies verification by a control center. But, "since we can know at most the rules observed by the elements of various kinds of which the structures are made up, but not all the individual elements and never all the particular circumstances in which each of them is placed, our knowledge will be restricted to the general character of the order which will form itself." The consequence of this abstract knowledge is that we shall "be able to influence only the general character and not the detail of the resulting order" (ibid., p. 41).

At this point, the dichotomous definition of orders may lead to misconceptions if it is taken at face value, as it would lead to overlooking the complementarities and interdependencies between organized and spontaneous orders. Hayek is fully aware of the limitations of this. For him, the spontaneous order of the market is made up of organizations that compete and/or cooperate with each other. Although managers mainly use commands to govern organizations, they could and should use abstract rules when their enterprise grows. In the process, they inevitably introduce spontaneous elements within organizations. Yet in spite of this, Hayek does not succeed completely in avoiding ambiguities on this question. Williamson, for example, agrees with Hayek that the central economic problem is adaptation. However, he considers his approach to be incomplete because it focuses exclusively on the role of markets. Williamson (1996) mentions Chester Barnard, who also stressed the importance of the same problem of adaptation in the 1930s. Paradoxically, says Williamson, unlike Hayek, Barnard emphasizes the role of organizations. Williamson finds both of these approaches partially correct but incomplete. He claims that both markets and hierarchies (and hybrid forms) are governance structures necessary to solve the problem of adaptation.[14]

Is it appropriate to say that Hayek is only in favor of spontaneous governance? As we have seen, Hayek rejects the dichotomy between organizations and markets and he clearly distinguishes between global organization (socialism) and local organizations (firms). Though Williamson exaggerates by saying that Hayek excludes organizations from his analysis, his conclusions contain a valuable element. This is what we will now try to show by reconstructing Hayek's system in two different directions. We will subsequently examine this phenomenon more closely by referring to two types of association between organized and spontaneous orders – atomistic orders and non-atomistic orders.

### Atomistic orders

As Jensen and Meckling (1992) observed, Hayek's argument of local and specific knowledge, pushed to its extreme, leads to an atomistic conception of organizations and markets. Effective decentralization requires autonomy and the creation of individual enterprises. This is true because each individual holds local and tacit knowledge which only he or she can successfully use. The final picture of the resulting spontaneous order is an order made up of atomistic organizations, which are made up of individuals only.

This atomistic vision of organized and spontaneous orders is, *a priori*, a better solution than the one defended by advocates of socialism. It emphasizes the fundamental links between the nature of knowledge, on the one hand, and autonomy on the other. However, this idea takes us dangerously close to pure and perfect competition. As Demsetz (1995) rightly observes, perfect competition is by no means a reflection of competitiveness but rather of perfect decentralization. In his original attempt to defend the neoclassical theory of the firm, Demsetz promotes the idea that this theory has the merit of showing the radical difference between two types of economic systems: closed and self-sufficient systems, and "separated" production systems (with specialization and indirect exchange). In the latter type of systems, firms and markets are not opposed because firms produce and markets make exchange possible. Both transaction cost theory and contract theory fail to make this distinction because they take markets and organizations to be analytically homogenous.

The idea of an atomistic order can clarify the essence of the complex market order and how drastically it differs from simple organizations. In this sense, even if it has no empirical content, the concept plays a heuristic role and is a good starting point for a more exhaustive analysis of historical capitalism. Indeed, capitalism as it has historically developed cannot be considered as an atomistic order because from its very beginning it is characterized by the existence of several organizations of different sizes, including large-size organizations.[15]

Considering orders as atomistic does not answer the various questions linked to a theory of firms: the existence of a firm, its limits, its internal organization, and the diversity of organizations. At best, the atomistic view could help to answer the question of the existence of an individual firm. A firm exists because there is an essential distribution of knowledge in complex economic systems and because each and everyone can benefit from this distributed knowledge by concentrating on one particular specialization, and by exploiting his own personal skills. But this alone does not explain why a firm – which goes beyond the limits of a single individual – exists. It is of the utmost importance to ask whether a single entrepreneur's firm, which turns into a larger firm, is the result of a simply quantitative increase in size, or rather if it modifies the nature of the business corporation.

Since firms are governed by commands, the question is why anyone would accept being under someone else's authority. This question is crucial because if an individual accepts such a contract, he or she loses his or her autonomy, which is the only guarantee of cognitive and economic efficiency according to Hayek (in his critique of socialist models). In other words, why does the employer–employee relationship exist at all? Is this relationship an intrinsic element of the capitalist organization (firm) and of the spontaneous order of the market? Why is it more efficient – not to say vital – to resort to a collective and hierarchically organized effort within one single firm, rather than to rely solely on individual and atomistic organization – in which case complementarities will be looked for on the market?[16] Before answering this question we must investigate non-atomistic orders.

## Non-atomistic orders

Hayek is far from being unaware of these questions. He acknowledges that capitalism encompasses individual firms but also large-size organizations. Every complex organization necessarily involves a large number of individuals. Every one of them has specific skills and privileged access to particular circumstances of time and place, be it in the internal or external environment of the organization. This is why the firm has to deal with the fact that knowledge within the organization exists in distributed form, which prevents it from being governed by the principles of command and hierarchy only. The cognitive arguments which prove that socialism is not feasible also apply to the firm: a completely centralized large firm is not feasible either. Hayek is right when he says that "in none but the most simple kind of organization is it conceivable that all the details of all activities are governed by a single mind" (1973, p. 49). Therefore, as is the case for all complex orders – particularly of the spontaneous variety – only abstract rules allow us to manage the internal dispersion of knowledge and continuous change:

> To some extent every organization must rely also on rules and not only on specific commands. The reason here is the same as that which makes it necessary for a spontaneous order to rely on rules: namely that by guiding the actions of individuals by rules rather than specific commands it is possible to make use of knowledge which nobody possesses as a whole.
>
> (Hayek, 1973, pp. 48–9)

In this case, abstract rules are indispensable and precious organizational tools capable of implementing decentralization and efficient autonomy that are necessary for adaptation:

> Every organization in which the members are not mere tools of the organizer will determine by commands only the function to be performed by each member, the purposes to be achieved, and certain general aspects of the methods to be employed and will leave the detail to be decided by the individuals on the basis of their respective knowledge and skills.
>
> (ibid., p. 49)

None the less, according to Hayek, organizational rules are relative and secondary since they are "rules for the performance of assigned tasks" and thus they are "subsidiary to commands" (ibid., p. 49), whereas spontaneous order rules are abstract, neutral (independent from objectives), and general (they can be applied to all the members of the system).

Since a firm is managed by command, and since all its members must direct themselves to achieving the same goals, one of the main organizational problems of the firm is the search for an equilibrium between control and flexibility, centralization and decentralization, between authority and autonomy. However, in order to reach this equilibrium, the head of the firm must possess strong organizational skills (strategies). This entails that the head of the firm is capable of organizing the exchange and interpretation of information and knowledge coming from all hierarchical levels. Nevertheless, this ability is likely to be limited, and possible obstacles are the cognitive limits of those in command. The limits of the firm are not determined by technological factors, as is the case for standard neoclassical theory, nor by transaction and incentive costs as in neo-institutionalist theories. First and foremost, the limits of the firm are determined by cognitive factors.[17] This is the main lessons from the debate on socialism.

### The limits of Hayek's theory of organizations

Despite Hayek's thorough contribution to the theory of organizations, his approach is too limited for various reasons. His discussion of non-atomistic orders keeps silent on the employment relationship. In some of his writings Hayek ponders problems related to labor and employment, but he treats these phenomena as if they were obvious and in no need of further explanation. Hayek concentrates mainly on the consequences of the large size of firms, and he does not study in depth how and why these firms have became big. He also concentrates on management only, and fails to discuss problems related to the theory of wages and labor. In fact, large firms are a very delicate issue for Hayek, and they lead him into contradictions.

By definition, firms are organized orders and as such they are governed by a commanding director and by deliberately created and imposed rules. Since labor is a major resource, if not the principal one, of an organization, it must be managed according to organizational principles (commands and deliberate rules), and thus wages become an organizational and strategic element. However, Hayek also believes that labor should be considered as a simple resource on the free market, as part of the spontaneous order and not as being a part of an organizational environment. So the wage is just an adjustment variable on the labor market. If we consider labor to be a commodity, and if we then consider wage as the price paid for it, labor becomes something that is objectivistic and homogenous. This was the implicit idea in Hayek's theory of business cycles in the 1920s and 1930s, but this was also the thesis he fiercely defended in the 1960s–1980s (Hayek, 1991).[18]

This commodity-like approach to labor, however, may be considered to be contradictory to the theory stating that cognition is subjective, tacit, heterogeneous, and not pre-established. Actually, in this cognitive perspective labor contracts cannot be seen as pure market contracts. If we try to apply radical subjectivism to the domain of labor we will find that decentralization and autonomy on the work floor are necessary conditions for encouraging workers to cooperate and to get involved in individual and organizational learning. At times, Hayek seems to be aware of this necessity, for instance when he states that "[o]rganizations encounter here the problem which any attempt to bring order into complex human activities meets: the organizer must wish the individuals who are to cooperate to make use of knowledge that he himself does not possess" (Hayek, 1973, p. 49). But he seems unaware that cooperation always comes at a cost: incentives and organizational justice. Giving workers the freedom to make decisions in order to adapt to particular circumstances is a very important necessary organizational condition. However, it is not sufficient. In exchange for their cooperation, workers must also receive incentives. Providing these is certainly one of the most difficult tasks of any organization, and it shows that the management of labor belongs, at least partly, to the domain of organization and its rules.

If we take the example of the security of employment and of all the measures and incentives which temporarily stabilize the situation of workers in a corporation we find Hayek maintaining ambivalent positions. On the one hand he rightly said that such measures are necessary for adaptation and learning in organizations:

> It may be in the interest of the corporation to tie its employees as closely to it as possible. ... The performance and very existence of a corporation is ... often bound up with the preservation of at least a certain continuity in its personnel, the preservation of at least an inner core of men right down the line who are familiar with its peculiar traditions and concrete tasks. The "going concern" differs from the material structure which will still exist after operations have ceased mainly by the mutually adjusted knowledge and habits of those who operate it.
>
> (Hayek, 1991, pp. 302–3)

On the other hand, Hayek rejects a scrutiny of the theoretical and practical consequences of this latter view:

> Nevertheless, in a free system (i.e., in a system of free labor) it is necessary in the interest of the efficient use of resources that the corporation be regarded primarily as an aggregate of material assets. It is they and not the men whom the management can at will allocate to different purposes, they which alone are the means which it is the task of corporations to put to the best use, while the individual must in the last resort himself remain free to decide whether the best use of his energies is within the particular corporation or elsewhere.
>
> (ibid., p. 303)

Thus, according to Hayek, measures taken to boost workers' competencies – which could help to solve the problems of adaptation and learning – slow down and prevent "healthy" liberalism from functioning well, and could even threaten civilization and freedom, and pave the way to socialism!

To be fair to Hayek, he does not completely ignore the problem of incentives since, according to him, they are the very reason of entrepreneurship and private ownership. The existence of incentives is one of the advantages of atomistic orders. For Hayek, incentives are necessary conditions to solve the problem of dynamic adaptation. We may conclude that in the end Hayek sketches a distinction not only between spontaneous and organized orders, but also between different types of individuals. On the one hand, entrepreneurs are seen as complex cognitive individuals who need private ownership and the impulse of profit in order to be autonomous, and in order to make the best use of their specific skills and local knowledge. On the other hand, workers are considered as just being simple technical quantities of objective and simple production power – far less complex than capital – and they do not need to be really autonomous.

Hayek must have been aware of this dilemma. In *The Constitution of Liberty* (1960) he writes that the capitalist civilization had been able to create a good substitute for private ownership, namely contracts. But this argument is weak: the autonomy of labor is no longer a requirement for local adaptation, and it consists simply in workers being free to either sign or breach an employment contract. Consequently, Hayek's critique of socialism loses some of its force. It does so not because it is not well founded, but because it is not completely and logically exploited by Hayek in his theory of liberalism.

## Conclusion

Hayek faces a dilemma. If he considers labor as a commodity, he is inconsistent with his own cognitive theory on which he bases his rejection of socialism. If, on the other hand, he takes his own cognitive theory to its logical consequences, he is led to a highly idealized notion of a very limited atomistic order, which, if applied to reality, would need a complete rethinking of the notions of organization and spontaneous market order. If Hayek had fully realized this, he would have arrived at a different theory of liberalism, if not at a different kind of preferred economic system. In order to explain Hayek's hesitations and ambiguous arguments, we propose the following simple thesis: in defending liberalism, Hayek's value judgements take the upper hand over scientific arguments. In the final analysis, his theory of liberalism rests on the moral rejection of totalitarianism.

Methodologically, Hayek's contribution is mainly negative. He only rejects a particular social system, socialism, but fails to give a satisfactory justification, either in descriptive-explanatory or in normative terms, of the liberal alternative. It may be possible to repair this, but in order to do so we would have to complete his cognitive theory, adding subjects worthy of research for economists in the Austrian tradition such as the role of emotions and fairness on the work floor and organizational justice. The direction to look for is an extrapolation of Hayek's fundamental contributions on adaptation, decentralization, and the comparative analysis of systems. "Austrian" economists would also need to include questions of labor and employment relationship in their research program.

## Acknowledgements

Jack Birner made useful comments on an earlier version of the chapter, as did the other participants at the conference, including the official discussant, Richard Aréna. I am indebted to them. The author also benefited from useful discussions with Pierre Garrouste, Mehrdad Vahabi, Frederic Lapeyre, and Nathalie Richebé. The usual disclaimer applies.

## Notes

1 See for example Foss (1998), Garrouste and Dulbecco (1999), Ioannides (1998), Langlois (1995).
2 The uncertainty which interests Hayek most is radical or structural uncertainty, as opposed to parametric uncertainty. Cp. Langlois (1994).
3 The peculiar character of the problem of a rational economic order is determined precisely by the fact that the knowledge of the circumstances of which we must make use never exists in concentrated or integrated form but solely as dispersed bits of incomplete, and frequently contradictory, knowledge which all the separate individuals possess, ( Hayek, 1948, p. 7).
4 In an exhaustive analysis conducted on a subjectivist basis, change, including technological change is mostly endogenous.
5 For an analysis of this notion see the excellent article by Birner (1996).
6 Under Marx's communism, the social division of labor is not a sign of progress, as is the technical division of labor; it is an institution that must be abolished.
7 Hayek made important contributions to the theme of tacit knowledge after this date, in his cognitive psychology (Hayek, 1967, 1978) and in his social philosophy (Hayek, 1960, 1973, 1988).
8 In Lange's model, what matters are not individual responses but their aggregate result. This is supposed to alleviate the cognitive task of the center.
9 One of the main roles of decentralized planning models from the 1950s to the 1970s – elaborated by Arrow, Hurwicz, Heal and Malinvaud, amongst others – consisted in establishing *tâtonnement* rules for a rapid and/or satisfying convergence toward equilibrium. Cp. Heal (1973).
10 An optimal performance is not required by Hayek; it is in planification models.
11 Here lies the origin of the incentive-compatibility theory, which is itself the origin of the principal–agent theory.
12 This issue is studied in depth in Janos Kornai's works in the 1980s and 1990s. Cp. Kornai (1991).
13 Cp. Langlois (1995) and Ioannides (1999) for interesting discussions of this aspect, particularly with respect to organizations.
14 It is necessary then, according to him, to use a criterion other than adaptation, such as asset specificity, uncertainty and the frequency of transactions. Cp. Williamson (1996).
15 We do not discuss here the role of the state as a particular form of organization which had an important role in the history of capitalism.
16 Along the same lines, with Hayek's theory in mind, how do we distinguish private firms governed by an employer–employee relationship from self-managed firms? See the important and provocative article by Prychitko (1996).
17 This does not exclude in the least that the impact of transaction or incentives costs must be considered in a complete theory. But first we must look at the problems put forth by the neo-institutionalist theories by focusing more closely on individual cognitive limits and the resulting dispersion of knowledge. Cp. Minkler (1993).

18 "[A]continuous adjustment of the various kinds of labor to the changing demand requires a *real labor market* in which the wages of the different kinds of labor are determined by demand and supply" (Hayek, 1991, p. 264).

## Bibliography

Birner, J. (1996) "Decentralization as Ability to Adapt," in B. Dallago and L. Mittone, eds, *Economic Institutions, Markets and Competition*, Cheltenham: Edward Elgar, pp. 63–89.

Demsetz, H. (1995) *The Economics of the Business Firm – Seven Critical Commentaries*, Cambridge: Cambridge University Press.

Dickinson, H.D. (1933) "Price Formation in a Socialist Community," *Economic Journal*, 47(170), pp. 237–50.

Foss, J.N. (1998) "Austrian Insights and the Theory of the Firm," in P. Boettke and S. Horwitz, eds, *Advances in Austrian Economics* 4, pp. 175–98.

Garrouste, P. and P. Dulbecco (1999) "Towards an Austrian Theory of the Firm," *The Review of Austrian Economics*, 12 (1), pp. 43–64.

Hayek, F.A. (1948) *Individualism and Economic Order*, Chicago: The University of Chicago Press.

—— (1960) *The Constitution of Liberty*, London: Routledge & Kegan Paul..

—— (1967) *Studies in Philosophy, Economics and Politics*, Chicago: The University of Chicago Press.

—— (1973) *Law, Legislation and Liberty*, London: Routledge.

—— (1978) *New Studies in Philosophy, Economics, Politics and the History of Ideas*, Chicago: The University of Chicago Press.

—— (1988) *The Fatal Conceit: The Errors of Socialism*, Chicago: The University of Chicago Press.

—— (1991) *Economic Freedom*, Oxford: Basil Blackwell.

Heal, G.M. (1973) *The Theory of Economic Planning*, Amsterdam: North Holland.

Ioannides, S. (1998) "Towards an Austrian Perspective on the Firm," *The Review of Austrian Economics* 11(1–2), pp 77–97.

—— (1999) "The Market, the Firm, and Entrepreneurial Leadership: Some Hayekian Insights," *Revue d'économie politique* 109(6), pp. 871–83.

Jensen M.C. and W.H. Meckling (1992) "Specific and General Knowledge, and Organizational Structure," in L. Werin and H. Wijkander, eds, *Contract Economics*, Oxford: Blackwell, pp. 251–74.

Kornai, J. (1991) "The Affinity Between Ownership Forms and Coordination Mechanisms: The Common Experience on Reform in Socialist Countries," *Journal of Economic Perspectives* 4(3), pp. 131–47.

Lange, O. (1938) "On The Economic Theory of Socialism," in B.E. Lippincott, ed., *On the Economic Theory of Socialism*, New York: McGraw-Hill.

—— (1967) "The Computer and the Market" in C.H. Feinstein ed., *Socialism, Capitalism and Economic Growth: Essays Presented to Maurice Dobb*, Cambridge, Cambridge University Press, pp. 158–61

Langlois, R. (1994) "Risk and Uncertainty," in P. Boettke, ed., *The Elgar Companion to Austrian Economics*, Cheltenham: Edward Elgar, pp. 118–22.

—— (1995) "Do Firms Plan?" *Constitutional Political Economy*, 6 (3), pp. 247–61.

Lavoie, D. (1985) *Rivalry and Central Planning: The Socialist Calculation Debate Reconsidered*, Cambridge: Cambridge University Press.

Minkler, A.P. (1993) "The Problem with Dispersed Knowledge: Firms in Theory and Practice," *Kyklos* 46(4), pp. 569–87.

O'Driscoll, G.P. and M.J. Rizzo (1985) *The Economics of Time and Ignorance*, New York: Basil Blackwell.

Prychitko, D. (1996) "The Critique of Workers' Self-Management: Austrian Perspectives and Economic Theory," in P. Boettke and D. Prychitko, eds, *Advances in Austrian Economics*, 3, Greenwich: JAI Press, pp. 5–25.

Roberts, P.C. and M.A. Stephenson (1973) *Marx's Theory of Exchange, Alienation and Crisis*, Stanford: Hoover Institution Press.

Williamson, O. (1996) *The Mechanisms of Governance*, Oxford: Oxford University Press.

# 10 The difference between order and organization and the foundations of Hayek's liberalism

*Pierre Garrouste*

## Introduction

Not all "Austrians" agree on the role liberalism plays in Hayek's thought. Some of them consider liberalism to be the cornerstone of his work and they think that all his theoretical contributions are devoted to the demonstration that it is the best social and political system. Others maintain that liberalism is only one possible consequence of Hayek's positive theory. According to the first interpretation Hayek's positive contribution is determined by his normative liberal *credo*, according to the second, Hayek's normative beliefs are the logical conclusions of his scientific contributions.

What both interpretations share is the idea that Hayek's liberalism is linked with a positive analysis which is based on the following systematic dichotomies:

*Table 10.1*

| *Philosophical foundations* | Evolutionary rationalism | Constructivist rationalism |
| --- | --- | --- |
| *Types of rules* | Abstract | Concrete |
| *Modes of coordination* | Spontaneous order | Organization |
| *Nature of coordination* | Competition | Cooperation |
| *Level of analysis* | Individualism | Holism |
| *Political system* | Liberalism | Socialism |

This system of dichotomies has been criticized "vertically" in the sense that the coherence of Hayek's thought is called into question, and "horizontally" by appraising its relevance. Both types of criticism, useful though they are, are partial or local because they only take into account one part of Hayek's thought.

In this contribution, my aim is to evaluate the whole system of dichotomies and to show that there is a gap between Hayek's positive and normative contributions. In other words, I want to challenge the way Hayek, starting from the level of types of rules, deduces the last line of the scheme.

The point of departure for Hayek is to find a solution to the problem of coordination. This problem is logically deduced from the fundamental Hayekian idea that knowledge is *essentially dispersed*. That idea in its turn follows from the theory Hayek develops in *The Sensory Order* (1952) and in the other publications he devotes to the analysis of the way individuals build up their cognitive capacities.

I will first focus on Hayek's concept of cognition.[1] My main objective is to show that the Hayekian assumption that there is a fundamental discrepancy between abstract and concrete rules can be challenged. I will then show that the opposition between those two kinds of rules lies at the basis of the distinction between organizations and institutions, even though Hayek sometimes says that this opposition is not always so clear. Finally, I will argue that Hayek's idea that liberalism is better that socialism either is based on a conception of those two political systems as ideal types – in which case it can be linked to his characterization of rules of conduct – or cannot be founded on the difference between orders and organizations.

## Abstract and concrete rules

According to Hayek, the problem of coordination arises out of the dispersion of knowledge. The problem exists because individuals do not have the possibility to transfer all they know. It is important here to take into account that Hayek's conception of knowledge is rooted in his analysis of the difference between the physical and the sensory order (Hayek, 1952). His problem is the following: what kind of relationship is it possible to set up between the human mind and the external world? As a matter of biography, Hayek hesitated in the beginning between psychology and economics, and he says that he devoted a great part of his time to psychology.[2] He was reacting to Mach's theory, and more particularly to the idea that "pure sensations" exist. According to Mach, sensations are relational, i.e. they need to be analyzed taking into account the set of connections that link them together. According to Hayek, sensations are themselves the result of a process of hierarchical classification:

> The main aim of the theory presented is to show that the range of mental phenomena such as discrimination, equivalence of response to different stimuli, generalization, transfer, abstraction, and conceptual thought, may be interpreted as different forms of the same process which we have called classification, and that such classifications can be effected by a network of connections transmitting nervous impulses.
>
> (Hayek, 1952, p. 147)

He adds that

> it deserves, perhaps, to be mentioned that, although the theory developed here was suggested in the first instance by the psychological views which Ernst Mach has outlined in his *Analysis of Sensations* and elsewhere, its systematic development leads to a refutation of his and similar phenomenalist philosophy: by destroying the conception of elementary and constant

sensations as ultimate constituents of the world, it restores the necessity of a belief in an objective world which is different from that presented to us by our senses.

(Hayek, 1952, pp. 175–6)

On the strength of this he concludes that individuals have perceptions just because they have "action patterns" that permit them to understand the external world. In this way "knowledge is primarily a system of rules of action assisted and modified by rules indicating equivalencies or differences of various combinations of stimuli" (Hayek, 1978, p. 41). In fact, if "action patterns" allow individuals to understand the external world (and then others' actions) the selection between the mechanisms producing those patterns permits those individuals to build up a system of rules of action.[3]

Within the framework of a system of abstract rules of action, each individual undergoes specific experiences that determine his own perceptions. In other words, each individual has his own perceptual history because his perceptions are the result of all the past confrontations with his environment. Individual perceptions are path dependent. Two conclusions follow from this. First, individuals who have the same kind of abstract rules of action can communicate because they can understand others' actions, even if they cannot explain those actions.[4] Second, they cannot communicate their system of rules of action (the main part of their knowledge) to others, because they do not know that they are using those kind of rules.[5] But they also cannot transfer to others some part of their knowledge because their perceptual histories are specific (idiosyncratic).[6]

What seems important here is that the Hayekian conception of the way the individual's mind functions is logically linked to the distinction he makes between abstract and concrete rules of conduct. Such a conception is essential because it constitutes the cornerstone of an important and fundamental dichotomy. Hayek distinguishes two kinds of rules. The first are abstract, i.e. they enable individuals to perceive the external world. They are abstract, but they are also tacit or implicit; we are unaware of them (in the following we will use the term "unconscious") because they are transcendental. The second type of rules are the concrete rules, i.e. according to Hayek, we are aware of them and can possibly even express and communicate their content ("conscious" rules).

What is then interesting to take into account is that abstract rules are unconscious, general and tacit, while concrete rules are conscious, specific and *codified*.[7] There is indeed a double dichotomy as far as the characteristic of the rules is concerned:

*Table 10.2*

| abstract | concrete |
|---|---|
| unconscious | conscious |
| general | specific |
| tacit | codified |

This set of dichotomies is important because Hayek's distinction between order and organization is based on it. However, even if the scheme seems coherent, one may still question whether it is relevant.

A rule is general if it can be applied whatever the case might be. On the other hand, a rule is specific inasmuch as it can be applied to some cases only. For example, a judge transforms general rules into specific ones by a process of verbalization. In this way, abstract rules can be transformed into concrete ones as far as their generality and "tacitness" are concerned. However, according to Hayek, there is no possibility for specific rules to become general; there is nothing that allows concrete rules to become abstract. Such a conception, which allows only one kind of transformation (abstract to concrete), may be challenged (Garrouste, 1999). One can identify three different kinds of process:

*Routinization,* a process in which conscious rules progressively become unconscious. The existence of routines can be considered to be the result of such a process.

*Generalization,* a process that extends the applicability of the rules.

*Codification,* the constitution of a support that is characterized both by an unambiguous semantic and by a precise and shared syntax.

One can challenge Hayek's strict distinction between abstract and concrete rules by showing that there is no gap between those two kinds of rules. If that is the case, the distinction between order and organization is weakened.

## The relations between order and organization

There are two ways of appraising Hayek's way of distinguishing between orders and organizations and of establishing the relations between those two modes of coordination. First, orders and organizations can be analyzed as two different and exclusive modes of coordination, i.e., as different in kind. Second, one may assume organizations to be contained in, or to be a subset of, orders.

### Order and organization as different kinds

What Hayek writes is not very clear on this point: "what distinguishes the two classes is not so much their origins as the nature of the rules they comprise. The rules of an order are abstract and independent of purpose, whereas the rules of an organization are concrete and directed toward a common purpose or purposes" (Langlois, 1993, p. 169). Such a distinction can be challenged for two reasons. First, if it is true that there is no link between abstract and concrete rules, the same is the case with the distinction between orders and organizations. This is because the latter distinction is based on the former. Second, Langois' criticism correctly shows that Hayek confuses the nature of the rules of conduct with their origin. If one distinguishes the nature and the origin of the rules of conduct, one may draw the following table (see Langlois, 1995):

*Table 10.3*

|  | Order | Organization |
|---|---|---|
| *Organic* | Organic order | Organic organization |
| *Pragmatic* | Pragmatic order | Pragmatic organization |

While the diagonal of this matrix is typically Hayekian, the NE and SW squares are not. On this basis it is then possible to point out that orders can be created and that organizations can emerge spontaneously. Accordingly, Hayek's sharp distinction between order and organization is only a special case that applies if one assumes the identities between order and abstract rules of conduct on the one hand and organization and concrete ones on the other. If, however, we consider that there is a continuum between abstract and concrete rules of action, then it can no longer be maintained that there is a difference in kind between orders and organizations. So, order and organization as defined by Hayek are only two extreme cases. Indeed, if we distinguish the nature and the origin of the rules of conduct, then it is possible to challenge the following Hayekian idea:

*Table 10.4*

| *Types of rules* | Abstract | Concrete |
|---|---|---|
| *Modes of coordination* | Order | Organization |
| *Origin* | Spontaneous emergence | Purposeful creation |
| *Nature* | Selective competition | Cooperation and comman |

Even Hayek himself admits that the strict distinction between the columns is difficult to maintain; he thinks that in all collections of individuals that have some minimal size collaboration needs both spontaneous order and deliberate organization. The problem is that he does not give any solution as to the ways in which these modes of coordination can be combined (Birner, 1996).

### Organizations as a sub-set of orders

Hayek writes that increasingly orders "will not be economies of individuals, but of such organizations as firms and associations, as well as of administrative bodies" (Hayek, 1988, p. 37). In this case, the problem is to define the boundaries of an organization *inside* an order. The difficulty is then linked to the definition of a criterion of demarcation. Hayek says that an organization is based on the fact that somebody (the entrepreneur) is commanding and that the rules he uses are compatible with the ones that are at the basis of an extended order. The problem is then the following: how can rules of a different nature coexist and be combined? The solution is not self-evident. It may be the case that individuals share the same set of abstract rules and that some concrete ones complete those abstract rules. This is the solution Vanberg proposes in his "constitutional" analysis of organization. He thinks that the difference between the two kinds of rules "reflects the difference in the nature of the problems they deal with" (Vanberg, 1994, p. 139). It is important to keep in mind that it is no longer a difference in the nature of the rules but a difference in the nature of the problems those rules permit to solve that is at stake. Accordingly,

> organizational rules are notably concerned with the two fundamental problems of corporate or organized action that I have mentioned above: the problem of how decisions are to be made on the use of the pooled resources, and the problem of how the social product of the collective endeavor is distributed or translated into separate returns of the individual members of the organization.
>
> (Vanberg, 1994, p. 139)

On the other hand, those two kinds of problems do not exist in the context of markets, and organizational rules are not relevant in this context. The solution is interesting because it enables us to solve Hayek's difficulty in giving an answer as to how the rules of conduct may be combined. Vanberg says that he is following Hayek on this point. What he actually does is to modify the very nature of the distinction between an order and an organization. As I have just argued, he transforms the problem by considering that the difference between the two types of rules is not a difference in their nature but a difference in the problems they permit us to deal with. This result is important as far as the distinction Hayek makes between liberalism and socialism is rooted in the distinction between order and organization.

## Liberalism versus socialism

Liberalism is the extension of the idea of spontaneous order into the social and political domains. Hayek considers the liberal society to be the result of an evolutionary process that enables us to pass from the archaic society to the extended one. The archaic society is based on cooperation while competition and selection characterize the extended one. According to Hayek, the error of socialism is that it conceives society as an organization that is based on concrete rules of conduct. In other words, individuals are thought to be capable of managing the coordination of their plans of action so as to attain definite desired collective objectives. According to Hayek, however, it is impossible to manage dispersed knowledge for the reasons that are presented below in the form of a logical argument. Hayek's demonstration goes as follows:

*Premise 1:* The distinction between abstract and concrete rules of action is the cornerstone of the difference between order and organization.

*Premise 2:* Liberalism is based on the assimilation of human society to an order although socialism considers this society as an organization.

*Premise 3:* Dispersed knowledge cannot be managed because of the problem of complexity.

*Premise 4:* An organization cannot be efficient, or is even impossible,[8] at the level of the whole of human society.

*Conclusion:* Socialism is not an efficient (or even a possible) political system.

This kind of argumentation is equivalent to an "if ... then" demonstration. In other words, if the distinction between abstract and concrete rules of conduct is ascertained and if due to the very characteristics of the abstract rules of conduct it is impossible to manage those rules, then liberalism is more efficient than socialism. However, a deductive argument may be valid without its premises being true. More specifically, the consequent may be true even if the antecedent is not. That liberalism is the best social and political system can be validly deduced from false propositions. However, it is not my aim to discuss in this contribution the methodological aspects of this kind of argumentation. What I want to discuss instead is the fact that Hayek wants to deduce the discrepancy between liberalism and socialism from his fundamental distinction between abstract and concrete rules of conduct. He wants to establish the consequent as well as the antecedent, or more exactly, he wants to explain that the consequent is true because the antecedent is true (*modus ponens*). If, as I tried to show above, the distinction between abstract and concrete rules of conduct is not relevant, then liberalism may be better than socialism but, if it is, this is not because of the truth of the first distinction.

We must then make a choice: either the Hayekian dichotomies are based on an analysis in terms of ideal types, or they are real types. If the former, then liberalism and socialism, order and organization, abstract and concrete rules of conduct are all ideal types and in between those opposite types a continuum of real types is possible. In this case the idea that liberalism and socialism are mutually exclusive real socio-political systems must be abandoned. If the latter, the dichotomies are conceived of as real, empirical ones. As I have tried to show, it is then impossible to follow the demonstration proposed by Hayek in the sense that the fact that the liberal system is more efficient than the socialist one needs to be founded differently because it is not due to the relevance of the distinction between abstract and concrete rules of conduct.

## Conclusion

The idea that Hayek's liberalism can be rooted in his conception of the rules of conduct as well as in his distinction between order and organization can be challenged. If Hayek's analysis of the way cognitive capabilities emerge is at the basis of his distinction between abstract and concrete rules of conduct, the fact that there is a strong discrepancy between those types of rules does not seem to be relevant. However, his conception of the difference between order and organization as well as his assumptions that liberalism and socialism are mutually exclusive political systems and that liberalism is more efficient than socialism are founded on this distinction of the rules of conduct. The results of this argumentation are, first, that liberalism and socialism are not necessarily real exclusive systems, and second, that if they are mutually exclusive, this must be demonstrated, and it must be explained why liberalism is more efficient than socialism.

## Notes

1 I am not going to present exhaustively the Hayekian conception of cognition. See for example Birner (1999).
2 "The upshot of it was that during the three years that I was officially enrolled as a law student, I divided my time about equally between economics and psychology, while my law studies were merely a sideline" (Hayek, 1992, p. 173).
3 "It seems to me that organism first develops new potentialities for actions and that only afterwards does experience select and confirm those which are useful as adaptations to typical characteristics of its environment" (Hayek, 1978, p. 42).
4 "The situation may be described schematically by saying that we know that the objects $a$, b, c, ..., which may be physically completely dissimilar and which we cannot exhaustively enumerate, are objects of the same kind because the attitude of X toward them is similar. But the fact that X's attitude toward them is similar can again be defined only by saying that he will react toward them by any one of the actions $a$, $\beta$, $\gamma$, ..., which again may be physically dissimilar and which we will not be able to enumerate exhaustively, but which we know to 'mean' the same thing" (Hayek, 1980, pp. 61–2).
5 "It would seem more appropriate to call such processes not 'sub-conscious' but 'super-conscious,' because they govern the conscious processes without appearing in them" (Hayek, 1978, p. 45).
6 "Nobody can communicate to another all that he knows, because much of the information he makes use of he himself will elicit only in the process of making plans of action" (Hayek, 1988, p. 77).
7 I use the term codified in order to make more explicitly the fact that according to Hayek those kind of rules need to be explicit, that is to say need to be supported by a shared semantic and a "social" syntax.
8 I do not enter here into the debate concerning the distinction between the possibility and the efficiency of socialism.

## Bibliography

Birner, J. (1996) "Decentralization as Ability to Adapt" in B. Dallago and L. Mittone (eds), *Economic Institutions, Markets and Competition. Centralization and Decentralization in the Transformation of Economic Systems*, Aldershot, Hants: Edward Elgar.

—— (1999) "The Surprising Place of Cognitive Psychology in the Work of F.A. Hayek," *History of Economic Ideas* 7(1–2): 43–84.

Garrouste, P. (1999) "La firme 'hayekienne' entre institution et organisation," *Revue d'Économie Politique* 109 (6): 885–902.

Hayek, F.A. (1952) *The Sensory Order: An Inquiry into the Foundations of Theoretical Psychology*, London: Routledge & Kegan Paul, reprinted in 1963.

—— (1978) "The Primacy of the Abstract" in *New Studies in Philosophy, Politics, Economics, and the History of Ideas*, London: Routledge & Kegan Paul.

—— (1980) *Individualism and Economic Order*, Chicago: University of Chicago Press.

—— (1988) *The Fatal Conceit: the Errors of Socialism*, W.W. Bartley (ed.), London: Routledge.

—— (1992) *The Fortunes of Liberalism: Essays on Austrian Economics and the Ideal of Freedom*, P.G. Klein (ed.), London: Routledge.

Langlois, R.N. (1993) "Capabilities and Coherence in Firms and Markets," paper for the conference on Evolutionary and Resource-based Approaches to Strategy, Copenhagen.

—— (1995) "Do Firms Plan?" *Constitutional Political Economy* 6(3): 247–61.

Vanberg, V. (1994) *Rules and Choice in Economics*, London: Routledge.

# Part IV
# Philosophy of law

# 11 The contradictions between Hayek's subjectivism and his liberal legal theory

*Theodore A. Burczak*

## Introduction

Is Hayek's theory of the development and implementation of the rule of law, especially as presented in his later works (1973, 1978c), consistent with the subjectivist understanding of human knowledge that underpins his economics? Some scholars argue that Hayek attempts to use the subjectivist insights derived from his economic theory to construct a broader defense of a liberal political order (see Boettke, 1995; Horwitz, 2000; Vaughn, 1998). However, the question arises whether his legal theory can be reconciled with his subjectivist emphasis on the limits of objective knowledge and human reason, because a considerable body of legal theory written from a broadly conceived subjectivist perspective, in particular legal realism, challenges the foundations of the rule of law and the notion of legal neutrality that Hayek makes so central to his liberalism. In this chapter, I adopt the perspective of the legal realists to point out some shortcomings of the argument that the subjectivist foundations of Hayek's economics can be successfully employed to support classical liberal political economy.

There are two reasons to investigate Hayek's legal theory and its relationship to his subjectivism. First, he suggests that markets cannot be defined independently of legal institutions because they determine what contracts are enforceable and how property may be used. Law is an important determinant of the legitimate domain of market relationships and the legitimate content of market exchanges, so that for Hayek the law determines whether the market works "beneficially" and "effectively" (Hayek, 1960, p. 229).[1] He claims that a common law process produces a neutral and apolitical method to determine the rules that constitute a beneficial and effective economic order, or the common good. However, a subjectivist perspective in legal theory might dispute this theory of the common good. Second, based upon the claim that a common law process, guided by the rule of law, can determine beneficial and effective rules for a market order, Hayek restricts the role of democratic policy-making. He fears that democratic majorities may threaten to usurp private property rights and erode the freedom of contract, thereby opening the door to totalitarian government. Hayek thus limits the legitimate role of democratic public policy in determining the rules and shaping the outcomes of the economic process by insisting that policies adhere to the rule of law and respect the wisdom of evolved, apolitical common law rules. But perhaps a subjectivist approach to social theory might give a larger role to democracy than Hayek is willing to grant.

For Hayek, the subjectivism of knowledge means that there is no necessary isomorphism between the objective world and human perception and knowledge of that world. His work in psychology (1952, 1967a, 1978a) attests that perception and knowledge are socially constituted. Perception depends upon the mental patterns that create and order meaningful experience. These patterns are constructed through experience, the acquisition of language, and the adoption of particular theories. I have argued elsewhere that Hayek's understanding of subjective knowledge is compatible with the postmodern assertion that all knowledge is discursive, by which I mean that human knowledge and meaning are irreducibly dependent on the languages, theories, and practices – all of which constitute discourse – adopted by diverse individuals (Burczak, 1994; see also Madison, 1989). The test of this individual and discursively constituted, or subjective, knowledge is not whether it somehow "mirrors" reality but whether a community agrees that this knowledge is useful.[2] By rejecting the mirroring nature of subjective knowledge, I am asserting that language, theory, and interpersonal communication are important constituents of our understanding of the world. A subjectivism that accepts the irreducibly discursive nature of knowledge is connected to a psychology that recognizes the creative and socially constituted nature of the human mind.[3]

One of the tenets of Hayek's legal theory, however, is that common law judges can *discover* neutral, universally applicable rules to adjudicate economic conflicts. This chapter contests Hayek's claim by tapping the subjectivist insights of the legal realists Jerome Frank (1970, 1973) and Karl Llewellyn (1960). A rigorous subjectivism, according to the legal realists, suggests that the judicial process is *creative*, and the possibility that law is created rather than discovered threatens Hayek's defense of the rule of law. As a result, to maintain a defense of the rule of law and legal neutrality, Hayek attenuates his subjectivism in his jurisprudence. He does this by resting his theory of the rule of law and the neutrality of the common law on judges who are able to obtain objective knowledge of legal facts and rules. A consistently subjectivist legal theory rejects this possibility and the corresponding belief that a common law process regulated by the rule of law establishes an objective, apolitical procedure to determine a neutral set of rules regulating market relationships, which might be thought to constitute the common good. This chapter argues that a subjectivist theory of knowledge calls into question Hayek's defense of the rule of law and his use of it to insulate the economy from activist public policy and a democratic determination of social welfare.

The chapter has four main sections. The first section discusses the character of Hayek's subjectivism and its connection to a view of the market as a creative process. The next section establishes the importance of the rule of law in his liberal political economy and describes the evolutionary character of his legal thought. It presents his explanation of the neutrality of the rule of law as the spontaneous result of a common law discovery process. The following section discusses the work of the legal realists Frank and Llewellyn, who highlighted the subjectivity of legal rules and facts and who emphasized the creativity of the judicial process, against Hayek's legal theory. Legal realism disputes Hayek's position that common law judges can discover objective, neutral rules, thereby undermining his defense of the rule of law. The final section concludes by exploring some of the implications of conceiving the legal process as irreducibly creative. If the legal process is a site of political debate and theoretical conflict over the definition of an effective and beneficial economic order, a common law system loses the privilege Hayek grants it relative to democracy, since the common law no longer can be understood as a neutral, disinterested process.

## The market as a creative process

Hayek is best known for his explanation of how a market economy coordinates the actions of diverse and dispersed individuals, who act according to their potentially unique perceptions of economic opportunity. The lure of profit activates producers to offer commodities for sale that are manufactured as efficiently as the producers conceive to be possible. If producers are able to sell these commodities successfully, they will earn an income that will allow them in their role as consumers to sample the commodities offered by others. While the consumers may not know precisely what they desire when they go to market, markets afford the opportunity to explore consumption possibilities and experiments in living that may both assist in and constitute the individual's quest for a good life. Production and consumption activity in a market economy are thus at its root "a voyage of exploration into the unknown, an attempt to discover new ways of doing things better than they have been done before" (Hayek, 1948, p. 101).

As has been noticed many times before, Hayek's market process does not facilitate the maximization of pregiven preferences (Hayek, 1967b), nor does it enable the movement to an objectively definable production possibilities frontier (Hayek, 1978b, p. 186). In the market process, sellers test their hypotheses about what things consumers may wish to purchase and how these things might be provided at low cost. These hypotheses are not based on objective, universally accessible knowledge but upon the individual seller's particular knowledge that may be partly articulate and partly tacit and that is contingent upon the seller's unique spatial and temporal location. If the sellers are able to persuade potential buyers that their wares are attractive at the asking price, then the sellers' hypotheses will yield a profit. If not, the seller will be forced to test a new hypothesis. The incentive of monetary profit and the hazard of monetary loss that exist in a market economy work to create an agreement among sellers of productive factors, producers, and consumers about which goods are scarce, what technologies might be appropriate, and which goods are pleasing (Burczak, 1994, pp. 47–50; Hayek, 1948, p. 106). The market process does not uncover knowledge of objectively existing production possibilities and pre-existing consumer preferences but creates an evolving intersubjective agreement about efficient methods to produce ever-changing desirable goods.

Hayek's vision of a market economy is similar to James Buchanan and Viktor Vanberg's (1991) understanding of the market as a non-teleological, creative process that they associate with the radical subjectivist perspective in economics. For radical subjectivists like G.L.S. Shackle and Ludwig Lachmann economic action is oriented toward an unknowable future that is itself dependent upon the decisions individuals make in the present. From this perspective, market economies are open-ended, evolving processes that are constituted by creative individual choice. Picturing the market as a creative process means that an omniscient observer, if one might be conceived to exist, would be unable to see all the economic opportunities that are possible, because those opportunities only exist after individual producers and consumers decide upon a course of action. Buchanan and Vanberg contrast this understanding of the market as a creative process with those who depict the market as a *discovery* process in which economic agents ferret out opportunities that an omniscient observer would know to exist. In the depiction of the market as a discovery process, market competition does not *create* an agreement about pleasing goods and effective technologies, it *uncovers* a reality that is already, in some sense, "out there." Despite some arguments to the contrary (e.g. Kirzner, 1979), this sort of discovery process view of market competition is not altogether compatible with Hayek's theories of knowledge and mind.[4]

If we understand the market economy as a creative process, then Buchanan and Vanberg (1991, p. 181) insist that we must recognize that the market, in the aggregate:

> neither maximizes nor minimizes anything. It simply allows participants to pursue that which they value, subject to the preferences and endowments of others, and within the constraints of general "rules of the game" that allow, and provide incentives for, individuals to try out new ways of doing things. There simply is no "external," independently defined objective against which the results of market processes can be evaluated.

In effect, Buchanan and Vanberg claim that a radically subjectivist perspective precludes any notion of the "common good" or any way to determine whether the market process serves the public interest in any sense other than that it enables those successful at earning an income the opportunity to explore consumption possibilities.

Hayek took a similar position. In *The Road to Serfdom* he defined the common good to be "limited to the fields where people agree on common ends." He suspected that "people are most likely to agree on common action where the common end is not an ultimate end to them but a means capable of serving a great variety of purposes" (1944, p. 60). In other words, in a modern economy with complex relationships among diverse and scattered individuals, people would only agree to respect the coercive power of government inasmuch as it was limited to enforcing agreed upon rules. But what would be the source and nature of these rules? Hayek believed the common law offered the appropriate arena in which to settle questions about the effectiveness and benefit of the market. He reached this conclusion because he understood the common law process to be a spontaneous order that articulated rules that people already implicitly accepted and because the common law generally satisfied the requirements of the rule of law.

## Hayek and the rule of law

For Hayek, the rules determining whether the market works effectively and beneficially – his notion of the common good – must be consistent with the rule of law. In his view, the rule of law is a device to limit government's ability to exercise its apparent monopoly on coercion. It is a meta-legal doctrine that should, in a free society, constrain the content of particular laws and, hence, the government's authority to enforce rules of conduct. The consistency of a particular law with the rule of law determines whether the government's authority to enforce rules is warranted, legitimate, and compatible with individual freedom, or whether the government's use of force is arbitrary, illegitimate, and a violation of individual freedom.

Hayek defines the rule of law as the restriction of government action to enforcing and legislating rules that are general, universally applicable, and well-announced (1960, pp. 205–10). By "general" Hayek means that law should take the form of long-term rules that will apply to unknown future cases. By "universally applicable" he means that everyone should be equal under the law, that the law cannot apply only to particular classes of people, and that the ruler as well as the ruled be subject to the same laws. Finally, law must be well-announced, or known and certain, so that individuals can predict the decisions of courts. Perhaps this is the most important attribute of the rule of law for Hayek, because the predictability of law enables individuals to have a good sense of the range of acceptable behavior. Legal certainty allows people to form expectations about how others will be permitted to act, and these expectations are essential to guide individual action in a manner consistent with social coordination.

Because the rule of law does not itself specify the content of any particular law, and because his subjectivism leads him to avoid locating the source of law in human reason, Hayek needs a theory of the determination of the content of specific laws that does not rely upon rational construction. He accomplishes this by pointing to the common law as a set of evolved rules that ordinarily satisfy the requirements of generality, universality, and certainty. Although he acknowledges that isolated rules can be created, the entire legal framework governing a market order cannot be viewed as the product of design because human reason does not have the capacity to foresee the unintended consequences of the imposition of a particular legal structure. Instead, a system of rules is discovered through a process of trial and error in which rules that are conducive to social order survive precisely because they help coordinate the actions and expectations of dispersed individuals. "Society," Hayek (1973, p. 44) writes, "can ... exist only if by a process of selection rules have evolved which lead individuals to behave in a manner which makes social life possible." Moreover, he maintains that in case law systems like the British common law, legal "development proceeded through a process of law-finding in which judges and jurists endeavored to articulate the rules which had already for long periods governed action and the 'sense of justice'" (Hayek, 1978c, pp. 78–9).

By the sense of justice Hayek refers to the "capacity to act in accordance with non-articulated rules" that are commonly accepted because they have proved useful in avoiding and adjudicating conflict (ibid., p. 81). When common law judges produce a legal decision, in general they merely are verbalizing those customary, previously inarticulate rules governing people's expectations of others' actions. For Hayek, the common law is at root an articulation of custom, of the pre-existing sense of justice. The judicial process is primarily a discovery process in which judges bring to light a previously inarticulate rule or a previous legal decision, itself based on custom that should have guided the conduct of the disputing parties. Common law judges discover precedents, either in past legal decisions or in commonly accepted behavior, that they apply to the case at hand. In this way, Hayek contends, social order is not so much a product of law as law is derived from the orderly, evolved interactions among individuals.

Hayek proposes not only that the content of the common law is rooted in custom, he also advances the provocative notion that the idea of the rule of law evolved through the common law process. He describes the rule of law as an evolved principle that emerged spontaneously in the attempt of common law judges to frame their legal opinions to be consistent with past rulings. In any particular case, a judge's decision is constrained by the existence of previously articulated rules, i.e. by precedent, and by the inarticulate sense of justice prevailing in society in order for that decision to be accepted by the disputing parties. The common law doctrine of precedent requires that new decisions be compatible with past decisions, so that judges do not have the discretion to decide cases according to their personal prejudices or values. "[I]t is part of the technique of the common law judge that from the precedents which guide him he must be able to derive rules of universal significance which can be applied to new cases" (Hayek, 1973, p. 86). The judge's task is to apply these general principles to the particular case at hand in order to reach a decision consistent with previously rendered judicial opinions, thereby giving the judge's ruling credibility. Hayek believes that "as a necessary consequence of case law procedure, law based on precedent must consist exclusively of end-independent abstract rules of conduct of universal intent which the judge and juries attempt to distil from earlier decisions" (1978c, p. 79). The doctrine of precedent thus ensures that the common law will display characteristics associated with the rule of law.

Hayek's common law judges are thus not creators of law. They merely *find* rules that are compatible with the existing common laws, that have themselves survived due to their superiority at coordinating human action. Adherence to common law precedent therefore enables judges to be neutral, objective referees. In addition, when judges follow precedent, their decisions are more likely to be accepted because these decisions are based upon past cases and conventional behavior that people accept as guides to action. Because Hayek supposes that precedent limits the creative power of judges, individuals are able to make rough predictions about what kind of action judges will find acceptable and unacceptable. The ability to make these rough predictions allows people to plan a course of action with some degree of confidence that the government will not interfere.

Hayek elevates the common law over democratic rule-making because evolved common laws generally conform to the requirements of the rule of law, while democratic rule-making has "no such built-in limitation" (Hayek, 1978c, p. 79). Democratic policy-making may well be inconsistent with the rule of law, and this inconsistency opens the door to what Hayek views as an illegitimate use of government coercion that will reduce individual freedom and result in the failure of all potentially coordinating, entrepreneurial activities to be undertaken.

Hayek does, however, admit there are occasions when the common law happens to develop in "very undesirable directions" (1973, p. 88). In such exceptional cases, corrective legislation may be necessary. He offers two general examples that might call for such legislation. First, economic transformation may occur more rapidly than the gradual evolution of the common law can accommodate. He supposes that because case law must always maintain consistency with precedent, by its very nature it changes slowly. Advanced market economies, on the other hand, can develop considerably more rapidly, so that social change may often outpace legal change. Second, he acknowledges that at times "the law has lain in the hands of members of a particular class whose traditional views made them regard as just what could not meet the more general requirements of justice" (ibid., p. 89). For example, he mentions the laws regulating interactions between masters and servants and between organized business and consumers as cases in which the law served the interests of a particular group rather than the more general interests of society. But to avoid deleterious consequences, corrective legislation must be consistent with the rule of law and be constrained by the prevailing sense of justice and custom embedded in the common law.

An important conclusion Hayek draws from his legal theory is that the rule of law precludes government action to obtain equality of opportunity, social justice, or any other substantive, results-oriented notion of the common good. If people conceive justice or the common good to depend upon "good" results, that would likely promote government action to achieve those results. But like Buchanan and Vanberg, Hayek believes that a good result cannot be objectively defined. The judgment of a good result is subjective, so that policy which aims at particular outcomes can only express the values of the people who make this policy, rather than some supposed common interest. Moreover, for a law or policy to be general and universally applicable, it cannot strive for a specific outcome, since such a policy must usually treat people differently. In Hayek's mind, this would constitute an arbitrary policy, since it directs the actions of some people according to the interests of others, rather than according to a general rule. Laws which abide by the rule of law, on the other hand, establish a neutral framework to guide and constrain government action, thereby preventing arbitrary coercion. For Hayek, a common law system guided by the rule of law provides a framework to ensure that the market works as beneficially and effectively as possible, which he defines as successful coordination that functions to the advantage of no person or group.

## Legal realism and the law as a creative process

Hayek reaches his conclusion about the possibility of obtaining neutral law through an evolved, common law process by casting judges as decidedly uncreative beings. He describes judges as "unwitting tools" whose decisions are limited and determined by the set of already existing rules (Hayek, 1973, p. 66). This conclusion seems odd considering that in his work in psychology he notes that a limited set of rules may be combined to produce an infinite array of actions.[5] Nevertheless, he supposes judges to be limited to making mechanical choices, and he regards this to be the essence of legal objectivity and neutrality: "it is because the judge who applies [rules] has no choice in drawing the conclusions that follow from the existing body of rules and the particular facts of the case, that it can be said that laws and not men rule" (Hayek, 1960, p. 153). Hayek's judges cannot decide cases based upon their sympathies and prejudices or upon the potential consequences of a particular decision, insofar as such consequence-oriented decisions might not cohere with past cases.

At first glance it might appear that judges must have either rational or empirical access to objective truth – legal facts and rules – in order to reach the neutral decisions Hayek suggests judges are able to pronounce. But, rather than viewing judges as rational fact- and rule-finders who are able to deduce the correct decisions based upon knowledge of these facts and rules, he describes judges as endowed with a special intuitive capacity, acquired through years on the bench, which enables them to reach the correct decisions:

> That the judge can, or ought to, arrive at his decisions exclusively by a process of logical inference from explicit premises always has been and must be a fiction. For in fact the judge never proceeds in this way.
>
> (Hayek, 1973, pp. 116–17)

Here Hayek approvingly quotes Roscoe Pound to describe his understanding of judicial reasoning: "the trained intuition of the judge continuously leads him to right results for which he is puzzled to give unimpeachable legal reasons" (ibid., p. 117). For Hayek, a judge tests hypotheses "at which he has arrived by processes only in part conscious" in order to arrive at a judgment (ibid., p. 120). He assures his readers that despite this intuitive reasoning process, judges are not usually swayed by their emotions and prejudices and generally discover the objectively correct, neutral result.

The conclusion that judges can discover neutral rules may not, however, be entirely compatible with a subjectivist approach to legal theory. The legal realists produced a body of literature broadly consistent with Hayek's subjectivism that challenged the traditional claims about the neutrality and predictability of law and of the ability of judges to pronounce objective, apolitical decisions. Most notably, the work of Frank (1970, 1973) and Llewellyn (1960) is especially corrosive of Hayek's account of the judicial process. Frank emphasized that judges did not have access to the objective facts of a case and thus had to rely on subjective "hunches" to determine the circumstances of a case. Llewellyn highlighted the indeterminacy of rules. He argued that the common view of precedent which pictured judges to be bound by previous decisions did not accurately convey the nature of judicial reasoning. Judges, according to Llewellyn, could easily discard previous rulings if they could show that the circumstances of the present case were different from past cases.

Frank used his analysis of the subjectivity of legal facts and Llewellyn used his discussion of the subjectivity of rules to argue that the judicial process was *creative* and not merely a matter of discovery, as Hayek argued. As a consequence, both maintained that legal decisions were less predictable than Hayek thought was possible, and their analyses of the legal process suggested the law was far less a neutral set of general, universal rules of just conduct than an instrument of public policy. Another implication of legal realism was that what Hayek viewed as exceptional – the development of law in directions beneficial to the interests of a particular group rather than to the interests of all – might be an ineradicable feature of the legal system. Legal realism suggested that the evolution of law is not as disinterested and idyllic as Hayek described.

### The subjectivity of facts

Frank drew attention to the inability of judges to obtain objective knowledge of the facts relevant to cases on which they had to pass judgment. Frank pointed out two reasons why objective facts were inaccessible. First, courts had to rely on the often-competing testimonies of antagonistic witnesses. And these testimonies are grounded in the irreducibly subjective perceptions of these witnesses. Second, courts must make subjective judgments about what portions of whose testimony will count as legally recognized fact. Frank wrote:

> The facts as they actually happened are therefore twice refracted – first by witnesses, and second by those who must first "find" the facts. The reactions of trial judges or juries to the testimony are shot through with subjectivity. Thus we have subjectivity piled on subjectivity. It is surely proper, then, to say that the facts as "found" by a trial court are subjective.
>
> (1973, p. 22)

The subjectivity of facts implies that a "trial court's facts are not 'data,' not something that is 'given'; they are not waiting somewhere, ready made, for the court to discover, to 'find'" (ibid., p. 23). Faced with the subjectivity of facts, Frank, like Hayek, believed that judges often relied on intuition and hunches to reach their decisions. Frank differed from Hayek, however, in that he made no presumption that judges' hunches were "correct." That is, he did not treat hunching as somehow reflective of some objective truth. Hunching was a creative activity rather than revelatory of an underlying reality. Rather than viewing legal facts as discovered, he considered it to be more appropriate to regard them as created through the legal process.

The most important conclusion Frank drew from the subjectivity of legal facts is that law is indeterminate and unpredictable. Since no one could know what the court would find as the facts of the case, there was no way to tell what or how existing rules would apply to the case. The law relevant to a particular case could not, then, be known until the court actually reached a decision. As a result, it was a "myth or illusion ... that law can be entirely predictable" (Frank, 1970, p. 37). Frank did not share Hayek's view that the unpredictability of judicial decisions would impede human action, however. He argued that the unpredictability of law did not present a serious obstacle to human action "since most men act without regard to the legal consequences of their conduct, and, therefore, do not act in reliance upon any given pre-existing law" (ibid., pp. 38–9). Unlike Hayek, Frank held that there was a gap between custom and law, which made it possible for people to act according to customary behavior and then to find this behavior deemed illegitimate by a law court. Frank's main point was that habits and customs, not law, guided human action, so that the unpredictability of judicial decisions did not prevent people from planning a course of action.

### The subjectivity of rules

Whereas Frank illustrated the indeterminacy and unpredictability of law by emphasizing the subjectivity of legal facts, Llewellyn demonstrated the indeterminacy and unpredictability of law by emphasizing the subjectivity of legal rules. Llewellyn challenged the common understanding that the doctrine of precedent bound judicial rulings to the decisions of past courts. He pointed out that precedent was "Janus-faced." By describing precedent as Janus-faced, he intended to bring to light the two, opposing approaches judges could adopt toward previous judicial opinions. Because judges had a choice about how to handle past cases, precedent became an instrument in the hands of skillful judges, not a bridle leading them toward a preordained result.

Llewellyn labeled the two approaches to precedent the "strict view" and the "loose view." The "loose view" of precedent is the one most commonly understood when judges say precedent determined their decision. "That is the view that a court has decided, and decided authoritatively, *any* point or all points on which it chose to rest a case" (Llewellyn, 1960, pp. 67–8). Having decided authoritatively, the court's decision becomes the standard for all future cases. To make use of the loose view of precedent is to use past decisions as the guide by which present decisions are reached. In the loose view of precedent, judges take the facts of the case before them to be similar to the facts of previous cases, so that if a similar case has been decided in a certain way in the past, so it should be decided in the present.

When judges exercise a strict view of precedent, they argue that previous judicial decisions do not apply to the case before them because the facts of the present case are different in some significant way, which invalidates the application of rules established in the past in seemingly similar cases. Previous decisions, in other words, do not automatically apply to the current case because those decisions might be deemed as relevant only to the unique constellation of facts surrounding those cases. Thus, the strict view of precedent "is in practice the dogma which is applied to *unwelcome* precedents. It is the recognized, legitimate, honorable technique for whittling precedents away, for making the lawyer, in his argument, and the court, in its decision, free of them" (ibid., p. 67). The notion that precedent binds the decisions of judges is not, in Llewellyn's view, a realistic description of the judicial process, since judges have a choice whether they would accept precedents as guides, or to reject them as irrelevant. As a result, Llewellyn concludes, like Frank, that it is difficult to predict the decisions of courts based upon knowledge of rules alone, because how judges will interpret the applicability of those rules is indeterminate.

Despite the inability to predict a court's decision based upon knowledge of rules, despite the creative potential of the judicial process, Llewellyn did not think it was impossible to form reliable guesses about the possible outcomes of a case. Lawyers who were familiar with the personalities of particular judges and with the kind of arguments these judges generally found persuasive would stand a better chance of winning a trial than lawyers who had little basis upon which to develop this knowledge. Lawyers were thus like Hayek's economic actors: they had subjective knowledge of time and place – specifically, the knowledge of judicial temperaments – which enabled them to present cases more likely to prove persuasive to particular judges and, hence, ultimately successful. Nevertheless, Llewellyn made it quite clear that those "who think that precedent produces or ever did produce a certainty that did not involve matters of judgment and of persuasion ... simply do not know our system of precedent in which we live" (ibid., p. 69). The subjectivity of rules further undermines Hayek's position that a common law system guided by precedent composed a method through which judges simply administered law rather than actively created it.[6]

### The implications of fact and rule subjectivity

Both Frank and Llewellyn agreed that the law relevant to a case did not precede the judge's decision. Judges continually created law. A legal system governed by the rule of law which promised that law, rather than men, ruled over people was inoperable in a world in which human actors – lawyers, judges, and juries – applied rules and determined facts based upon their subjective interpretations of events and of the applicability of rules. There is no reason to believe judicial decisions must reflect the customs regulating behavior or an inarticulate sense of justice, as Hayek proposed. A common law system then may not necessarily fulfill the requirements of objectivity and neutrality Hayek believes the rule of law ensures. Law may always be the instrument of particular interests. The facts and rules which judges "find" to be relevant are filtered and shaped by their values, theories, and preconceptions, so that their decisions will, in part, be expressions of those values, theories and preconceptions. For the realists, common law decisions cannot be disinterested pronouncements of some objective interest made by judges who cloak their subjectivity behind the robes of justice.[7]

A subjectivist legal theory informed by legal realism thus challenges the atheoretical, evolutionary claims Hayek makes about the common law. As we have seen, he understands the common law to have progressed through a process of trial and error, so that the laws establishing the assignment of contested property rights and the enforceability of contracts are those which have survived a long evolutionary process directed by no one. Significantly, he depicts the common law as operating independently from theoretical influence to reach a neutral, apolitical resolution of what rules determine whether the market works beneficially and effectively. But we might also question Hayek's claims about the neutral evolution of the common law by noting that judicial decisions are constituted, in part, by the theories of justice judges implicitly hold. Since we have seen that judges are not "bound" by precedent and can generally choose whether or not past cases are relevant to the case before them, the theoretical perspectives adopted by judges play a critical role in shaping their decisions. Legal judgment, then, is always theory-laden, which implies that the common law is partly the creation of particular philosophic assumptions and notions of justice.[8]

The realist account of the legal process raises an important question, a question Hayek would likely ask of it: If it is the case that law is as unpredictable as Frank and Llewellyn describe, and if law is often used as an instrument of social change, change that is difficult to portray as in the common interest, why do so many people, judges and citizens alike, accept law as a stable, authoritative system of rules? Why, for instance, do judges insist on describing their task as the discovery of consistent rules, as a task bound by precedent? Hayek doubts that accounts of legal change as instrumental could be accurate because people would not tolerate the aggressive and interested uses of law to promote social change. For Hayek, the legitimacy of law flows from its internal consistency and its consistency with custom, requirements which he believes the common law generally fulfills. He claims people's allegiance to law depends on whether the law satisfies certain expectations concerning the general, consistent, purpose-independent character of rules, allegiance which will vanish when these expectations are disappointed (Hayek, 1973, p. 92). From his perspective, it would be difficult to reconcile the widely perceived consistency of law with judicial creativity, particularly creativity expressed in the interests of specific interests.

Edward Levi (1964) answers the question of why law is generally perceived as stable and consistent by observing that the law is a "moving classification system." By describing law as a moving classification system, Levi draws attention to the possibility that the legal system is able to retain the appearance of consistency even while new laws are continually being created. This is because legal texts are filled with ambiguous rules and malleable language which can be mined and interpreted in support of a variety of judicial decisions. Judges are able to describe themselves as merely discovering and applying already existing law, rather than actively creating policy, since legal texts are open to multiple and creative interpretations. Levi (1964, p. 272) writes:

> movement in the [legal] system frequently will not be apparent. When it is apparent, it is often justified obliquely on the basis that this policy step was taken some time ago and is reflected in prior decisions. The system permits a foreshadowing of results and therefore has built into it the likelihood of a period of preparation so that future decisions appear as a belated finding and not a making of law. The joint exploration through competing examples to fill the ambiguities of one or many propositions has the advantage of permitting the use in the system of propositions or concepts saved from being contradictory because they are ambiguous, and on this account more acceptable as ideals or commonplace truths.

In Levi's view, the perceived consistency of law is partly a function of the persuasive efforts of judges, who exploit the polysemy of legal texts to underpin the decisions they reach, and partly a function of the theoretical perspective adopted by observers of the legal system. However, Levi's characterization of law as a moving classification system implies that the legal system could as easily be perceived as inconsistent as it is perceived to be consistent.

## Democracy and the creation of the common good

The crux of Hayek's argument against democratic policy is that it often attempts to obtain interested goals, for instance distributive justice. To accept goal-oriented policy-making as legitimate, he insists, poses a grave threat to individual freedom, because it opens the door to the use of government power to direct or limit the actions of specific individuals in order to achieve these goals. If, however, government power is restricted to ensuring that all people obey the same set of abstract, universal rules rather than used to achieve particular goals, Hayek maintains that individual freedom is protected. The common law achieves this goal, because Hayek believes it generally evolves into a system of mutually consistent, universal rules which aim at no particular result and are equally applicable to all. A legal system regulated by the rule of law ensures that law, rather than a group of people, rules equally over all.

But Hayek's legal thought is not consistently subjectivist. While he acknowledges that the people controlling the government may well use government power in the effort to achieve their subjective goals, he does not recognize that common law judges may also act according to their subjective, theory-laden perceptions of just outcomes. Hayek does not recognize this because he imagines judges are somehow able to *discover* correct, commonly accepted rules appropriate to the objective facts of the case. A subjectivist account of the judicial process inspired by legal realism emphasizes the subjectivity of rules, facts, and even the perception of consistency in the law itself, and pictures the judicial process as irreducibly *creative*. To understand the judicial process as creative, partly, if not completely, erodes the barrier Hayek places between democratic, and sometimes interested, policy-making and the supposedly disinterested, evolved common law. From a subjectivist perspective, common law rules may well be as interested as Hayek thinks democratic policy-making is prone to be.

Others reach a similar conclusion. Hasnas (1995a) calls the rule of law a potentially dangerous myth. He accepts the realist critique of legal neutrality and worries that widespread belief in the rule of law leads to the public's acceptance of illegitimate uses of state power. Christainsen (1990) agrees that judges in government courts cannot know all the circumstances of time and place that would be necessary to pronounce objective decisions. Because "common law judges are decision-makers of enterprises – government courts – for which rights are not transferable, and sometimes not even defined," Christainsen (p. 503) maintains that "they are in the position of central economic planners." As such, there is no discovery process in a common law court system to ensure "efficient" judicial decisions (ibid.). Both Hasnas and Christainsen believe the solution to the potentially inefficient and biased nature of a common law system can be solved if we end the state monopoly over the provision of legal decisions and allow the development of a private court system with competing providers of adjudication services.

Private adjudication may have its merits in some cases, but I am unpersuaded that private courts provide the best forum to determine the constitution of the common good. While extensive comment on the nature and benefits of a private court system would require another paper, it is readily apparent that wealth can influence the outcomes of government court trials, even when some minimal efforts are made to provide legal representation for the poor. In a setting where adjudication is exclusively marketed, it would not be surprising to see an even greater correlation between wealth and the interests served by the decisions of private courts. Arthur Okun (1975) calls the threats that wealth and income pose to substantive equality before the law "the transgression of dollars on rights," a transgression that Okun believes might be checked by limiting the domain of the market, rather than expanding it, and invigorating the democratic sphere of social life.

The main point is that if law courts are as political as legal realism suggests, Hayek's defense of a common law system as a neutral method to discover the sense of justice and the rules that constitute the common good is called into question. Perhaps the chief difficulty with Hayek's legal theory is that a singular sense of justice, or the common good, like economic opportunity and true knowledge, is not "out there" waiting to be found. Perhaps the common good needs to be created. As several critics of Hayek have argued, democratic government provides a framework where the nature of the common good might be debated and forged.

Unfortunately, finding a compelling defense of democracy in Hayek's thought is difficult. As Juliet Williams (1997, p. 108) points out, "the real problem for Hayek is not that his commitment to liberalism conflicts with his desire to limit democracy, but rather that his version of central liberal principles does not entail democracy in the first place." Hayek tends to emphasize the problems with democracy rather than recognizing that perhaps democratic institutions have evolved to help negotiate an agreement about the nature of the common good in a world in which knowledge is limited and subjective.

Gus diZerega's work on democracy as a spontaneous order is instructive in this regard. DiZerega follows Hayek in claiming that spontaneous orders "are rooted in the principle of voluntary consent." But as diZerega (1989, p. 206) argues in contrast to Hayek, democratic institutions aim to create "consent over community values and practices." Democracy involves a set of non-instrumental procedures – one person–one vote, free speech and other rights of citizenship, separation of powers, etc. – that establish a framework permitting a collective conversation about the nature of the common good, an ideal type that would exist "if citizens were to come to a free and uncoerced agreement about public policy" (ibid., p. 225).[9]

Some might argue that the real world outcomes of democratic politics are dramatic departures from any ideal type notion of the common good.[10] For instance, in *The Political Order of a Free People*, Hayek tags "the so-called approval by the majority of a conglomerate of measures serving particular interests" that he believes characterizes modern democracy as a "farce" (Hayek, 1979, p. 134). Yet earlier in the same book, he explains that it is legitimate for government to use coercion to supply collective goods, even if those goods are not demanded by a "considerable majority." From his perspective,

> it will clearly be in the interest of the different individuals to agree that the compulsory levying of means to be used also for purposes for which they do not care so long as others are similarly made to contribute to ends which they desire but the others do not. Though this looks as if the individuals were made to serve purposes for which they do not care, a truer way of looking at it is to regard it as a sort of exchange: each agreeing to contribute to a common pool according to the same uniform principles on the understanding that his wishes with regard to the services to be financed from that pool will be satisfied in proportion to his contributions.
>
> (ibid., p. 45)

Yet, since there is no way for Hayek to know how others value collective goods provided by democratic political action, it is not clear why a subjectivist should accept his portrayal of modern democracy as a farce.

Admittedly, real world democracy may be imperfect and messy, but given the contestable nature of questions concerning justice, democracy has an attribute the common law lacks: democratic politics institutes a forum for multiple, competing views of justice to be heard and debated.[11] In his critique of Hayek, Brian Crowley (1987, p. 291) argues that democratic "politics relies on procedures to make possible and to encourage critical analysis in the constant search for agreement on the meaning of the good life and how it is to be pursued." If we accept the subjectivist position that all facts, interpretations, and judgments are theory dependent and socially constituted, the evaluation of what is an effective and beneficial economic order, or what is the common good, is open for discussion. That is, the common good needs to be created.[12] Hayek, though, wishes to silence debate over the natures of justice and the common good by asserting that justice involves little more than the establishment of universal rules through a neutral case law procedure. Rather than following Hayek's failed path (if the legal realists are right), we might better conceive justice to be a goal – not a given – of an ongoing and collective conversation about the meaning of social welfare. In such a world, democratic policy-making is attractive because it often allows the possibility of a plurality of visions of distributive and procedural justice to be inspected. It permits the definition of a beneficial and effective economic order to be created in an open, dialogical process.

## Acknowledgments

Thanks are due to Peter d'Errico for many hours of conversation about the ideas in this chapter and to the Denison University faculty reading group on "Social Theory and the Mind."

## Notes

1  An extract from *The Constitution of Liberty* is instructive: "The decision to rely on voluntary contracts as the main instrument for organizing the relations between individuals does not determine what the specific content of the law of contract ought to be; and the recognition of the right of private property does not determine what exactly should be the content of this right in order that the market mechanism will work as effectively and beneficially as possible" (Hayek, 1960, p. 229).

2  Kuhn (1970) and Rorty (1979) are of course two well-known philosophers who have made this point. But see also Hayek (1967a, p. 54; emphasis added): "So far as the recognition of the particular conditions is concerned to which a theoretical statement is applicable, we always have to rely on *interpersonal agreement*, whether the conditions are defined in terms of sensory qualities such as 'green' or 'bitter,' or in terms of point coincidences, as is the case where we measure."

3  It is clear that Hayek understands the mind to be socially constituted. According to Hayek, "what we call mind is essentially a system of rules conjointly determining particular actions" (Hayek, 1978a, p. 42). These rules are acquired through experience with particular objects, people, languages, and human cultures. Although the mind is a socially constituted system of rules that generates particular actions, the "various combinations of abstract propensities [or rules] ... makes it possible for a causally determined structure of actions to produce ever new actions it has never

produced before" (ibid., p. 48). As Hayek notes, "[e]ven a relatively limited repertory of abstract rules that can thus be combined into particular actions will be capable of 'creating' an almost infinite variety of particular actions" (ibid., p. 49).

4 Not all would accept the claim that Hayek's market process is creative. Littlechild (1986) argues that Hayek suppresses the creative dimension of entrepreneurship and implicitly harbors a notion of entrepreneurs as individuals who are able to penetrate the dark void of time and ignorance in order to discover objective opportunities consistent with economic coordination. See also Burczak (1994, p. 54) for my earlier views on this question.

5 See note 3.

6 We can also challenge Hayek's legal thought by noting how rule and fact subjectivity blur the line between facts and rules. Kim Lane Scheppele (1990) draws on the legal realist literature to argue that the distinction between law and fact is impossible to uphold because interpretation of facts necessarily involves interpretation of law, and vice versa. The radical legal historian Morton Horwitz (1977, pp. 28–9) describes how the emergence of a supposed distinction between law and fact at the turn of the nineteenth century in the United States was due, in part, to the desire of judges to limit the ability of juries to decide the law of a case. Judges wanted to retain the authority to pass judgment on the law relevant to a case, so that they could encourage economic growth through the legal system. The distinction between law and fact limited the power of juries to the determination of legal facts, thereby minimizing a jury's ability to reach decisions hostile to commercial and industrial interests.

7 As an example, Horwitz (1977) describes how American common law judges used their creative ability to recast the common law in the interests of industry and commerce during the first several decades of the nineteenth century. During this period, the US economy shifted from being primarily based on agriculture to become increasingly industrial and commercial. Until 1800, however, the common law generally reflected agrarian interests. Horwitz describes how judges came to identify with the industrial and merchant classes and began to decide cases in order to promote industrialization and economic growth. According to Horwitz, judges consciously manipulated the common law to be more supportive of the emerging commercial order rather than the old agricultural order. Horwitz (1977, p. 255) writes: "The basic system of tort and property law ... was judicially created. And, by and large, it was strongly geared to the aspirations of those who benefited most from low cost economic development." We do not necessarily have to endorse all the details of Horwitz's legal theory to recognize that the legal system can in fact serve particular interests.

8 James Gordley illustrates how theories of justice have shaped the development and structure of modern law. His work thus disputes Hayek's claims about the apolitical, atheoretical evolution of the common law and that theories of justice (i.e. the rule of law) are derived from the practice of common law jurists. Gordley finds that modern contract law was not produced by a slow process of trial and error in the English common law, as Hayek supposes, but rather owes its origins to the attempts of the sixteenth-century Spanish scholastics to integrate Aristotelian and Thomistic notions of justice with Roman legal texts. Gordley (1991, p. 246) notes that some legal theorists, like Hayek, think that:

> The "great elementary conceptions, ownership, possession, contract, tort and the like," seemed to have emerged without benefit of theory from an English legal tradition that stressed the practical and particular. But ... it did not happen that way. The great elementary conceptions of contract law came out of a Greek philosophical tradition grafted on to Roman law by moral philosophers.

The Spanish scholastics sought to establish a consistent doctrinal system for deter-mining whether or not courts should enforce a contract. Gordley shows how the structure of modern contract law is shaped by this endeavor, and he concludes that a court's determination of the validity of any contract, or its rulings more generally, are saturated with theory.

9  See Boettke (1997) for a discussion of Hayek's use of market equilibrium as an ideal type that parallels diZerega's understanding of the common good as an ideal type.

10  Hasnas (1995b, pp. 112–32) believes public choice economists expose real-world polit-ical processes to produce inferior results when compared to real-world markets. Yet Hasnas's conclusion misses the point insofar as the standard one uses to evaluate markets is precisely what the realist critiques of legal neutrality and of a disinterested determination of the common good by the common law calls into question.

11  Of course, the legal process also institutes a forum to air the competing legal argu-ments and perspectives on justice of disputing parties. But the disputants do not attempt to persuade each other of the merits of their views, and the judge has sole authority to decide who presents a better argument. The legal process, in other words, offers a quite constrained arena for competing visions of justice to be articu-lated. See, however, Levi (1964, pp. 280–1) for a more favorable evaluation of courts as a site to debate political and moral issues.

12  In an earlier paper (Burczak, 1996/7), I argued that conversations about justice might be oriented toward determining whether market outcomes effectively meet human needs. Hayek suggests that we might consider the nature of a just society by asking in what kind of society would we like our children to live (1976, pp. 188–9).

## Bibliography

Boettke, P. 1995. "Hayek's *The Road to Serfdom* Revisited: Government Failure in the Argu-ment Against Socialism." *Eastern Economic Journal* 21 (1): 7–26.

—— 1997. "Where Did Economics Go Wrong? Modern Economics as a Flight From Reality." *Critical Review* 11 (1): 11–64.

Buchanan, J. and V. Vanberg. 1991. "The Market as a Creative Process." *Economics and Philosophy* 7: 167–86.

Burczak, T. 1994. "The Postmodern Moments of F.A. Hayek's Economics." *Economics and Philosophy* 10: 31–58.

—— 1996/7. "Socialism after Hayek." *Rethinking Marxism* 9 (3): 1–18.

Christainsen, G. B. 1990. "Law as a Discovery Procedure." *Cato Journal* 9 (3): 497–530.

Crowley, B. L. 1987. *The Self, the Individual, and the Community. Liberalism in the Political Thought of F.A. Hayek and Sidney and Beatrice Webb.* Oxford: Oxford University Press.

diZerega, G. 1989. "Democracy as a Spontaneous Order." *Critical Review* 3 (2): 206–40.

Frank, J. 1970. *Law and the Modern Mind.* Gloucester, MA: Peter Smith.

—— 1973. *Courts on Trial.* Princeton: Princeton University Press.

Gordley, J. 1991. *The Philosophical Origins of Modern Contract Law.* Oxford: Basil Blackwell.

Hasnas, J. 1995a. "The Myth of the Rule of Law." *Wisconsin Law Review.* 199–223.

——1995b. "Back to the Future: From Critical Legal Studies Forward to Legal Realism, or How not to Miss the Point of the Indeterminacy Argument." *Duke Law Journal* 45 (1): 84–132.

Hayek, F. A. 1944. *The Road to Serfdom.* Chicago: University of Chicago Press.

—— 1948. "The Meaning of Competition." In *Individualism and Economic Order.* Chicago: University of Chicago Press.

—— 1952. *The Sensory Order.* Chicago: University of Chicago Press.

—— 1960. *The Constitution of Liberty*. Chicago: University of Chicago Press.

——1967a. "Rules, Perception and Intelligibility." In *Studies in Philosophy, Politics and Economics*. Chicago: University of Chicago Press.

—— 1967b. "The Non Sequitur of the Dependence Effect." In *Studies in Philosophy, Politics and Economics*. Chicago: University of Chicago Press.

—— 1973. *Law, Legislation and Liberty. Vol I. Rules and Order*. Chicago: University of Chicago Press.

—— 1976. *Law, Legislation and Liberty. Vol. II. The Mirage of Social Justice*. Chicago: University of Chicago Press.

—— 1978a. "The Primacy of the Abstract." In *New Studies in Politics, Economics and the History of Ideas*. Chicago: University of Chicago Press.

—— 1978b. "Competition as a Discovery Procedure." In *New Studies in Politics, Economics and the History of Ideas*. Chicago: University of Chicago Press.

—— 1978c. "The Confusion of Language in Political Thought." In *New Studies in Politics, Economics and the History of Ideas*. Chicago: University of Chicago Press.

—— 1979. *Law, Legislation and Liberty. Vol. III. The Political Order of a Free People*. Chicago: University of Chicago Press.

Horwitz, M. 1977. *The Transformation of American Law, 1780–1860*. Cambridge: Harvard University Press.

Horwitz, S. 2000. "From *The Sensory Order* to the Liberal Order: Hayek's Non-rationalist Liberalism." *Review of Austrian Economics* 13 (1): 23–40.

Kirzner, I. 1979. "Hayek, Knowledge, and Market Process." In I. Kirzner, *Perception, Opportunity, and Profit*. Chicago: University of Chicago Press.

Kuhn, T. 1970. *The Structure of Scientific Revolutions*, 2nd edition. Chicago: University of Chicago Press.

Levi, E. H. 1964. "The Nature of Legal Reasoning." In *Law and Philosophy*, ed. Sidney Hook, 263–81. New York: New York University Press.

Littlechild, S.C. 1986. "Three Types of Market Process." In *Economics as a Process*, ed. Richard Langlois, 27–39. Cambridge: Cambridge University Press.

Llewellyn, K. 1960. *The Bramble Bush*. New York: Oceana Publications.

Madison, G. B. 1989. "Hayek and the Interpretive Turn." *Critical Review* 3 (2): 169–85.

Okun, A. 1975. *Equality and Efficiency. The Big Tradeoff*. Washington, D.C.: Brookings.

Rorty, R. 1979. *Philosophy and the Mirror of Nature*. Princeton: Princeton University Press

Scheppele, K. L. 1990. "Facing Facts in Legal Interpretation." *Representations*, no. 30 (Spring): 42–77.

Vaughn, K. 1998. "Hayek's Implicit Economics: Rules and the Problem of Order." *Review of Austrian Economics* 11 (1–2): 129–44.

Williams, J. 1997. "Hayek, Democracy, and the Rule of Law." *Critical Review* 11 (1): 101–20.

# 12 The norm and the judge in Hayek's liberalism

*Bruno Deffains*

## Introduction

Hayek has traditionally distinguished between law and legislation by under-lining that law came before legislation. Not all the rules within society are of a legal nature but individuals are required to follow the rules because each person makes decisions in situations of limited information and rules change in such a way as to enable society to manage this "state of ignorance". In the long term, the emergence of and the changes in the rules will ensure the survival of society. Hayek comments that a free society will work well only where free action is guided by strongly held beliefs (Hayek, 1973, p. 229). Rules, then, are the product of strong moral beliefs. This is the basis for the statement of rules of conduct enabling the setting up of the legal system. Here Hayek derives his inspiration not only from common law (law created by the judge) but also from the Romano-Germanic tradition (the judge pronounces the law on the basis of the codification of norms). Of course, the development of legal systems is a continuous process "within which each stage produces unpredictable consequences" (Hayek, 1973, p. 34). According to Hayek, the problem is one of producing a system of rules exhibiting an internal coherence capable of managing the different problems with which society is confronted. The role of the legal system thus appears as central to the thinking of Hayek as it is this system which selects the "right rules" and applies them to particular cases.

Hayek is opposed to legal positivism which insists upon the idea of a constructed law as opposed to a natural law:

> judicial positivism holds the essentially anthropomorphic view which considers all rules of justice as the product of an invention or of a deliberate design and even boasts of having finally escaped all influence of this meta-physical conception of natural law, the search for which is the source of all theoretical intelligence on social phenomena. If we were aware that law is never totally the result of a thought, but is judged and tested on the bench of a set of rules invented by no-one ... we would obtain a criterion enabling us, via the progressive elimination of rules which are incompatible with the

rest of the system, to steadily approach absolute justice (perhaps without ever reaching it).

(Hayek in Rueff, 1967, p. 207)

For the positivists, however, law is produced in the sense that it constitutes a set of norms resulting from the activity of "law-makers". Who are these law-makers? At times it is the legislator who produces laws whilst at others it is the judge who takes part in the creation of law by providing legal solutions to the cases for which he is required to make a decision. Judges are therefore among the main sources of law because when courts of law give rulings they create legal solutions which are then expressed in the form of rules. Several interpretations can, however, be made according to whether one considers that the judge restricts himself to applying the solutions of positive law or whether he derives solutions from the legal tradition. In the second instance, law would be the object of continuous change driven by the jurisprudence of the courts. In England or America jurisprudence has long been the major source of law by designating the set of non-codified rules as common law. The courts, of course, are forced to apply the laws (statute laws) but the latter do not theoretically have any other role than that of completing or correcting common law. In this sense, law exists quite independently from all codification and one may truly speak of a primacy of judge-made law (as opposed to judge-said law).[1]

However, it is obvious that, since the middle of the twentieth century, the role of the judge has also been considerably reinforced in countries having a Romano-Germanic tradition. He is now far from remaining at the service of the law on the model of the act of pronouncing law (*juris dictio*). Legal activism appears through the multiplication of the judge's missions, particularly in the field of economics: he administers goods, values them, and manages companies. The idea of a crisis situation in the justice system generally refers to the fact that the increase in the number of tasks has not been matched by an adequate number of judges and that the courtrooms have not been modernized. Enhancing the role of the judge could also be linked with the quantitative explosion of cases in the courts. Justice has become a consumer good but has also produced a qualitative change in the demand for justice. The judge is increasingly required to act as a referee.

Everyone appears to agree then that the function of the judge has undergone profound changes which have repercussions upon the status of the judge, upon the methods he uses, and upon the procedure he follows. To emphasize this we shall quote the distinction drawn by Ost (1985, p. 7) between models of justice which are "liberal-legalist" and "technocratic-normative". These models are based on the classical distinction between the judge-referee, pronouncer of law, and the judge-leader, creator of law. By highlighting the limits of these models, we will bring out the interest of Hayek's approach based on the recognition of a judge-discoverer of law.[2] The object of this note is to present and discuss Hayek's arguments regarding the role of judges in the evolution of social norms. This discussion will enable us to underline the present-day importance of

Hayek's work at a time when the "power of judges" has been brought into question in countries having common law as well as in those having civil law.

## Producing law and the judge's behaviour: referee or leader?

The legalist-liberal model will develop in liberal states that exhibit a separation of powers and the primacy of the legislature. Justice is formal and logical, deduced from general rules and abstract concepts. However, in the technocratic-normative model, power is partly held by possessors of specialized knowledge who define technical norms justified by their efficiency. Justice is, above all, instrumental, progressive, and pragmatic in the sense that it shows the fair solution as being the most adequate in relation to a given objective (i.e. the norm adopted by the social planner).

The economic context plays a decisive role in the presentation of the functions of law. In the liberal-legalist model, the economy is one of free exchange in which the state does not intervene beyond its prerogative as a policeman of human activity. The main function of the judge is one of arbiter of economic and social exchange in the context of a spontaneous and evolving order. In the technocratic-normative model of post-industrial societies, the state goes well beyond this as it has become involved in interventionism, especially in the realm of redistribution (welfare state). This transformation has obviously affected the functions of law as it has become an active instrument for economic and social change. Henceforth it has become "a management technique aimed at the promotion of the optimum social and economic development of society" (Ost, 1985, p. 7). The consequence of these new conditions for the promotion of welfare through law is a considerable increase in the norms of objective law aimed at fixing the restrictive framework for economic and social activities.

One consequently understands that the major source of law has been modified. In the liberal-legalist model, the law, being abstract and general, dominates the legal sphere.[3] The exception lies in contracts whose extreme flexibility is particularly well suited to the development of exchanges. In the technocratic-normative model, the law is always omnipresent but it is increasingly negotiable so as to be applied as a contract whereas the contract itself can fulfil a regulatory function (e.g. in the area of the control of natural monopolies). Such an observation leads us to insist upon the changes affecting the status and the role of the judge.

### The judge as referee

The traditional distinction of the liberal-legalist model is drawn between *lex data* (law which is applied by the judge) and *lex feranda* (law which is created by the legislator). It is this distinction which is responsible for the subordinate position of the judge. He can only express himself via decisional types in an impersonal and bureaucratic manner. So much so that a number of judges can succeed one another until a case has been settled.

The principle of the judge as a pronouncer of law is at the heart of legal positivism. Indeed, he does not recognize any other law than that emerging from the legislator. Hence, jurisprudence is not a source of law. An assimilation is made between the rules and the law.

Positivist authors refer, in the first instance, to the thinking of Montesquieu according to whom the judge has no power. The spirit of the law indeed testifies to a clearly unambiguous approach to the role of the judge: "the judges of the Nation are but the mouth which utters the words of the law, inanimate beings who can neither alter its force nor its rigor". The author logically deduces that "the power of judgement is not an active force, neither would it be a political force, as are legislative and executive power" (Montesquieu, *De l'esprit des lois*, p. XI).

In the twentieth century, the positivist view has been perfectly summarized in the analysis of Kelsen. The legal value of a norm comes from the manner in which it is presented rather than from its contents. The validity of a rule of law depends essentially on the way it conforms to a fundamental legal norm (the Constitution) taken as the standard of legal values. By extension (and in a pyramidal logic), the rule must also conform to the other norms regularly enacted by the authorities and validated with regard to the fundamental norm. Bentham, the founder of utilitarian philosophy, defended a similar approach. He does not justify the law other than by its utility; the law is a technique for maximizing net pleasures: penal law, for example, consists in applying punishments to offenders which are greater than the satisfaction that the latter have derived from their illegal activities.

It must be emphasized that Bentham draws a very clear line between the task of the judge and that of the legislator. The former should not concern himself with the contents of the texts. This is the task of the legislator. The judge is simply there to apply the texts imposed by the state. Two arguments will therefore be used to prevent the judge from having any creative power. First of all, the judge is an organ for the implementation of the will of the legislator, his function being subordinate to the will of a higher power. If, in certain cases, the judge is able to interpret the rule of law, he must always refer to the will of the legislator. Secondly, and by the very nature of the function, the judge cannot be considered as a political power.

According to the positivist doctrine, a rule only qualifies as being law if it is deliberately laid down by the political authorities. This approach is coupled with a specific conception of jurisprudence. Positivists do indeed adhere to an "instrumental view" of the judge. He merely applies the rules of law. Consequently, his task is purely technical. In a certain way, the activity of a judge is programmed by the legislator, each case being classified in a legal catalogue and defined once and for all. This exhaustive catalogue would leave the judge no room to manoeuvre. His only task would be to carry out two rather simple operations: the first is to identify the case submitted to him so as to place it in his repertoire.

Such a task requires no particular skills except perhaps a sound knowledge of positive law. The second is to read and apply the law as it has been planned by "the code". In these conditions it is easier to understand why this view of the judge allows for nothing other than legislative production: if all cases have been foreseen then no change is appropriate.

For the positivists, the judge should limit himself to applying the use of the method of "subsumption of facts". Each fact should be classified under the competence of its corresponding jurisdiction which, following this, will apply the appropriate law. As for method, the judge-referee then applies the general will of the law based upon "a logical and formal method built around chains of syllogisms whose law presents the major element, facts the minor element and judgement the conclusion" (Beccaria, 1764). Certainly, any application of the law supposes an interpretation but the margin for the judge is, in theory, strongly influenced by implicit rules.

### The judge as leader

In the technocratic-normative model, the judge now takes political action in the widest sense of the word. He is no longer necessarily an agent for the conservation of texts of law but becomes the co-author of legal, economic, and social change. The result of this is a need for increasing specialization on the part of the judge, more frequent use of experts, and the development of alternative modes of dispute settlement.

The emergence of the technocratic-normative model in fact marks the passage of the judge-referee to the judge-agitator (or from he who pronounces the law to he who creates the law). The judge-referee was content to apply the general will of the law to particular cases; it was not up to him to advise nor to foresee the consequences of his rulings. The judge-leader, on the other hand, brings about the passage from the *judicature* (judicial function) to the *magistrature* (politico-judicial function). He continues to settle disputes by applying the law, but his intervention can take place before or after the ruling. In other words, his mission is henceforth one of prevention and orientation which is not restricted to the closed field of subjective rights determined by the law. He is responsible for the conservation and the promotion of interests finalized by socio-economic objectives and regulated by the systems of corresponding technical and behavioural norms. This model is largely dominant when, as in the USA, the courts impose real standards of conduct upon economic agents outside any pre-established context.

The formalism of the liberal-legalist model has given rise to numerous reactions amongst which that of the School of Free Law is certainly the most radical. Erhlich, the German jurist, founded the expression of free law at the end of the nineteenth century. The general idea is that of a spontaneous invention of law. He considers the judge to be at the origin of law and not the legislator. Later on, factualist positivism developed in the USA, stimulated by the work of the movement for sociological jurisprudence.[4] Except for Pound, a Harvard professor, the heads of this movement were mainly supreme court judges: Holmes, Brandeis, and Cardozo. Their names remain associated with major decisions in the realm of anti-trust legislation or civil law. Each of them went to great lengths to link law to other social phenomena by highlighting the effects of laws and court rulings upon the economic and social environment. Most of the advocates of this approach pronounce the famous formula of Holmes: "law is nothing more than the forecast of what the judges will in fact decide in the future" (quoted in Villey, 1984, p. 78).

The current of sociological jurisprudence subsequently gave birth to movement of "Law and Economics" directed at the economic evaluation of the legal rules. The general idea is to actually provide the jurist with a method enabling him to give a description of reality (via the evaluation of the consequences of the application of the rules) and to suggest legislative changes in cases where the rule is inadequate when compared to its objectives. Conceived in this way, the "Law and Economics" movement represents the final development of factualist positivism based upon an instrumental and dynamic conception of law.[5] In other words, the judge would be in a position to shape law *ex nihilo* with the aim of reaching certain goals.

At the outset, the economic analysis of law was a movement of economics towards law as it proposed using the tools of economic analysis to study questions relevant to the field of law. To be more precise, it can be defined as the application of the theoretical hypotheses and evaluation criteria of economists for the explanation and appraisal of legal rules. Generally speaking, the rules of law put in place within the framework of the Anglo-Saxon legal system are considered as exogenous rules the effects of which we seek to understand. Reasoning is generally carried out in terms of partial equilibrium in a context of rationality of the agents, these being the judges and those being judged. Therefore, the changes observed in individual behaviour can be attributed to the changes in constraints to which the individuals are submitted via legal norms (Cooter, 1984).

With the publication of Posner's book in 1972, the economics of law became a dominant current of thought in American legal doctrine. Economic reasoning was to be applied to an increasingly varied number of fields: property law, civil liability (contract or criminal), penal sanctions, or indeed alternative dispute resolutions. Henceforth, the economics of law has provided the jurist with a global method destined to provoke thought on the functions of the various legal institutions. However, the problem posed by Posner goes beyond this as he defends the thesis of the economic efficiency of common law. This thesis seeks to have common law explained (but not perfectly) as a system enabling the maximization of the wealth of society, i.e. the judges from Anglo-Saxon courts would make their rulings as if their implicit aim was economic efficiency. But what are these objectives? In which direction does the judge usher the law? The authors are unanimous on this: judges operate so as to maximize social well-being. This well-being is measured in purely quantitative terms as the goal is to "maximize social wealth".

Two particularities are thus present in Posner's approach. First of all, a rule must be able to be violated as soon as its inefficiency has been proven. The judge is not to punish rational behaviour. Secondly, the law should encourage individuals to make efficient decisions. In the case of the law of accidents, the judge will have to evaluate to what extent the individual having caused an accident has taken the economically justified preventive measures (application of the rule of judge Hand). The role of the judge is to "mimic the zero costs transaction" because the question of the search for efficiency via coercion can only be put if the parties are unable to conclude directly (the theorem of Coase). In fact, when the judge-eader takes the place of the judge-referee, considerable adjustments to procedure are to be observed to the extent that the formal respect of procedural rules is no longer satisfactory but there is a quest for efficiency as well as for rapidity and flexibility in the intervention of the judiciary. On both sides of the Atlantic, the best proof is to be seen in the considerable development of alternative types of dispute settlement (arbitration, mediation, conciliation), which are supposed to lighten the load of the courts and minimize the social cost of justice.[6]

Finally, the judge's method is also affected by the change of model. The method of the judge-leader who collaborates on the application of particular policies is instrumental and teleological. The judge solves the dispute of rights or interests by gathering inspiration from economic or social ends. Indeed, it happens that these aims (as well as the rules supporting them) are not clearly defined or that conflicting interests exist so that the intervention of the judge also means defining referents or arbitration (e.g. in the field of biotechnology, genetics, or law of accidents). Certain authors therefore warn against this type of system deviating. Firstly, when the judge is unable to serve as a referee, power will fall into the hands of the technician or engineer. This idea is reflected in the argument developed by Habermas that in advanced capitalist societies, science takes the place of ideology. Secondly, government by the judges and the contentious society will develop (Terré, 1988). Our aim here is not to comment on these risks of deviation but rather to emphasize the interest of Hayek's analysis, beginning with the limits of the models described above.

## Hayek and the judge as "extender-discoverer" of law

The majority of the criticisms aimed at the economics of law concern the argument of Posner rather than the overall object of the economics of law. Indeed, the basic aim is to highlight the limits of the judge as a "creator" of law. On the one hand, the realism of the rules prompting the action of the judge is criticized by saying that there are to be no objective criteria capable of providing him with optimal conduct. On the other hand, the fact of reducing the magistrates' decisions to the consequences of their sentences is criticized because it is unlikely they will be aware *ex ante* of the effect of the rules they have applied. In reality, the Posnerian conception is too restrictive to account for the wealth of the economic analysis of law as a dynamic approach to law.

Hayek's conception of the judge stands apart from the two others. The judge neither simply applies the law nor does he create it: he is a producer of law but within a legal continuity. He extends existing law by following the tradition. Hence the law should be discovered by the judge and not made by him. This holds in the countries of common law as well as in countries where the law is codified (even if this task is easier in countries of common law, as Barry points out). In Hayek's view, the judge is an extender-discoverer of law to the extent that he ensures that the new rules converge with spontaneous order. This observation is based upon a double criticism.

### Criticism of the legalist-liberal model

The approach of the judge-pronouncer of law rests on the hypothesis of an infallible and omniscient legislator, capable of drawing up a list of all future situations. However, such a catalogue does not exist and cannot be drawn up. This is why Hayek considers the judge to be indispensable. In an uncertain universe, it is necessary to have judges who are responsible for settling disputes. If all cases could be imagined beforehand and if everyone knew the solution for all types of trial, like a price indicator, then there would be no need for a judge. Any agent representing the state would be able to find a solution to a dispute between two parties. The problem of positivism thus comes from the assimilation made between the rules and the law. Kelsen defends this attitude which is akin to forgetting the theoretical and empirical difficulties. In fact, no-one can *ex nihilo* draw up a complete catalogue of legal rules.

In Hayek's approach, law is spontaneous by nature and the role of the judge is to bring rules into being which will lead to a stable and orderly society, an order within which the expectations of economic agents have a strong chance of being accurate. Identifying the rules with law means getting rid of all those rules which do not have a legislative origin. In reality, this means denying that rules initially appear through practice before being codified. In fact, the conception of a judge as a person who applies the law is unsatisfactory. It reduces the power of the judiciary to a mere annex of legislative power. Such a violation of the principle of the separation of power means entrusting one single sovereign institution with the production of law, this institution then being a monopoly.

This view rests on an improper conception of the role of the judge. The judge's role can in no way be restricted to this function of arbitrator. In a liberal economy, according to Hayek, no spontaneous order can be conceived of without the judiciary. The production of law by the judge is the very process of the emergence of rules compatible with a spontaneous order. It is via the settlement of disputes that information is spread and that parties can build converging expectations. It then becomes possible to confront the liberal-legalist with another model we will call "liberal-normative", with reference to the place of the rules of conduct in Hayek's work. In this model, the function of the judge is very different from that of the referee. The questions judges will have to answer will not be those of deciding whether the parties have obeyed the will of a particular authority, but whether their actions were in line with what could reasonably be expected of them.

We see that Hayek offers a vision which is far removed from the "catalogue" of the positivists that the judge has to apply scrupulously. Through his ruling, the judge will confirm the "legitimate" expectations of those concerned, i.e. those predictable in a liberal economy. Consequently, the judge should not be an agent of the executive power. The characteristic attitude of the judge is thus derived from this particularity that he should not have to bother with what any particular authority would like to see happen in a given situation, but with what private individuals have legitimate reasons to expect. In fact, the judge has an essential part to play in spontaneous order. He facilitates the convergence of expectations by throwing light upon harmful and reprehensible acts. By repeatedly forbidding certain behaviour, he will uphold the opinions of economic agents as to what is and what is not allowed. From this point on, they can expect illegal practices not to spread and this in itself is precious information. Should the need be felt to call upon an impartial judge, it will be because such a person is considered as being capable of deciding on the outcome of the case as if it had occurred elsewhere and at any other moment; consequently, in a manner which will respond to the expectation of anyone who finds himself in a similar position.

Hence, people call upon the judge because he has the experience of a large number of similar cases. However, even if the cases are similar they are never identical. Determining what is comparable and what is not is a very important function. The intervention of the judge is thus particularly necessary in unusual cases in which the parties may, in all good faith, have totally opposite opinions. By definition the judge is an experienced player as his role consists in solving disputes within the framework of a recurrent game. Going before the judge is thus a simple application of the principle of the division of labour. As he has specialized knowledge about the rules and practices, he is better suited making a ruling on a dispute than inexperienced individuals. The argument of Hayek is based upon an essential premise: rules exist as practices before being codified. The role of the judge is to sanction rules which are unwritten yet respected. This is of course true in countries of unwritten law but can also explain the evolution of jurisprudence in countries having written law.

### Criticism of the technocratic-normative model

In the Austrian vision, the concept of the judge creator of law is insufficient for two reasons. Firstly, if one considers the judge to be a creator of law *ex nihilo*, then one will seek out the rules governing his activity. This is the whole meaning of the criterion of maximizing social wealth. However, the rules granted to the judge are not realistic. There is no satisfactory objective criterion that can enforce optimum behaviour on the judge. Secondly, the "justice" of the judge is reduced to the consequences of his sentences. What counts the most in Posner's approach is the concrete result of the sentence of the rule and not the justice of the procedure or the initial distribution of the rights (Coase's theorem). Making a ruling in relation to its consequences supposes that it is possible to know *ex ante* the result of a rule of law. Such a supposition is obviously unrealistic. The insufficiencies attached to this conception of the judge lead us again to insist upon the role of the judge as a discoverer of law.

In Posner's concept, the judge is seen to be at the origin of largely autonomous rules and detached from all tradition. Hayek does not see this presentation of things as relevant for at least two reasons. Firstly, social order exists before the activity of the judges and secondly, the function of a judge supposes the negation of particular objectives.

On the first point, the argumentation is based upon the fact that no-one is capable of conceiving a legal system in its entirety. The judge is no exception to this idea. His role is not to build up a legal system with a precise aim. On the contrary, he is to give meaning to the existing rules and, if necessary, to rectify the shortcomings of the law by making a ruling which is compatible with the judicial tradition. Following Hayek, it will often be impossible to distinguish between the simple utterance of rules which, up until this point, have existed in the form of practices, and the formation of rules which have never been used as a basis for action but which, once formulated, will be accepted as reasonable by almost everyone. But in neither case will the judge be free to pronounce any rule he likes. The rules he announces must fill a precise gap in the already established system of rules, in such a way that the new rules serve to maintain and improve the order of actions that the already existing rules make possible. The judge is not at the origin of social order but of the spontaneous rules observed. By settling disputes, his role consists in improving and preserving an order whose logic he helps to be discovered.

On the second point, two arguments are to be considered. First of all, the judge must favour neither of the parties: he must restrict himself to the task of discovering the law (Barry, 1998) and send information concerning the rules of conduct to the whole of society. According to Hayek, there is no greater danger for society than the search for objectives by the judge, such as the maximization of social wealth. Something which may be beneficial to parties in conflict may be harmful for all the other individuals in society. Indeed, the search for particular objectives may well increase legal uncertainty. This instability of the system also gives rise to inflation of trials as soon as the expectations based on current practices are unfulfilled. Hayek explains that the changes in jurisprudence often seem due to the fact that the courts make favourable rulings for one category of the population compared to another: consumers versus producers, pedestrians versus drivers, employees versus employers.

The task of the judges is not to turn themselves into planners of social order. As Hayek comments: the only public good with which the judge should concern himself is to ensure that the rules upon which the parties could reasonably rely have been respected. He should not consider the distant goal on which one may have wished the rules to converge and of which he can be but largely unaware;

he must enforce the respect of the rules even where, in the pending case, the probable consequences appear to him to be undesirable.

### *Jurisprudence as an evolutionary process*

Within the framework of the "liberal-normative" model and the concept of the judge as a discoverer of law, it is tempting to introduce the judge as an agent defending established order whose target is the status quo. In reality, the judge does not defend society's concrete order but what Hayek calls "abstract order" (in the sense of general traits of social coordination). Only in this sense can the judge ensure the protection of the law designed as being a set of abstract rules. Contrary to the structural view of Lachmann, Hayek defends an aggregate view of the rules characterized by the fact that in each period there is a stock of legal rules. It is always possible to add new rules to this stock without destabilizing the whole system. For this the judge needs to intervene to verify that they are coherent with the existing stock. A given rule can thus be rejected or accepted into the existing stock after going through the hands of the judge.

The set of abstract rules gives rise to a highly mobile and fluctuating concrete order providing all actors with considerable room for manoeuvre. The judge, far from working in favour of this status quo, takes part in the definition of this margin for manoeuvre by improving the predictability of behaviour. Through his deliberate action, the judge attempts to maintain and improve the social and dynamic order. The reason why the judge will be asked to intervene will be that the rules procuring this mutual adjustment are not always respected or not clear enough or inappropriate for the avoidance of conflict when one obeys them. As circumstances continually arise for which the rules will no longer be adequate, the task of foreseeing disputes and increasing the compatibility between activities by appropriately restricting the effect of authorized action is obviously never over.

The fact that abstract order is, by definition, evolutionary explains the fact that it can never be perfectly coherent and exempt from gaps (there is a tendency towards equilibrium without ever attaining it). But if the law evolves, it will always fall within a legal tradition; this explains why it is so important for the judges to justify their rulings. The justifications will inform not only the parties but also all individuals about the tradition into which the ruling fits. This supposes that the judge clarifies the tradition to which he is referring.

Hence, from the three concepts presented here, the third seems to be the most appropriate for the real activity of the judge: neither an applicator nor a creator *ex nihilo*, the judge is at the origin of the spontaneous evolution of the legal system where, in the words of Hayek, he participates in the mechanism of the immanent criticism of law: given that any system of established rules of conduct is always based upon experiences of which we are only partially aware, and produces an order of activities which we only partially understand, we cannot hope to reconstruct the whole thing. If we are to fully profit from all the experience which has only been transmitted in the form of traditional rules, any criticism and effort to improve particular rules must take place within a given framework of values which, to attain the goal sought, should be considered as not requiring justification. We will describe as immanent criticism this type of discussion which evolved in a given system of rules and which evaluates such and such a rule in relation to its coherence or compatibility with all the other rules converging to form an order of activities of a certain kind.

## Notes

1  The characteristics of common law can only be understood through the history of the rule of law. This was the distinctive sign of the English legal system which was marked by the predominance of the courts over political power as far as everything regarding the content of law was concerned. The judge was bound by traditional rules and by a set of principles emanating from natural law which were incorporated within these traditional rules. In this sense, the rule of law is not a rule of law but a rule about law, a meta-rule or rather a political ideal. The *rule of law* does not therefore correspond to the supremacy of legislation (whoever the legislator may be), but to its opposite: to the subordination of the legislator to common law observed by the courts. Today, quite to the contrary, when the term *rule of law* is used, it is often meant that the government and the judge are bound by the law voted by parliament; the *rule of law* is thus reinterpreted as a sort of principle of legality. But the *rule of law* was not just a simple political or philosophical ideal; it constituted positive law. In other words, until the seventeenth century, English positive law was a sort of natural law in the sense that it was not wrapped up in the laws or the orders of the Sovereign, but was derived by the judge from a set of traditional principles of material justice and from good reasoning. Natural law was thus law as it is, whereas what for a good number of contemporary theorists of law is positive law was, at that time, law as it should have been for a few philosophers.

   This change in the sense of the concept of the *rule of law* highlights the passage from the liberal state to the state of law. According to Hayek, this change is the one which goes from one concept of the *rule of law* where law is conceived in a material manner, to a concept where law is only considered in a formal sense. In the material concept of law, the latter must conform to the substantial requirements of justice: it must be fair; according to the formal concept, on the other hand, a law is as such only if it conforms to procedural and formal requirements, i.e. if it is correctly adopted.

2  The distinction drawn by Ost is based on the concept of ideal types defined by Max Weber. In practice, the two models of justice can co-exist as is shown by the example of the alternate modes of dispute settlement which have formal and informal justices co-existing.

3  It is interesting to emphasize that Bentham was one of the most ardent protagonists of codification in England.

4  It was present in Europe, however, with sociological positivism which, in the heritage of Montesquieu had a certain influence in the Germanic countries through E. Erhlich or in France through L. Duguit.

5  The influence of the sociological jurisprudence movement was also strongly felt in the work of the advocates of Legal Realism (Llewellyn and Frank), who have conceived of a science of law aimed at the observation of the consequences of rules, especially in the manner in which they fare after the judge's ruling. These authors indeed reject the idea of the certainty of law and the predictability of the decisions of justice (see Severin on this and the previous points).

6  This does not mean, however, that the welfare state is less preoccupied by access to
    the judicial system that the police state tends to show through the development of
    legal aid or the admission of collective action before the courts.

## Bibliography

Barry, N. P. (1998) "Limited Government, Individual Liberty and the Rule of Law",
    *Selected Works by Arthur Asher Shenfield*, Editions Elsevier.

Beccaria, C. (1764) *Des délits et des peines*, Edition Cujas, 1975.

Cooter, R. (1984) "Prices and Sanction", *Columbia Law Review*, 61 (3), pp. 1,523–59.

Gérard, F., Ost, F. and Van de Kerchove, M. (1985) *Fonction de juger et pouvoir judiciaire: trans-
    formations et déplacements*, Bruxelles: Bruylant.

Habermas, J. (1981) *Between Facts and Norms: Contributions to a Discourse Theory of Law and
    Democracy (Studies in Contemporary German Social Thought)*, Frankfurt Am Main: Suhrkamp
    Verlag.

Hayek, F.A. (1973) *Law, Legislation and Liberty*, London: Routledge & Kegan Paul, vol.1,
    *Rules and Order*.

Kelsen, H. (1979) *Allgemeine Theorie der Normen Manzsche*, Wien: Verlag und Universität-
    buchhandlung.

Lachmann, L.M. (1973) *Methodological Individualism and the Market Economy*, London: Insti-
    tute of Economic Affairs.

Montesquieu, C.L. de S. (1748) *De l'esprit des lois*, Paris: Garnier Flammarion, 1979.

Ost, F. (1985) "Les transformations de la fonction du juge", in Gérard, F., Ost, F. and Van
    de Kerchove, M., *Fonction de juger et pouvoir judiciaire: tranformations et déplacements*, Brux-
    elles: Bruylant, pp. 95–121.

Posner, R.A. (1997) *Economic Analysis of Law*, Boston, Little, Brown & Company, 4th
    edition.

Rueff, J. (1967) *L'ordre social*, Paris: M.T. Génin, third edition.

Serverin, Evelyne (1999) *Philosophie du Droit*, La Découverte, Repéres.

Terré, François (1988) *Introduction générale au droit*, Paris:Dalloz.

Villey, M. (1984) *Philosophie du Droit*, Paris: Dalloz , p. 78.

# Part V

# Norms from facts?

# 13 Coordination, survival and normativity

## A Hayekian perspective revisited

*Thierry Aimar*

This brings me to what in my personal development was the starting point of all these reflections, and which may explain why, though at one time a very pure and narrow economic theorist, I was led from technical economics into all kinds of questions usually regarded as philosophical. When I look back, it seems to have all begun, nearly thirty years ago, with an essay on "Economics and Knowledge" in which I examined what seemed to me some of the central difficulties of pure economic theory. Its main conclusion was that the task of economic theory was to explain how an overall order of economic activity was achieved which utilized a large amount of knowledge which was not concentrated in any one mind but existed only as the separate knowledge of thousands or millions of different individuals. But it was still a long way from this to an adequate insight into the relations between the abstract rules which the individual follows in his actions, and the abstract overall order which is formed as a result of his responding, within the limits imposed upon him by those abstract rules, to the concrete particular circumstances which he encounters.

(Hayek, 1965, pp. 91–2)

## Introduction

Contrary to the opinion of numerous commentators, it is far from clear whether normative elements are part of Hayek's thought. Certainly, Hayek has always pleaded in favor of market mechanisms and laissez-faire. However, nothing in his writing enables us to *directly* claim that his liberalism may be identified with a normative position. The aim of this chapter is to show that Hayek's liberal discourse is not merely a value judgement. A review of Hayek's intellectual career would seem to offer the elements necessary for *indirectly* establishing a *normative Austrian economics*. Our argument will be developed in two parts. In the next section we will analyze the analytical content of the notion of a tendency toward equilibrium. Very early ("Economics and Knowledge," 1937), Hayek attributed an empirical dimension to the notion of tendency toward equilibrium: "It is only by this assertion that such a tendency exists that economics ceases to be an exercise in pure logic and becomes an empirical science; and it is to economics as an empirical science that we must now turn"

(Hayek, 1937, p. 44). But the theoretical and empirical significance of this tendency toward equilibrium has created numerous debates within the Austrian tradition. We will examine to what extent a number of these debates determined the course taken by Hayek and brought him from his work on the economy of rules to the argument developed in his last publication, *The Fatal Conceit* (1988). In this book, Hayek defines survival as the empirical criterion of a coordination that is guaranteed by the functioning of liberal societies. In the following section we will attempt to demonstrate that this argument for survival allows for the definition of a normative principle which is based on a purely economic approach. Despite recent attempts toward this aim, Austrian authors (Kirzner, 1976, 1988, 1998; Cordato, 1992) have not succeeded in actually defining a doctrinal norm which is constructed with the tools of economic theory. We argue that the Hayekian perspective enables the foundations for a normative Austrian economics to be established.

## Survival as a criterion for coordination

The argument for coordination is a permanent feature of the Austrian tradition. In various forms, this argument has been present in all periods of this economic tradition and has concerned all of its protagonists. Yet in relation to the market economy, this argument has provoked a series of debates in contemporary literature. It is from this perspective that the analysis that Hayek develops in his last work, *The Fatal Conceit*, appears to us to constitute a fundamental stage in this process.

### *The "tendency toward equilibrium": the history of an analytical enigma*

Although attempts to develop a principle of coordination can be found in the initial period of the Austrian School (Menger, 1871, 1883; Wieser, 1914), it was only at a later date that this became an obbject of inquiry in its own right. This inquiry was developed along two main lines. The first is related to the foundation of an Austrian welfare economics (Rothbard, 1956; Kirzner, 1976, 1988; Cordato, 1992). This perspective was developed in a series of stages, all of which converged in a representation of market processes as producing a general form of coordination. The second line of thought was developed in Hayek's work. He answered the questions he himself had formulated in "Economics and Knowledge." In doing so, from the 1960s onwards, Hayek developed an interpretation of the coordination of expectations which focused on the idea of the rules of just conduct. Added to the market mechanism, the rules of just conduct seem to have the function of stabilizing individuals' preferences and of regulating their behaviors. Thus they facilitate forecasting and the organization of agents' expectations.

The aim of the Austrian welfare economists (Rothbard, Kirzner and Cordato) is to show that exercising market processes is associated with individual satisfaction for all agents concerned (cf. Aimar, 1998). Here, the production of utility takes place via the definition, which varies according to the authors, of the coordinating *virtues* of the market. All these contributions naturally took place within the subjectivist framework, which, despite its diversity, represents one of the common axes of the Austrian tradition. For an author such as Rothbard (1956), this Austrian subjectivism imposes two constraints: on the one hand, it prevents common preferences of agents from being expressed and thereby forbids any objective definition of welfare; on the other hand, it is opposed to any inter-personal comparison of gains and costs.

For Austrian welfare theoreticians, the market (catallaxy) is the institution that carries out this double task. The rules of voluntary exchange allow the wants of all exchange partners to be satisfied. This does not require an inter-personal comparison of gains and costs: "the very fact that an exchange takes place demonstrates that both parties benefit (or more strictly, expect to benefit) from the exchange" (Rothbard, 1956, p. 250); and that the expected utility of a market transaction is always derived from the *subjective* aims of the partners. In the final assessment, it would thus be possible to use these lessons to construct an *Austrian welfare economics* associated with a principle of coordination of individual interests and based on the working of the market: "The obvious example of coordinated action is voluntary inter-personal exchange in which each participant acts to improve his position, with such improvement possible only because each participant's action is coordinated precisely with that of his trading partner. In using the coordination criterion as the theoretical basis for evaluating social efficiency, the individuality of purposes is not lost sight of" (Kirzner, 1976, p. 85).

In "Welfare Economics: A Modern Austrian Perspective" (1988), Kirzner does not establish an effective symmetry between market exchange and the production of utility. Indeed, and as Mises and Rothbard had already ascertained, any exchange necessarily takes place within time, and the inability to know future conditions prevents market exchange from ensuring in advance that satisfaction will ensue *ex-post*. As for Kirzner, he emphasizes an ignorance which "is not attributable to the costs of search, or of learning or of communication. In such cases the decision-maker's ignorance is *utter* ignorance – i.e., it is a result of his ignorance of available, cost-worthy, avenues to needed information, which includes, of course, the possibility of his being altogether unaware of the very existence of valuable information" (Kirzner, 1988, pp. 85–6). The functioning of the market does not therefore guarantee the success of individual plans formed at the basis of the transaction. To this extent, it is much more a question of updating the economic conditions that will maximize the *opportunities* for the success of the plans than to guarantee the production of utility via exchange. In fact, as far as Kirzner is concerned, the advantage of the market is to mobilize and to transmit information as rapidly as possible. Should these mechanisms be allowed to be performed freely, the opportunities to eliminate agents' errors will be maximized, thereby creating *a tendency toward equilibrium*, such that "initially clashing, discoordinated activities, are somehow being hammered out in a manner such as to approach a more smoothly dovetailing pattern of activities" (Kirzner, 1988, p. 87).

Finally, Cordato (1992) centered his defense of market coordination around the question of the formation of individual plans. The theme of property returns to the limelight. In Cordato's view, private property is not sufficient for plans to succeed. But it is a necessary condition for their construction as "No meaningful means ends framework is even possible without the ability to access and control physical resources" (1992, p. 65). Catallactic competition to obtain scarce resources thus makes exercising individual property rights indispensable. Given that the goals vary, the resources do as well and the possibility of obtaining new ones is important ("an act of exchange is an act of giving up less appropriate means for more appropriate means," ibid., p. 63). To this extent, market transactions are assimilated to a procedure providing welfare. The legitimacy of entitlements to resources thereby spreads to that of the product of inter-personal exchange. Respect for individual property rights and freedom of market exchange allow Cordato to forge the concept of *catallactic efficiency* which simultaneously expresses the idea of a control over resources and the possibility to obtain new ones.

This Austrian analysis of welfare is not totally satisfactory. Both Kirzner's and Cordato's approaches run into difficulties. Even if the improvement in information effectively enables agents to redirect their activities as fast as possible, it does not reinforce coordination as certain existing plans are rendered obsolete and guaranteed situations are challenged. Opportunities that were exploitable at particular levels of information may cease to be exploitable under different conditions. The process of the diffusion of existing information can therefore be interpreted both as a "tendency toward equilibrium" and as a "permanent endogenous disequilibrium."

In "Coordination as a Criterion for Economic 'Goodness'" (1998), Kirzner attempted to bypass this pitfall by formulating the process of coordination as a simple adaptation to constantly changing information, and not as an actual evolution toward an increasing compatibility of plans:

> The innovator competitor who, entering the industry and pushing out the older firms, is disrupting the earlier plans, is replacing a less coordinated set of market activities, by a better coordination set. In the "dynamic" sense of the term "coordination" … this brash, aggressive competition is coordinative. The disruption it causes in earlier plans of the inefficient producers is the evidence for and manifestation of the earlier state of discoordinatedness which has generated the changes (of which this disruption is part). The apparent earlier calm which, as a result of the aggressive new competition, has been followed by sudden disruption, was in fact utterly misleading. That calm was a fact expressing the presence of as yet undiscovered (but very real) discoordinatedness; dynamic competition shat-

tered that calm, replacing the earlier uncoordinated sets of activities by better-coordinated set.

(Kirzner, 1998, p. 297)

In this perspective, the entrepreneurial activity would only be a reply to the observation of a lag between the structure of activities and the structure of knowledge. This will necessarily result in the non-realization of certain individual plans. Leaving the market free would thus amount to giving to the structure of activities maximum opportunities to adjust to the structure of information. Kirzner is aware that the reduction of certain disequilibriums via the market will necessarily give rise to new disequilibriums as it will create new information and new opportunities. But the argument seems to be the following: interfering with the catallactic process would be nothing more than endorsing and reinforcing the lag observed at the beginning of the process and would therefore increase the degree of discoordination. However, this gradual move toward this restricted definition (for want of something better) of the coordinating tendencies of the market has a negative side: defining an increasingly blurred relation with the very notion of welfare. In the same article Kirzner, surprisingly, goes as far as admitting that: "In fact, the well-being is not referred to in the coordination criterion at all" (ibid., p. 297).

### *Rules as a response to the ignorance of the future*

In Hayek, the coordination of subjective expectations thus requires at least a predictability of objective data,[1] if not a constancy, which could not, in itself, be encouraged by the market. The origin and nature of this predictability are, at the time of "Economics and Knowledge," questions having no answers as far as the author is concerned. He is thus obliged to admit "I am afraid that I am now getting to a stage where it becomes exceedingly difficult to say what exactly are the assumptions on the basis of which we assert that there will be a tendency toward equilibrium and to claim that our analysis has an application to the real world" (Hayek, 1937, p. 48). It is only much later on, thanks to the concept of rules of just conduct (1967a and b, 1964, 1973, 1976 etc.), that Hayek is to offer an explanation of the principles for the coordination of plans. These rules indeed play the role of a complement to prices to produce an intertemporal coordination of activities.

In a previous article (Aimar, 2000), we examined the literature on the concept of rules of just conduct. Most comments highlight that these rules permit both an economy and an accumulation of a capital of information: an economy of information to the extent that these rules incorporate abstract knowledge and crystallize a quantity of individual knowledge, the sum of which would be inaccessible to an individual mind; as capital of information in the sense that this synthesized knowledge is a wisdom and experience accumulated across centuries which benefit agents. We have observed that this literature has neglected an essential aspect of Hayek's thought on this subject, viz. the idea that rules of just conduct are relevant to the management and regulation of ignorance about the future. Because they are general, these rules allow agents who follow them to respond to unpredictable situations in advance, and increase the probability that their plans will come true. But above all, they permit the stabilization of a social environment, which without them would represent the kaleidic universes, to use Shackle's term, whose configuration is indetermined (cf. also Birner, this volume). In our opinion, here lies the essential point of Hayek's argument: the predictive dimension of rules corresponds to the theoretical explanation of the empirical assessment of a tendency toward equilibrium, established by Hayek initially in "Economics and Knowledge."

Social coordination through its various elements (market, rules, institutions) corresponds to an order of activities uncontrolled and uncontrollable by the individual mind and whose rationalization *ex-ante* is a hopeless quest. Hence, the "constructivist" will to improve the overall structure of the existing rules in a conscious and deliberate manner is not feasible:

> Since our whole life consists in facing ever new and unforeseeable circumstances, we cannot make it orderly by deciding in advance all the particular actions we shall take. The only manner in which we can in fact give our lives some order is to adopt certain abstract rules or principles for guidance, and then strictly adhere to the rules we have adopted in our dealing with the new situations as they arise.
>
> (Hayek, 1965, p. 90)

This structure of rules constituting, in Hayek's view, the architecture of social cooperation represents a spontaneous order. He defines this order as

> a general method of indirectly creating an order in situations where the phenomena are far too complex to allow us the creation of an order by separately putting each element in its appropriate place. It is a sort of order over the particular manifestation of which we have little control, because the rules which determine it determine only its abstract character, while the detail depends on the particular circumstances known only to its individual members.
>
> (Hayek, 1965, p. 92)

There is, as such, a correspondence, a symmetrical principle, between spontaneous orders and abstract rules, enabling them to exist and function. The correspondence between *the structures of prediction* formed by the rules of just conduct and the existence of *pattern prediction* resulting from their application thereby enables an explanation of the fact "that there must be some discernible regularity in the world which makes it possible to predict events correctly" (Hayek, 1937, p. 49). The difficulty is that in the 1970s and 1980s, Lachmann minimized the interest of this theoretical explanation by stressing the stakes of the *structural* nature of the norms of behavior and the influence brought about by their change.

Indeed, if Hayek himself stresses that "this interplay of the rules of conduct of the individuals with the actions of other individuals and the external circumstances in producing an overall order may be a highly complex affair" (1967b, p. 71), he would appear to under-estimate the difficulties involved. The obsolescence of a rule of just conduct inevitably means a loss of efficiency of the set of other rules due to their inter-dependence.[2] In the same way as a change in a particular price will necessarily involve a change in the structure of relative prices, a marginal change in rules will lead to their overall restructuring: "It seems therefore that the need for coherence and permanence on the one hand and for flexibility on the other hand cannot be easily reconciled" (Lachmann, 1971, p. 89). From here onwards, the theory of the rules of just conduct as an interpretation of a structure of coordinated expectations is, in the form of an explanation of principle, brought into question.

Using this approach, it seems useful to address the analysis that Hayek developed in his last publication, *The Fatal Conceit* (1988). Often overlooked or misunderstood in the literature, this text contributes to highlighting the logical trajectory of Hayek's work. It serves indirectly as a response to Lachmann, by offering an empirical criterion of coordination. The aim of this criterion is to permit the corroboration of an explanation of principle that is formulated around the idea of rules of just conduct.

## The Fatal Conceit: *the argument of survival*

The Austrian lit erature examined above has not been able to define an empirical definition of coordination. No doubt the major obstacle to this definition lies in subjectivity, which would appear to go against the definition of individual common values. This constraint has led the Austrians to refer to a procedural dimension of the question of coordination via the theme of information. Yet, this approach itself poses certain analytical problems. Above all, however, it does not enable one single empirical criterion to be identified which would make possible the differentiation between situations of coordination and those of discoordination. The approach Hayek has adopted in *The Fatal Conceit* seems to us to provide an answer to this problem.

In the "Theory of Complex Phenomena" (1964), Hayek has already explained that the definition of an abstract structure requires a reference to general features, to "the minimum number of elements of which an instance of the pattern must consist in order to exhibit all the characteristic attributes of the class of patterns in question" (Hayek, 1964, p. 25). The idea of a tendency toward equilibrium thus reflects the existence of a structure of coordinated expectations. Of course, due to the constraints of the complexity that accompanies all social phenomena, the aim is not to take account of all forms of coordination. The objective is simply to address the general form of coordination, that is, the characteristics common to all forms of social coordination.

*The Fatal Conceit* is an attempt to define the general features of coordination. In the chapter devoted to "The Extended Order and Population Growth," Hayek brings together the elements scattered throughout his earlier work (especially in *Law, Legislation and Liberty*) which he proceeds to organize in a systematic and coherent analysis. In it, Hayek deals with population, the division of labor and survival. On the one hand survival unquestionably belongs to the sphere of the common characteristics of coordination to the extent that, for plans to be satisfied, whatever their particular content, the agents must stay alive. This objective element necessarily transcends all subjective conceptions of coordination one can imagine. On the other hand, in a situation of division of labor, the survival of growing populations necessarily reflects the existence of coordinating mechanisms. If individual activities were not coordinated on a wide scale, there could not have been such a degree of specialization of functions and the level of output of goods providing sufficient food for the populations could never have reached present proportions: "If we ask what men most owe to the moral practices of those who are called capitalists the answer is: their very lives" (Hayek, 1988, p. 130). Indeed, on the basis of experience, Hayek notices a symmetry between capitalist societies (the *Great Society*) and the survival of increasingly numerous populations.

Of course, one could object to Hayek that population increase could, in the long term, involve an objective cost reducing the chances of survival by intensifying competition to obtain the available goods. However, Hayek would have none of this. Quite the contrary. The factor of labor is linked to increasing returns: the dispersion of knowledge and of skills correlated to population increase, the interaction of individual subjectivity linked to an increasingly richer and diversified human capital, the intensification of the process of knowledge acquisition all explain that "[s]tep by step, momentary impediments to further population increase are penetrated, increases of population provide a foundation for further ones, and so on" (ibid., p. 127). Thanks to the idea of survival, the definition of this empirical criterion for coordination will allow Hayek to corroborate his conjectural theory of rules of just conduct, which he in fact connects to an evolutionist framework. It is indeed via a system of selection, competition and imitation that market-based societies and the rules of just conduct have steadily imposed themselves and been generalized on an international scale: "Yet if the market economy did indeed prevail over other types of order because it enabled those groups that adopted its basic rules the better to multiply, then the calculation in market values is a calculation in terms of lives: individuals guided by this calculation did what most helped to increase their numbers, although this could hardly have been their intention" (ibid., p. 132).[3]

Many authors have criticized Hayek for proceeding with his analysis not in terms of individuals but of groups and for making use of a holistic concept. These attacks, however, reflect an ignorance of epistemological constraints surrounding the understanding of extended social phenomena. Indeed, it is forgotten that here, "Explanation and prediction of course do not refer to an individual event but always to phenomena of a certain kind or class" because "the more we move into the realm of the very complex, the more our knowledge is likely to be of the principle only, of the significant outline rather than of the detail. Especially where we have to deal with the extreme complexity of human affairs, the hope of ever achieving specific predictions of particulars seems vain" (Hayek, 1955, pp. 9, 20). Because "the extended order [is] probably the most complex structure in the universe" (Hayek, 1988, p. 127), apprehending individual situations cannot thus be undertaken at this level of the analysis. Certainly, the degree of falsifiability of the theory in question may be seen as low. There is an infinite number of particular circumstances which have conditioned, and may continue to condition, the survival, preservation and development of economic societies. Yet, very early, Hayek notes:

> our difficulty is precisely that we are unable to ascertain by observation the presence and specific arrangement of the multiplicity of factors which form the starting point of our deductive reasoning. Neither the assumption that factors of the kind assumed are present, nor of course the validity of the deductive reasoning need, therefore, be regarded as disproved if the conclusions at which we arrived are not borne out by observation. But though observation of such complex situations cannot decide whether our conditional ("if then") statement is true, it will help us to decide whether to accept it as an explanation of the facts which we observe.
>
> (Hayek, 1955, p. 10)

Thus the connection between an empirical criterion of coordination, via the idea of survival, and an explanation in principle (theory), based on the idea of rules of the *Great Society*, allows Hayek to establish his representation of social order. *The Fatal Conceit* ends a program of research that began with "Economics and Knowledge." At the same time, this piece of work provides a true criterion of normativity based upon economic analysis.

## Survival as a criterion of normativity

The idea of a relation between the criterion of coordination and of survival finally leads us to the second part of our chapter, that is to say the foundation of an Austrian normativity. Indeed, we shall attempt to show that the element of survival may be used as a foundation for a normative Austrian economy. For a decade now, numerous attempts have been made within the Austrian tradition to establish a coordination-normativity symmetry. All of them have failed, not really because of insufficiencies already observed in the analysis of coordination, but more due to the constraints of the subjectivist paradigm which prevents an area of common interest between individuals from being defined substantively. The analysis offered by Hayek circumvents these difficulties. By precisely explaining an objective element of coordination, which itself corresponds to a value shared by all agents (market or not market), it provides a principle of normativity based on economic analysis. Nevertheless, we would emphasize the fact that this normativity (which reflects a sphere of common values) does not necessarily correspond to a prescription (i.e. the idea of a necessary choice by individuals in favor of the socio-economic conditions which would permit the maximization of the satisfaction of these common values).

## Coordination-normativity: the failure of a traditional perspective

Kirzner and Cordato took upon themselves the task of founding the liberal doctrine via their analysis of welfare. For both authors, the presentation of the advantages of the market enables a normativity in its favor to be established, whatever the nature of the goals pursued. For Kirzner, the market maximizes the use of available information from which all individuals within its sphere will benefit; indeed, it is from this point that it is possible to "reconcile Mises's strong normative position in economics with his declared insistence on *Wertfreiheit*" (Kirzner, 1976, p. 80). In "Coordination as a Criterion for Economic 'Goodness'" (1998), he considers in the same order of ideas that "Economic science is thus, through the notion of coordination, able, we shall maintain, to provide an objective criterion in terms of which the economic goodness and badness of economic situations or economic policies, may be judged" (Kirzner, 1998, p. 292); for Cordato, the market expresses the respect of individual property rights, which themselves condition the formation of plans. It thus allows for a definition of "normative economics" and for the definition of liberalism as "ideal institutional setting" (Cordato, 1992, p. 64).

This analysis presents problems. Beyond the loss of substance of the theories of coordination, the difficulty is that the field of the analysis of welfare creation is reduced to the question of the market: only the preferences of the actors present on the market are taken into account. Certainly, this reduction is supported by the principle of demonstrated preference as defined by Mises. This principle means that action alone teaches us about the preferences of agents to the extent that it is linked to choice. But *de facto*, the Austrian analysis of welfare does not take into account feelings of envy which may characterize certain individuals. Individuals remaining with their initial endowments may not be neutral as far as the exchanges of others are concerned, and may develop an aversion to the market. In this case, the market could have negative psychological external effects on those agents who do not exchange. The production of utility by market agents can produce negative effects on the agents who remain outside the market. In this respect, it cannot be stated at the social level that all exchanges bring an increase in satisfaction, or that respecting property rights is beneficial to all. Defining a normativity, which imposes itself upon each individual within the social area (and not only the cata-lalaxy), is therefore not scientifically acceptable. In parallel, Kirzner himself admits that if "we do not need any help from moral philosophy in order to identify the coordination concept and associate specific economic policies with an either greater or lesser likelihood of generating coordination ... we certainly need moral philosophy to help judge the goodness (or badness) of greater degrees of coordinatedness" (Kirzner, 1998, p. 292).

This assessment was furthermore acknowledged by Rothbard himself, even though he was a pioneer in the Austrian analysis of welfare (1956): "It must not be thought that we have, in our discussion of welfare economics, been attempting to set forth any ethical or political program. On the contrary, the proposed welfare economics has been put forward without inserting ethical judgments" (Rothbard, 1956, p. 261). Hence, Rothbard refuses to grant a normative character to the Austrian welfare economics. For this reason, Rothbard chose a different avenue with *The Ethics of Liberty* (1982). He introduced a normative dimension into the Austrian problematic by the use of a philosophical approach based upon the theme of natural law. Up until this moment, the neo-Austrian position had been governed by a principle of neutrality toward values (*Wertfreiheit*), which prevented a doctrinal position from being truly transformed into a political norm. Rothbard, as opposed to the other heirs of Mises' thought (Hayek, Lachmann, Kirzner), seeks to liberate Austrian analysis from the reign of *Wertfreiheit*. By defining a rational *ethics* of human behavior, thus reflecting the ontological nature of property and of individual freedom, he thereby presents a normative defense of economic liberalism which, apparently, is independent of its efficiency. As individual freedom and property are natural rights as far as Rothbard is concerned, the market must necessarily be respected to the extent that it represents the sphere of ontologically based voluntary transactions of endowments. In the final analysis, it expresses "the full exercise of his natural self-ownership" (1982, p. 45). But this normative approach contains a certain negative counter-argument: *the abandoning of all references to economic analysis.*

Consequently, as far as this literature is concerned, there is no true *normative Austrian economics*. Faced with these shortcomings, Hayek's contribution, based upon the idea of survival, opens up a new perspective which restores the foundations of a laissez-faire-coordination-normativity trilogy. Nevertheless, to demonstrate its legitimacy requires that we return to the teachings of Mises.

### The definition of a new Austrian normativity

The relationship between the theme of survival and that of normativity has already been considered by Shearmur. In a recent contribution, *Hayek and After* (1996),[4] Shearmur states that "the biologically based is not a bad starting-point. We can, indeed, talk about gains in well-being in terms of people's not being frustrated in their biologically based desires; or, if they wish not to eat, drink, live in decent conditions and so on, of this being a matter of their choice, rather than something that is forced upon them by their circumstances" (Shearmur, 1996, p. 174).

Biological factors alone are not enough for Shearmur; they need to be supplemented by particular nuances. This has an enormous effect on their impact. Indeed he immediately points out: "I should stress, in view of my earlier emphasis upon the biological, that I do not mean to limit what we can say about well-being to the biologically based" (Shearmur, 1996, p. 174) because "as part of this theory, the insights of subjectivism should be recognized: it is important that individuals may prefer to choose not to eat or to copulate, and may even, in some circumstances, prefer to die" (Shearmur, 1996, p. 175). By highlighting this point, Shearmur is well aware that he is putting the cat amongst the pigeons of normativity, as no objective hierarchy between the element of survival and the subjective goals of agents is established in his theoretical model. From here on, any assertion of a normativity focusing on the idea of survival necessarily falls within the realm of value judgements. In fact, Shearmur appears to see this as nothing more than an element of possible evaluation, a "second best" solution aimed at filling the space left by the absence of an economic criterion of normativity.

Seen at this level of the analysis, it is indisputable that the argument of survival cannot be defined as a true norm. Nevertheless, Shearmur appears to provide the prelude to a solution to the problem of the Austrian normative economy. Restoring the coherence of his analysis, however, requires a return to the work of Mises. Indeed, Shearmur is unaware of the advantages brought by the praxeological schema and of the manner in which it can be linked to the question of survival. As Mises defines it, praxeology is defined as "a theoretical science of human action, i.e., a science that aims at the ascertainment of universally valid laws of human conduct" (Mises, 1933, p. 68). Action constitutes the fundamental axiom upon which the construction of all economic theory is ultimately based. Action is thus the "ultimate data" for social knowledge because the human mind is incapable of moving beyond the concept of action.

In all of his epistemological writings (1933, 1957, 1962, 1966), Mises argues for the apodictical characteristic of praxeological principles, meaning that their validity and applicability are independent of circumstances of time and place. At the same time, Mises has always defended the idea of a praxeological subjectivity, by claiming that praxeological theorems "are valid for every human action without regard to its underlying motives, causes, and goals" (Mises, 1966, p. 21). The principles of praxeology are, by definition, directed toward actors, i.e. individuals functioning within a means–end structure. What is the relationship between the praxeological model and the idea of survival? Certainly, for Mises, the goal of action is not necessarily to preserve one's life as "To live is for man the outcome of a choice, of a judgment of value" (Mises, 1966 p. 20). However, life is an inevitable condition of action. Indeed, the means–end relation expressed by the latter requires the use of life which can hence be defined as a non-substitutable factor for the production of action. Consequently, there is a logical correlation between the process of action on the one hand and, on the other, the promotion of resources enabling life to be preserved and conserved until the plan has succeeded. This implies no hypothesis concerning the particular subjective ends of agents, and in no case implies that the aim of action is preservation of life.[5] In this respect, we may speak of an "apodictical value" in the sense that this valorization of survival is independent of circumstances of time and place; we prefer to speak of "praxeological values" in the sense that their presence in *each* actor is established by the pattern of human action, no matter what the nature of the ends may be – marketable or non-marketable. Admitting the existence of these praxeological values in no way means that there will be a reduction in the sphere of subjectivism nor an abandoning of the principle of *Wertfreiheit*. Each individual will continue to be considered as a singular being, whose aims are contingent and changing (praxeologically indeterminated).

In *The Ethics of Liberty* (1982), Rothbard, too, defines life as an objective value but his naturalist approach leads him to establish the irrationality of certain individual objectives:

> If Crusoe had eaten the mushrooms without learning of their poisonous effects, then his decision would have been incorrect – a possibly tragic error based on the fact that man is hardly automatically determined to make correct decisions at all times. Hence his lack of omniscience and his liability to error. If Crusoe, on the other hand, had known of the poison and eaten the mushrooms anyway – perhaps for "kicks" or from a very high-time preference – then his decision would have been objectively immoral, an act deliberately set against his life and health.
>
> (Rothbard, 1982, p. 32)

Rothbard refers to the idea of human nature so as to lay down an objective ethic of values, essential to his defense of liberalism. But the praxeological schema shows that a reference to any form of naturalism is unnecessary and that there is no need to abandon the Austrian principle of subjectivism in order to establish the existence of values that are *common and permanent* to the actor-individuals, whatever the particular aims of their actions.

In our view, the interest of the Austrian analysis of welfare, as it had been formulated up until that time, was limited by two elements: on the one hand, respect for subjectivism prevents a common and universally acceptable content, acceptable by all individuals, from being attributed to the concept. This constraint has led all the protagonists of the debate to reduce the understanding of welfare to a procedural mode via the intermediary of market exchange; on the other hand, the attempt to establish a symmetry of principle between the market and true creation of utility has failed. Indeed, even if the idea of a preference is demonstrated by inter-personal exchange, the production of welfare *ex post facto* by the market is not, due to the ignorance of the future, the contingency of evaluations and utter ignorance.

In our opinion, the reference to survival enables us to get around these two difficulties. With regard to the first, the apodictical content of this praxeological value provides us with a universal criterion for welfare, whether or not the actors are present on the market. Hence we are not required to limit the analysis to any particular, arbitrarily defined field. As for the second difficulty, that is to say the creation of utility, the criterion we retain for welfare is not procedural but substantive. It reflects the existence of "praxeological goods," i.e. the resources necessarily conditioning the practice of any process of action through the element of survival. Praxeological goods can be clearly defined as they are derived quite simply from the satisfaction of physiological needs. The welfare index thus easily becomes measurable and corresponds to the production level of praxeological goods.

Our approach is closely related to that of Rawls (*A Theory of Justice*, 1971) in terms of primary goods.[6] But while it shares the advantages of Rawls' theory, it is not marred by the difficulties encountered by Rawls. Our formulation enables us to circumvent two of the logical problems presented in Rawls' theory that critics often note: on the one hand, the heterogeneity of the set of primary goods as defined by Rawls, which leads him to logical contradictions in the presentation of his theorems of justice (Boudon, 1977). Conversely, praxeological goods, due to the strictly physiological dimension of the needs they satisfy, relate back to a homogeneous sub-set of material goods; on the other hand, numerous authors (Roemer, 1993; Sen, 1982, 1985) have questioned the ability of individuals to use (derive a psychological income from) these "Rawlsian" primary goods. Should individual asymmetries be observed in the ability to "consume" the latter, the validity of the theorems of justice will be affected and Rawls' rule of equity will lose all relevance. Conversely, within the framework of our praxeological approach, this criticism is unjustified. Indeed, the answer to the problem of knowing whether individuals are capable of deriving satisfaction from having such goods at their disposal will necessarily be affirmative. Praxeological goods are apodictically valued by each actor as they are a precondition to *any* type of action.

Mises' reference to the pattern of human action enables us to provide the idea of valorizing survival with a universal content. Maximization of welfare, defined substantively through survival, is necessarily derived from the rule of the maximization of the production of "praxeological goods." By consequence, all individuals, be they present or not on the market, value "praxeological goods" as much as they value the socio-economic condition enabling the probability of them being produced to be maximized. As an institutional mode that maximizes the level of production of praxeological goods, the *Great Society* in Hayek's terms (the Extended Order) is identified with the socio-economic state allowing individual hopes for survival to be maximized. Thus, with the rules of just conduct, we have access to a principle of normativity that favors a liberal organization of societies, on the basis of an economic criterion of coordination. In our formulation, the definition of a Hayekian normativity thus takes account of the existence of a zone of agents' common values. However, our definition does not mean that individuals must *necessarily* choose in favor of social conditions maximizing the production of goods permitting their satisfaction.

### Normativity without prescriptions

Indeed, the definition of this normativity does not necessarily imply that agents must develop a doctrinal preference in favor of the market. When considered in the field of survival, the formation of the doctrinal preference depends upon the

situation of each agent and, in particular, on their initial endowment of "praxeological goods." Thus, Austrian normativity could not possibly reflect a symmetry
between individual rationality and a preference for the market. By the same
token, this form of normativity does not assume any aspect of prescription.

The schema in Figure 13.1 enables us to understand the distinction drawn
between normativity and prescription. In fact, and to quote Sen (1977), "judgements" must be distinguished from "interests." The indifference maps[7] of the
two representative individuals are identical. In accordance with praxeological
laws, they reveal a lexicographical nature and identical "judgements" on the part
of the two individuals. But differences in budgetary constraints involve different
"interests." Whereas it is in the interest of individual 1 to witness the development of praxeological goods so that his budgetary constraint may give him the
chance to increase satisfaction (the passage from A to B), the second individual
already possesses sufficient praxeological resources enabling him to develop
action processes and to valorize other subjective goods which are not necessarily
produced by the market: social justice, solidarity, egalitarianism (the broken
sections of the budgetary constraints R2 and R2'). His "interest" is therefore to

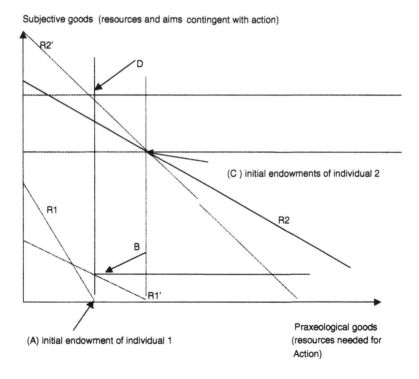

*Figure 13.1*

witness a reduction in his opportunities to consume praxeological resources in favor of other goods and thereby to attain a higher indifference curve (the passage from C to D). The two individuals represented on the graph above have identical common values but their doctrinal preferences will be different: one favors the market whereas the other will possibly favor different socio-economic situations.[8] Consequently, the doctrinal preference of an individual will not be dependent upon his "judgements" but upon his "interests" which depend here upon his initial endowment in praxeological goods.

Other cases could be imagined where, for example, agents are unaware of their initial endowments in praxeological goods, are similarly unaware of their subjective values but benefit from information on their individual skills. Hence, an individual who is aware of the market's capacity in terms of production of "praxeological goods" may well prefer an economic structure in which there is a certain degree of redistribution if he considers, through his aptitude for rent-seeking, that he can take advantage of the opportunities to obtain more goods than he would have had in the case of a free market.

At this point, it is possible to clearly define what Austrian normativity might be. It is based on the condition of impartiality defined by Rawls as the position of an ideal observer:

> A rational and impartial sympathetic spectator is a person who takes up a general perspective: he assumes a position where his own interests are not at stake and he possesses all the requisite information and powers of reasoning. So situated he is equally responsive and sympathetic to the desires and satisfactions of everyone affected by the social system.
>
> (Rawls, 1971, p. 217)

This condition of impartiality presented by Rawls is in itself a theory having its origins in the axiom of the original position highlighting the idea of "a veil of ignorance." The definition of an Austrian normativity works in the same way when referring to individuals aware of the lexicographical nature of their indifference map, but unaware of their endowments in praxeological goods, their idiosyncrasies (values other than praxeological) and their particular skills. In short, a "judgement" should quite simply be made whilst putting aside one's "interest."

Continuing the comparison with Rawls' reasoning, the criterion of normativity we have just defined is the Austrian translation of the Rawlsian criterion of maximin.[9] The Austrian version is, however, notably different from that of Rawls and this is in two ways: on the one hand, it takes account of intrapersonal criteria – and not inter-personal – as in *A Theory of Justice*. Indeed, in Rawls' version the maximin implies a classification of social alternatives starting from the situation of the worst-off individual. From an Austrian point of view, he is simply expressing the fact that satisfaction of praxeological needs (minimal or prior conditions for action) is characterized by a lexicographical order priority over other types of needs. The classification of socio-economic conditions should therefore fall in favor of the one which best promotes the minimal or prior conditions to any action; on the other hand, the principle of maximin in the theory of Rawls corresponds to a theorem of justice which has its roots in the original position. Within our Austrian framework, it is of an axiomatic nature because it reflects a praxeological reality.

## Conclusion

At the present stage of the literature, the terms of a normative Austrian economics have not been satisfactorily defined by the contemporary authors who are explicitly working toward this goal. The reconstruction of the Hayekian model seems to open a new perspective. In *The Fatal Conceit* (1988), Hayek confirms the superiority of spontaneous institutions in the competition between economic systems, by insisting on their historical ability to enable growing populations to survive.

Moreover, using this approach, Hayek appears to reconcile the old and the new Austrian traditions. His argument seems close to that of Carl Menger, as the latter defines the field of economics as "the precautionary activity of humans directed toward covering their *material needs*" (Menger, 1883, p. 65) and constantly refers to "the common good." This approach, up until then considered as simplistic compared to a more generic conception of the "economic point of view" (Kirzner, 1960), is nevertheless the key to a universal definition of welfare as it may be defined thanks to the praxeological scheme laid down by Mises. The fusion of these two perspectives within the Hayekian theoretical framework appears to us to be remarkably productive as far as the normative Austrian economics is concerned.

## Notes

1  Indeed, increasing coherence of expectations can only be guaranteed from the moment that existing prices enable future prices to be indicated in one way or another. In *Law, Legislation and Liberty*, Hayek takes up the question to explain the nature and conditions of the process: "The correspondence of expectations that makes it possible for all parties to achieve what they are striving for is in fact brought about by a process of learning by trial and error which must involve a constant disappointment of some expectations. The process of adaptation operates, as do the adjustments of any self-organizing system, by what cybernetics has taught us to call negative feedback: responses to the differences will be reduced. This will produce an increased correspondence of expectations of the different persons so long as current prices provided some indications of what future prices will be, that is, so long as, *in a fairly constant framework of known facts, always only a few of them change*; and so long as the price mechanism operates as a medium of communicating knowledge which brings it about that the facts which become known to some, through the effects of their actions on prices, are made to influence the decision of others" (Hayek, 1976, p. 125).

2  For Lachmann, certainly, "Knowledge of concrete circumstances is more often likely to be affected by obsolescence than the presumably more durable truth enshrined in generalizations." But "The ramifications of obsolescence depend on the degree of

complementarity between the part of the stock of knowledge affected by obsolescence and other parts. The invalidity of a general rule must have considerably more far-reaching consequences than that of one particular circumstance" (Lachmann, 1986, p. 52).

3 In "Notes on the Evolution of Systems of Rates of Conduct," Hayek had already emphasized that "The individual may have no idea what this overall order is that results from his observing such rules as those concerning kinship and intermarriage, or the succession to property, or which function this overall order serves. Yet all the individuals of the species which exist will behave in that manner because groups of individuals which have thus behaved have displaced those which did not do so" (Hayek, 1967b, p. 70).

4 This work constitutes, in part, the development of a previous article, entitled "From Menger to Hayek: Biology, Subjectivism, and Welfare" (Shearmur, 1990).

5 The majority of goals pursued by individuals implies remaining alive. The majority of ends targeted by individuals implies remaining alive: "Notwithstanding all declarations to the contrary, the immense majority of men aim first of all at an improvement of the material conditions of well-being" (Mise,s 1966, p. 96). But this intuitive remark is not praxeological. The aim of an act may be to suppress one's life. "The impulse to live, to preserve one's own life and to take advantage of every opportunity of strengthening one's vital force is a primal feature of life, present in every living being. However, to yield to this impulse is not – for man – an inextricable necessity" (Mises, 1944, p. 25). However, what a priori is certain is that all actors necessarily value life as a means and not as an end. As strange as this may seem, the action of an individual whose goal is suicide remains within the framework of our analysis: between the moment when the decision to commit suicide is taken and the moment it comes into being, the individual will promote all the resources enabling him to carry out his act.

6 In *A Theory of Justice* (1971) Rawls seeks to establish a criterion of justice which may be used to evaluate socio-economic states. To this end, he defines an axiomatic by referring to a state of nature (*original position*). The aim of this axiomatic is to highlight common preferences amongst agents to which the primary goods correspond. Rawls uses this axiomatic of the original position to deduce his theorems of social justice ("equity"), which are identified with a rational criterion of endowments distribution.

7 It may appear surprising to introduce the idea of indifference into an Austrian reasoning. Mises himself often pointed out the conceptual impossibility of imagining a perfect human being, i.e. perfectly indifferent. Imagining this situation indeed necessarily implies the *act* of thinking, i.e. the manifestation of a preference. It is well-known that "Indifference can never be demonstrated by action" because "Every action is necessarily a choice, and every choice signifies a definite preference. Action specifically implies the contrary of indifference" (Rothbard, 1956, p. 237). Absolute Indifference is therefore not conceivable. If we were to graphically depict an area representing overall possible and imaginable actions, no actor could legitimately claim that each of the points located within this area brings him the same level of satisfaction. Nevertheless, an individual is capable of mentally imagining, at any given time, situations of indifference between *certain* actions or situations and thereby to consider (rightly or wrongly) that *certain* particular points within this area would procure himself the same level of satisfaction. Hence, there is nothing to prevent one from using indifference maps as a psychological representation by the actor of his own subjectivity.

8 In the case of individual 1, judgement and interest take the same direction. For individual 2, there is an asymmetry between judgement and interest.

9 In *A Theory of Justice* (p. 115), Rawls is intent on distinguishing the principle of difference from the economist criterion of maximin. This distinction is of no consequence in our analysis.

# Bibliography

Aimar, T. (1998) "L'économie autrichienne du bien-être: quelle définition possible?" *Revue d'Economie Politique*, septembre–octobre, 5, pp. 691–709.

—— (1999) "Equité versus coordination? Une controverse autrichienne soulevée par Rothbard," *Revue Economique*, 50 (2), pp. 301–21.

—— (2000) "Time, Coordination and Ignorance: a Comparison between Hayek and Lachmann" in *History of Economic Ideas*, 7 (1–2), pp. 139–68.

Block, W. and Rockwell, L. H. (eds.) (1988) *Man, Economy and Liberty: Essays in Honor of Murray Rothbard*, The Ludwig von Mises Institute, Auburn University.

Boudon, R. (1977) *Effets pervers et ordre social*, Paris: Presses Universitaires de France.

Cordato, R. (1992) *Welfare Economics and Externalities in a Open-Ended Universe: a Modern Austrian Perspective*, Boston: Kluwer Academic Publishers.

Hayek, F.A. (1937) "Economics and Knowledge" in (1948) *Individualism and Economic Order*, Chicago: The University of Chicago Press.

—— (1948) *Individualism and Economic Order*, Chicago: The University of Chicago Press, 1980.

—— (1955) "Degrees of Explanation" in (1967a) *Studies in Philosophy, Politics and Economics*, Chicago: The University of Chicago Press.

—— (1964) "The Theory of Complex Phenomena" in (1967a) *Studies in Philosophy, Politics and Economics*, Chicago: The University of Chicago Press.

—— (1965) "Kinds of Rationalism" in (1967a) *Studies in Philosophy, Politics and Economics*, Chicago: The University of Chicago Press.

—— (1967a) *Studies in Philosophy, Politics and Economics*, Chicago: The University of Chicago Press.

—— (1967b) "Notes on the Evolution of Systems of Rules of Conduct" in (1967a) *Studies in Philosophy, Politics and Economics*, Chicago: The University of Chicago Press.

—— (1973) *Law, Legislation and Liberty, Rules and Order*, London: Routledge & Kegan Paul (1993).

—— (1976) *Law, Legislation and Liberty, The Mirage of Social Justice*, London: Routledge & Kegan Paul (1993).

—— (1988) *The Fatal Conceit: The Errors of Socialism*, Chicago: The University of Chicago Press.

Kirzner, I. (1960) *The Economic Point of View*, New York: Sheed & Ward, Inc. (1976).

—— (1976) "Philosophical and Ethical Implications of Austrian Economics" in *The Foundations of Modern Austrian Economics*, Dolan, E. (ed.) *The Foundations of Modern Austrian Economics*, Kansas City: Sheed & Ward, Inc.

—— (1988) "Welfare Economics: A Modern Austrian Perspective" in *Man, Economy and State, Essays in Honor of Murray N. Rothbard*, Ludwig von Mises Institute, pp. 77–89. Reprinted in *The Meaning of Market Process, Essays in the Development of Modern Austrian Economics*, 1992.

—— (1998) "Coordination as a Criterion for Economic 'Goodness,'" *Constitutional Political Economy*, 9: 289–301.

Lachmann, L. (1971) *The Legacy of Max Weber*, Berkeley: Glendessary Press.

—— (1986) *The Market as an Economic Process*, Oxford: Basil Blackwell.

Menger, C. (1871) *Principles of Economics*, New York and London: New York University Press (1981).

—— (1883) *Investigations into the Method in Social Sciences, with Special Reference to Economics*, New York and London: New York University Press (1985).

Mises, L. (1933) *Epistemological Problems of Economics*, New York and London: New York University Press 1981.

—— (1944) "The Treatment of Irrationality in the Social Sciences" in *Money, Method and the Market Process*, 1990, pp. 16–36, Norwell: Kluwer Academic Publishers.

—— (1957) *Theory and History*, Auburn, Alabama: The Ludwig von Mises Institute (1985).

—— (1962) *The Ultimate Foundation of Economic Science*, Sheed Andrews & MacMeel, Inc. (1978).

—— (1966) *Human Action, A Treatise on Economics*, Chicago: Henry Regnery Company.

Rawls, J. (1971) *A Theory of Justice*, Cambridge: Harvard University Press.

Roemer, J.E. (1993) "A Pragmatic Theory of Responsibility for the Egalitarian Planner," *Philosophy and Public Affairs*, 22: 146–66.

Rothbard, M. (1956) "Toward a Reconstruction of Utility and Welfare Economics" in *On Freedom and Free Enterprise*, Princeton: D. Van Nostrand Company, Inc.

—— (1982) *The Ethics of Liberty*, Atlantic Highlands: Humanities Press.

Sen, A.K. (1977) "Social Choice Theory: A Re-examination," *Econometrica*, 45, pp. 53–90.

—— (1982) "Ethical Measurement of Inequality: Some Difficulties" in *Choice, Welfare and Measurement*, Oxford: Basil Blackwell.

—— (1985) *Commodities and Capabilities*, Amsterdam: North Holland.

Shearmur, J. (1990) "From Menger to Hayek: Biology, Subjectivism, and Welfare" in *Carl Menger and his Legacy in Economics*, Durham and London: Duke University Press.

—— (1996) *Hayek and After*, London and New York: Routledge.

Wieser, F. von (1914) *Social Economics*, New York: Augustus M. Kelley (1967.)

# Index

Printed in the United States
by Baker & Taylor Publisher Services